To: Jeremy
& Jim
Bon Appétit!
Mike
9/28/16

Easy Gourmet Recipes
for the Frugal Cook:
Mikey Likes It!

Volume II

By
Michael P. Burwen

KUDOS

"Too often, cookbooks present recipes that are silly exercises in undisciplined creativity, watered down vanilla versions of quality originals, or full of things that are nice to look at but will never get made. Michael Burwen's book thankfully does none of these. "Mikey Likes It" takes the reader down the author's memory lane of solid American-format, protein-based meals from a variety of cultural flavor profiles. The recipes are straightforward, clear, and as the author indicates, easily accomplished by an enthusiastic amateur cook in a normal kitchen. The ingredients and techniques are interesting enough without proving overly exotic, rare or difficult. I especially like the backbone of Continental Cuisine dishes that everybody likes but have fallen out of vogue with flavor-of-the-moment chefs and authors more enchanted by Vegetarian North Vietnamese street food and other such drivel. If you're looking for a go-to cookbook that can put a little weekend in your week, or improve your dinner parties with little extra work or money, this would be a great way to go." --- Daniel H. Scherotter, Chef's Council for the Center of Culinary Development, President of the Golden Gate Restaurant Association and Culinary Arts Instructor, San Francisco Schools

"Like most home cooks, I love making delicious, flavorful food for family and friends. Elbows on the table, napkins on laps and the dog begging for morsels. In addition, I revere an author that has the ability to put their cooking experience in writing the clear, thoughtful, organized way Michael Burwen has. Being a 50 year collector of cookbooks with a library of over 300 of 'em, along with every single issue of Saveur Magazine from its inception, I can say that this aptly titled book will be a top favorite of mine for time honored, go-to, easy-to-make recipes. We've savored many of these internationally inspired recipes, look forward to enjoying them all and think you will as well. All of the ingredients are easily available for home cooks who love wonderful food! I especially like the insightful author's notes of experience. Therefore, I highly recommend this book!" --- G'ma Carol

"I read this cover to cover over one very long night into the wee hours of the morn. That's how good this book is. I can't wait to shop soon and try a number of new recipes that in the past seemed too difficult to tackle. Some gave me the courage to cook again those sophisticated foods I cooked with my mother many years ago before marriage. Mr. Burwen's easy writing style takes daunting foods, seeming OH so complex to construct, and makes it seem very easy. He grants lots of literary license to tease & play around with alternatives ingredients. On a last note he gives HINTS & TIPS on where to find groceries not necessarily seasonal or in close proximity to where you live. He the kind of Chef I'd love to meet. He does not seem too self absorbed but genuinely interested in cooking & teaching. Bravo for a first book. I can't wait to read the next." --- Susan Tydings Frushour

"What a wonderful idea! Great concept and great recipes. I know everyone will enjoy it. The recipes look easy and full of good ingredients to make fabulous meals!" --- Cathy Rogers, Cooking Instructor and Author

Fortunately for us, Michael Burwen is willing to share his versatile and comprehensive array of favorite recipes. My wife and I are eager to start using this as our go-to cookbook. And yes, you can print out your Kindle recipes from your Mac, protecting the Mac from the adversities of the kitchen environment. At the very least, check out Mike's version of beef stroganoff. Maybe even comparing it to Julia's famous, but labor-intensive, recipe of Julie and Julia fame. Hardly anyone needs another cookbook, but this is a great addition anyway!" --- John S

So interesting and knowledgeable I was taken aback. Can't wait for the second book. The recipes are so easy anybody can do it." --- Sara J

"Mike Burwen's writing style and commentaries make this collection of recipes so appealing I'm almost tempted to turn on my stove during this summer heat wave! I'm flattered that Mike chose to include my recipe for chicken livers and mushrooms, which he begged of me several years ago, after I served the dish with scrambled eggs and spinach soufflé at a New Year's Day brunch. The same recipe is a great, frugal dinner item when enhanced with sherry or marsala wine and served over rice." --- Barbara Marks

"This cookbook stands well above an already crowded pack. The organization makes it easy to browse and then follow your fancy. The recipes are skillfully pared down to their basic elements and the anecdotal tips along the way are both instructive and amusing. The book adds a significant new contribution to the genre." --- Allan Retzky

"I cook extensively but rarely use cookbooks or recipes as I love to experiment. However, after browsing through this book, I found so many delicious sounding ideas that, like the author, I plan to "adapt" many of the recipes. Thank you Mikey." ---Michael (Cleveland)

"If you are looking to add some pizzazz to your cooking this is the book. You won't find boring food here, food cooked in the standard way. Recipes are tweaked with an extra ingredient or two and perhaps a different technique to produce great dishes that only look complicated. In addition to recipes there are great sections on cooking equipment and ingredients, including advice. The book is easy reading, written in a pleasant conversational style. It's a worthwhile addition to your cookbook library." --- Al Cattalini

Caveats and Legal Stuff

If I can remember where I got a recipe, I mention it. Usually, I've doctored the recipe to suit my own tastes or to simplify it, so it isn't exactly the same as the original. Unfortunately, in the early days, I didn't bother to write down the source, so many recipes don't have attribution. I suppose it doesn't really matter, because I read that one cannot copyright a recipe, so hopefully I won't get sued. The U.S. Government says:

"Copyright law does not protect recipes that are mere listings of ingredients. Nor does it protect other mere listings of ingredients such as those found in formulas, compounds, or prescriptions. Copyright protection may, however, extend to substantial literary expression—a description, explanation, or illustration, for example—that accompanies a recipe or formula or to a combination of recipes, as in a cookbook."

I purchased a royalty-free license to use the front cover graphic, "Chef Hug", from CanStockPhoto.com. It was designed by someone with the moniker *cthoman,* and I want to thank him or her.

Words of Appreciation

I hope you enjoy this book, my second cookbook. Rather, I hope you enjoy making the recipes contained therein. It took Julia Child seven years to write and publish her *Mastering the Art of French Cooking, Volume I,* and she had help. I collected the recipes in this book over more than 40 years, so I've got her beat hands down (smirk). I admit, however, that Julia had a great influence on my love of cooking – and eating. I even stole some of her creations for my books.

Volume I was published in late 2013. I sold a few and gave away a lot to charitable organizations. Although I didn't get rich, my customers were effusive in their praise, and that praise stimulated this second book, Volume II. Thanks to all of you who like my work.

It is no coincidence that I married a woman named Sherry, one of my favorite ingredients. She gave me several ideas that I think have gone a long way to improving the content and presentation of this book. I resisted most of her ideas at first. After all, how could I write anything less than perfect? Eventually, I came around to accept her advice. Thanks, Sherry.

I also want to thank my progeny, Jill, Marcy and Ross, my grandchildren, Naomi and Jordan, and my baby sister, Elisabeth, who have eaten my food and lived to tell about it.

As was Volume I, this Volume II is dedicated to my father, Charles Burwen, who taught me that great food is not important, and my mother, Charlotte Burwen (née Freedman), who taught me that it is. You be the judge of whose teachings survived.

Mike Burwen

Petaluma, California

August 2015

Table of Contents

Chapter 1: Introduction   1

Background and Purpose 1

Who Should Read This Book.. 2

Ingredients 4

Cookbook Organization 8

A Few Words About Equipment 9

Servings, Yield, Prep Time, Cook Time and Measurements 13

What to Have in the Pantry and Where to Get It 14

Abbreviations and Shorthand Notations 20

Chapter 2: Appetizers, Tapas and First Courses   21

Asparagus and Artichokes with Lemon Aioli............................... 21

Asparagus Wrapped in Prosciutto 22

Baby Eggplants, North Beach Style... 23

Bay Scallop Appetizer... 24

Clams Casino.. 25

Cucumber, Fennel and Gravlax 26

Filipino Chicken Wings.. 27

Garlic Calamari Rings 28

Grilled Shishito or Padron 29

Pintxos with Peppers, Anchovies and Garlic 30

Roasted Peppers Stuffed with Frying Cheese............................. 31

Shrimp with Sherry Sauce 32

Spanish Tortilla 33

Tempura... 34

Chapter 3: Breakfast and Brunch   36

All-in-one Breakfast.. 36

Baked Apple Puff 37

Blintz Pie with Blueberry Sauce 38

Cardamom French Toast 40

German Pancakes 41

Matzoh Brie... 42

Omelet Soufflé 43

Omelet Stuffed Bread 45

Schnecken 46

Shirred Eggs with Mushrooms, Ham and Cheese 48

Chapter 4: Desserts and Pastries 49

Bananas Foster 49

Chocolate Hazelnut Tart in Filo Cups 50

Chocolate Mousse 51

Chocolate Truffles 52

Classic French Apple Tart 54

Floating Island 55

Home-made Baked Donuts 56

Melons Macerated in Wine 58

No-Bake Cheesecake 59

Puff Pastry Berry Tart 60

Roasted or Sautéed Fruit 61

Sabayon, Zabaglione, Custard or Whatever 62

St. Clement's Pie 63

Chapter 5: Hors d'oeuvres and Finger-foods 64

Angels on Horseback 64

Bacon-wrapped, Cheese-stuffed Dates 65

Bagel Chips 66

Brined Garlic Shrimp 67

Bruschetta with Prosciutto and Other Stuff 68

Caviar and Cucumbers 69

Ceviche 70

Cheese Crisps (Fricos) 71

International Chips 72

James Beard's Onion Sandwiches 73

Mini Quiches 74

Nuts to You 75

Onion Apple Bites 76

Stuffed Mushrooms 77

Chapter 6: Main Dishes: Beef 78

Beef Braised in Red Wine 78

Beef Stroganoff in One Pan Revised 80

Braised Beef Cheeks 81

Bruce Aidell's Steak with Pepper Sauce 82

Catalan Beef Stew 83

Churrasco 85

Filet of Beef, Low Temperature Method 86

Individual Beef Wellingtons 87

La Genovese 88

Marinated Tri-Tip Roast 89

Michael Jordan's 23 Delmonico Steak 90

Oxtails, Caribbean-Style 91

Sherry's Brisket Pot Roast 92

Spanish Steak Stir-Fry 94

Sukiyaki 95

Thai Beef and Peppers Stir-fry 97

Chapter 7: Main Dishes: Chicken and Game Hen 99

Best Chicken Stew 99

Braised Herbed Chicken Thighs 101

Catalan Chicken Picada 102

Chicken and Mushrooms 104

Chicken Cacciatore II 106

Chicken Paprikash 108

Chicken Thigh Escalopes 109

Chicken Vesuvio with Potatoes and Artichoke Hearts 110

Chicken with 40 Cloves of Garlic 111

Cider-braised Chicken Legs 112

Moroccan Chicken Tagine 113

Saffron Chicken Breasts in Cream Sauce 115

Sweet and Sour Glazed Game Hen 116

Tandoori Chicken 117

Chapter 8: Main Dishes: Duck and Game Birds 119

Asian Quail 119

Braised Guinea Hen 121

Brined and Steamed Duck 123

Brined and Roasted Pheasant 124

Chinese Glazed Squab 126

Citrus Braised Duck 127

Roast Glazed Duck, Low Temperature Method 128

Turducken 130

Chapter 9: Main Dishes: Lamb and Goat   131

Berbere Lamb 131

Grilled Goat Chops 132

Grilled Lamb Shoulder 133

Jamaican Goat Curry 134

Lamb Ragù 135

Madras Lamb Curry 136

Roast Leg of Lamb 138

Stuffed Seared Lamb Tenderloin 139

Chapter 10: Main Dishes: Pork   140

Baby Back Ribs a al Greque 140

Braised Pulled Pork 142

Chinese Pork and Noodle Stir-fry 143

Creole Paella 144

Orzo with Sausage, Peppers and Tomatoes 146

Pasta alla Carbonara 147

Pork Adobo 148

Roast Pork Loin 149

Sausage, Artichoke and Sun-dried Tomato Pasta 150

Spareribs with an Asian Flair 151

Stinco 153

Tuscan Sausages and Grapes 155

Chapter 11: Main Dishes: Seafood   156

Baked or Grilled Lemon Halibut, With or Without Crust 156

Grilled Fish Filets with Citrus Sauce 157

Mediterranean Shellfish with Fennel and Tomato 158

Pan-seared Filet of Sole Meunière 160

Red Curry Steamed Mussels 161

Salmon en Croute 163

Scallops Gratinée 164

Shellfish Ravioli with Olive Oil Poached Tomato Cream Sauce 165

Shellfish with Ptitim 166

Singapore Noodles 167

Sole Rolls with Asparagus 169

Spaghetti con Vongole 170

Stir-fried Shrimp 171

Chapter 12: Main Dishes: Veal   172

Moroccan Veal Stew 172

Swedish Meatballs (Fricadella) 174

Veal Marengo with Truffles 175

Veal Marsala 176

Veal Martini 177

Veal Medallions with Mushrooms 178

Chapter 13: Main Dishes: Vegetarian   180

Cheese Fondue 180

Linguine with Onion Sauce 182

Pasta with Mushroom Sauce 183

Stuffed Peppers 184

Tomatoes Stuffed with Mushrooms and Onions 185

Chapter 14: Salads and Salad Dressings   186

Arugula Salad with Figs, Bacon and Cheese 186

Blue Cheese Dressing 187

Caprese Salad 188

Chicken Salad with Roasted Bell Peppers 189

E.A.T. Tomato Salad 190

Greek Salad 191

Grilled Lettuce Salad 192

Kicked Up Cole Slaw 193

Kohlrabi and Carrot Salad 194

Moroccan Beet Salad 195

Panzanella 196

Pickled Cucumber and Onion Salad 197

Potato Salad with Roasted Red Peppers 198

Roasted Fennel and Onion Salad 199

Wilted Spinach Salad 200

Chapter 15: Sauces, Dips, Spreads, Marinades and Rubs   201

Asian Marinade 201

Beurre Blanc 202

Black Currant Mustard Sauce 203

Brown Butter 204

Chocolate Sauce 205

Crème Anglaise 206

Cuban Citrus Salsa 207

Green Peppercorn Sauce 208

Honey Balsamic Sauce 209

Lime Sour Cream 210

Lobel's Coffee Steak Rub 211

Mango or Peach Chutney 212

Mediterranean Yogurt Sauce 213

Pomegranate Molasses 214

Port and Dried Fruit Sauce 215

Red Wine Sauce Rapide 216

White Clam Sauce 217

Chapter 16: Soups   218

Avgolemono Soup 218

Cold Berry Soup 219

Exotic Mushroom Soup with Goat Cheese 220

Onion Soup 221

Pho 222

Roasted Tomato Basil Soup 224

Thai Coconut Chicken Soup 225

Chapter 17: Starch Side Dishes 227

Baked Orzo with Mushrooms and Peas 227

DIY Foccacia 228

French Potato Casserole 229

Jamaican Rice and Peas 230

Kasha Varnishkas 231

Kicked Up Champagne Risotto 232

Mashed Potatoes with Celeriac 234

Moroccan Couscous 235

Piadine 236

Pooris 237

Potato Kugel for Gourmets 238

Spaetzle 240

Sweet Potato Casserole 241

Chapter 18: Vegetable Side Dishes 242

Broccoli with a Thai influence 242

Cauliflower "Twice-Baked Potatoes" 243

Fennel Confit 244

Fried Green Tomatoes 245

Gin and Orange Juice Braised Endive 246

Ginger Sesame Carrots 247

Green Beans and Curly Celery 248

Grilled Marinated Vegetables 249

Moroccan Cauliflower Latkes 250

Mushroom Ragoût 251

Mushrooms with Red Wine Sauce 252

Parmagiano Zucchini Rounds 253

Quick Ratatouille 254

Sugar Snap Peas with Thyme and Shallots 255

Sweet and Sour Onions 256

Tomatoes Stuffed with Cheese, Herbs and Breadcrumbs 257

Chapter 19: Sandwiches 258

Fast Pork Fajitas 258

Grilled Cheese Sandwiches 259

Hong Kong Pork Wraps 260

Merguez Burgers 261

The Ultimate Steak Sandwich 263

The World's Best BLT 265

Vegetable Panini 266

Chapter 20: Miscellaneous 267

Clarified and Brown Butters 267

Kreplach, Wontons and Purses 268

Macerated Berry Topping 269

Mock Clotted Cream 270

Phony Mascarpone 271

Poor Man's Seafood Stock 272

Preserved Lemons 273

Ras El Hanout 274

About the Author and This Book 275

Chapter 1: Introduction

Background and Purpose

Why, you may well ask, publish a Volume II, especially when I sold only a few hundred of Volume I? Frankly, I'm not entirely clear on the reasons, but I did have fun writing and publishing Volume I, and, besides, I have nothing better to do. I belong to an organization called the Bay Area Independent Publishers Association (BAIPA). A lot of professional editors, book designers and publishers are members, and they all tell me that anybody who sells a hundred copies of an independently published book should consider it a great success. I find this hard to believe since really successful cookbooks sell in the millions, but it is encouraging to hear nonetheless.

Although I didn't sell millions, I tried. I sent a copy to the book department of Costco, which I was told is the second largest bookseller in North America. I got a polite note stating that, although my book was among the best they have seen content-wise, they didn't think they could sell enough to make money on it. I got similar responses from bookstores, Wal-Mart and other retailers. Some stores wanted glossy paper and lots of color photos. The argument that the world's greatest cookbooks including *Larousse*, the *New York Times Cookbook*, *Mastering the Art of French Cooking*, the *Joy of Cooking* and others didn't have photos got me nowhere. Pros in the business advised me to get Oprah to endorse my book. I sent her a review copy, but she never responded. C'est la vie.

I had some recipes that I wanted to share that I didn't put into Volume I, mainly because I thought Volume I was big enough as it was. In addition, I've been watching some TV cooking shows lately and they stimulated a number of Mikey Likes It recipe ideas that, in many cases, I was able to improve (or copy – thank goodness recipes cannot be copyrighted). You will find some of them in this book as well.

Much of the information in this introductory chapter duplicates that contained in Volume I. I did that intentionally in case you didn't buy Volume I (shame on you). In any event, I think the information on ingredients and equipment is current and bears repeating. I've included some new information that I think you will find useful

If you are like most cookbook junkies (including me), you undoubtedly want to go immediately to the recipes, which, after all, are the heart of this book. It's your book and you can do as you please, but I urge you to at least skim through this introductory chapter. I think you will find some useful information on subjects like buying ingredients and equipment. First, a bit of background:

When I was growing up, my typical evening meal consisted of meat, cooked well-done without gravy, baked potatoes (with butter, no sour cream), canned stringbeans and green salad without dressing. This is basically what my father would eat, much to my mother's consternation, since she liked to cook. As a result of this diet, I never thought much about food. I ate to live; I did not live to eat.

I got married in my early 20s, right after college graduation. On my first day of work following the honeymoon, I came home, expecting to find dinner ready. To my utter surprise, I learned that the extent of my wife's cooking experience was making tea – with teabags. She was, literally, terrified of the kitchen. (But she later became a great cook!) I was left with two choices: starve to death or learn to cook. I chose the latter.

From that inauspicious beginning, I developed an affinity for food. Throughout an adult lifetime spanning more than 50 years, I've been cooking – and happily so. My cooking bent is to make dishes that allow for tossing in a little of this and a little of that without resorting to the use of measuring devices. Not only is it more fun than slavish adherence to a recipe, but it gets the creative juices flowing and makes the dishes you create your very own.

I've been collecting, modifying and inventing recipes for more than fifty years. About twenty years ago, I started using a recipe management computer program. That program enabled me to capture my favorite recipes, sort them and search them. It was a great aid, enabling me to get rid of the 3x5 cards that were once de rigueur in home kitchens.

After I retired, I started to think about putting my collected recipes in a cookbook so that they could be shared with others. Cookbooks usually have a theme such as a country or region like Italy or Latin America, a type of food like bread or beverages, or a class of food like desserts or appetizers. But my recipe collection is all over the map and includes all kinds of cuisines, courses, and types of food.

The criteria I used for deciding what recipes to include in my cookbooks are:

- I like it – a lot; i.e., Mikey Likes It
- The dish is relatively easy to make (there are a few exceptions)
- It has a small number of ingredients, not counting spices and herbs
- Anybody familiar with basic techniques such as sautéing, braising and grilling can master the dish
- The recipe allows latitude on ingredients and proportions (excluding some baked dishes).

Who Should Read This Book

I wrote (in Volume I) "I suspect that this book is going to appeal more to men than women." That turned out to be a false assumption. Many more women than men bought the book, and they all were complimentary. That said, a majority of the recipes are for hearty dishes. If you are looking for steamed broccoli, fat-free, gluten-free, or sugar-free, this is not your cookbook.

In general, I excluded recipes that require expensive or hard-to-find ingredients. If a recipe does call for something that is beyond your budget or difficult to find, I suggest alternatives in many cases. As much as I love them, there are no recipes that call for imported white truffles, foie gras, or Caspian caviar. That said, I realize that the word "frugal" that appears in the title of this book can mean different things to different people. I include recipes that call for such things as steak, veal medallions and pheasant. Those are certainly not cheap, but they aren't in the caviar/truffle category, and, I think that most people who read cookbooks are willing to prepare dishes with these ingredients at least once in a while.

Many of the recipes leave decisions on the choice of ingredients and their proportions to the reader. Anyone can follow an explicit recipe, but there isn't much intellect involved in doing that. In addition, many of the recipes suggest or provide alternatives to consider. I've tried to challenge you to make it up as you go along, just as I am inclined to do. If you need recipes that contain precisely measured ingredients and detailed step-by-step procedures, you probably won't care for this book. On the other hand, if you are looking for something that stimulates your creative juices (no pun intended), you may very well find it here.

With a few exceptions, every recipe is easy to prepare, and, although there are some that are time-consuming, most are not. This is a cookbook for people who want to serve up great meals without having to invest a lot of time in the process.

In this Volume, I've included several classics like green peppercorn sauce, onion sandwiches and clams casino. There is a reason recipes become classics; namely, they are terrific. However, sometimes they seem to get lost – a generational thing I guess. In any event, I hope you try a few of them and see what you may have been missing!

A note about heat: Many of my recipes call for heat in the form of chilis, red pepper flakes, cayenne, sriracha, etc. Although I used to love hot, spicy food, I can't take it any longer. Therefore, all of the recipes that call for heat make it optional. If you like your food hot, I encourage you to include those ingredients.

Finally, I guarantee that each of the 219 recipes in Volume I and the 215 recipes in this book will create something delicious that will appeal to most palates, even though their ethnicity is all over the map. India, Southeast Asia, China, France, Italy, the Mediterranean, Latin America and North America are all grist for my mill. I encourage you to mix and match. As I said in Volume I, to make one of the best meals you will ever have, grill a New York steak and serve it with a French Sauce Diane, Israeli couscous, Chinese sesame stringbeans and a Moroccan tomato salad. Follow it with strawberries topped with Italian balsamic vinegar.

My books are subtitled *Mikey Likes It*. That sums up the message I want to convey.

Ingredients

When it comes to ingredients, I've tried to stick with stuff that can be bought in an average American market. That said, quality of ingredients is of paramount importance to any dish. If you use poor-quality ingredients, your dishes will be poor-quality. First-quality ingredients can be bought online today, so you can always resort to that source if you can't find what you need locally.

Here are a few ingredient tips – in alphabetical order:

Bread

Although there aren't any bread recipes in this book, I consider bread a must-have accompaniment to almost every meal. Go out of your way to find excellent quality bread. I live in Northern California, where eating good bread is commensurate with a religious experience, but not everybody has the choices I do. Nevertheless, it will pay you to look around for artisan breads. As much as good bread can enhance a meal, lousy bread can ruin it.

Some of the recipes suggest accompanying the meal with Indian naan bread. If you have an Indian restaurant in your neighborhood, you can get it as takeout. If not, look for frozen naan in your local market. Naan freezes well, and the frozen stuff is pretty good. I just warm it up in the microwave and smear it with butter. You can also heat it up in a toaster.

Butter

Although you can get by with the conventional salted butter, I strongly recommend that you use only unsalted butter that has low water content. This quality butter is often imported from Europe, but the imported stuff is expensive. Instead, look for an American-made butter that says something like "made in the European tradition" on the label.

Cheese, Grated

Many recipes call for grated cheese. If you can afford it, use imported Parmagiano Reggiano. If not, Grana Podano, Pecorino Romano, or Asiago can be substituted. Costco usually has the best price for Parmagiano Reggiano, but you have to buy a lot of it. I cut it up into chunks and freeze them; otherwise it will dry out if you don't use it within a couple of weeks. Stay away from anything labeled "parmesan."

Demi-glace

Demi-glace is highly concentrated stock made from beef, chicken, veal or even vegetables. It is an indispensible ingredient to many sauces. I recommend that you buy it rather than make it. (It is easy to make, but very time-consuming.) If you are only going to buy one kind, I suggest you buy the one made from veal as it goes well with everything.

Flour

All wheat flours are not created equal. The main difference is the amount of a protein called gluten. There are four general categories of flour based on the percentage of gluten: Bread flour 13-14%; all-purpose flour 11-12%; pastry flour 9-10%; cake flour 7.5-9%. If you have only all-purpose flour, don't despair because you can lower the gluten content by mixing in flours like cornstarch or potato starch that have no gluten or raise the gluten content by adding pure gluten which can be purchased. For example, to make cake flour (and save money), sift together 8 parts of all-purpose flour with 2 parts of cornstarch.

Self-rising flour has baking powder mixed into it. Not a good idea because you have no control, and, after being stored for a few months the baking powder will lose its effectiveness.

Garlic

Although garlic is one plant, the way it is prepared can greatly influence its flavor contribution to a dish. Crushing or pressing the garlic releases strong oils. Chopping or slicing garlic with a sharp knife does not release those oils, and the flavor contribution will be relatively mild. Roasting the garlic gives it a nutty flavor that melds beautifully with many dishes.

Herbs and Spices

Don't keep any dried leafy herbs longer than 6 months or ground spices longer than a year. Over time, they oxidize and lose their pungency. Dishes made with old herbs and spices taste blah. Use them and your good work will be good for nothing. You have no idea how long an herb or spice has been on a market's shelf, so I recommend that you buy your herbs and spices from a purveyor that guarantees freshness. Always smell the herb or spice if you aren't confident about the quality. If it smells strong, use it. If not, toss it.

Fresh herbs rarely stand up to long cooking, but for some dishes they are a requirement. The prices they charge for fresh herbs in markets these days are absurd. There is no excuse for not growing your own, even if you live in a dark apartment. I grow fresh basil, oregano, rosemary, tarragon, thyme and mint from seedlings purchased at a local nursery. Basil is an annual and needs to be replanted every year, but the rest are perennials, so you never have to buy them again.

Meat and Fish

I love the cooking shows where the chef goes to his/her butcher or fishmonger and gets exactly what he wants, custom cut by trained craftspeople. Unfortunately, outside of a few big cities, those skilled people don't exist today. Some local markets will special order, but that tends to be expensive. Your only recourse is to shop around until you find the best deals. If you live in an area that has a large Latino population, you may find some terrific meat and fish bargains in Latino markets. For example, not one of the supermarkets in my town sells oxtails, but I can get very good oxtails at my favorite Latino market, and they are inexpensive. Remember, if you are going to braise your meat, inexpensive cuts taste best. Fat and gristle are your friends in braised dishes.

Fish and shellfish have become expensive. When I was a kid, lobsters were $.35/lb and scallops were a poor man's food. Coupon hunting pays off in this category. Find the loss leaders and you can save a ton of money. It doesn't matter if you buy your fish fresh or frozen. The key with frozen fish is to defrost it slowly in the refrigerator. Also stay away from frozen fish if you can see ice crystals in the package. That means the fish is old. Some markets sell fish that was once frozen in the defrosted state. While most meat can be refrozen once or twice without harm, fish will suffer from refreezing.

Olive Oil

I use only extra virgin olive oil (EVOO) when olive oil is called for in a recipe, because it adds flavor. If you don't want that flavor (for example in an Asian stir-fry or for making French fries), use canola or peanut oil. There are artisan EVOOs that are expensive. Save them for dipping and salad dressings, not cooking. If you are going to cook the EVOO, use the least expensive you can find.

Onions

I prefer to use sweet onions such as Vidalias. There isn't anything wrong with the standard yellow onions, but the sweet ones are more versatile, and, when cooked, I can't tell the difference.

Pasta

All of my pasta recipes can use either fresh or dried pasta. With a few exceptions, the only fresh pasta served today in restaurants and homes in Italy is sheet pasta used for dishes like ravioli. If the dried stuff is good enough for Italians, it's good enough for me. That said, not all brands of American-made dried pasta are good. If you don't know what a given brand is like, buy the dried pasta imported from Italy. It turns out that some of the imported pastas aren't very good either, so do your homework.

Peppers, Roasted

Making roasted peppers is a pain. If you want to make your own (and I certainly wouldn't discourage you), the easiest method is as follows: Heat oven to 500°. Quarter the peppers and remove seeds and membranes. Place the peppers on a baking sheet, skin side up and roast until the skin turns black. Let cool and peel away the charred skin. Sometimes the charred peel is difficult to remove. Try peeling under running water – it might help. Another method is to put the peppers in a paper bag when hot and allow them to "sweat" in their own steam before peeling them.

You can buy peppers roasted and peeled in jars or cans. The canned peppers will be preserved in acidic brine, and they will taste differently from the ones you make yourself, so hunt around for a brand you like. Amazon.com sells four 28-oz cans for $17, a very good deal if you have the free shipping service.

Puff pastry

Some of my recipes are essentially fruit pies. Not being much of a baker, I don't like to make pie crust dough. Instead, I buy frozen puff pastry, usually the Pepperidge Farm brand, which is available everywhere. Although it does come in sheets, your market may carry only the pre-formed puff pastry tartlet shells. No matter. You can roll the shells into a ball and flatten out a sheet with a rolling pin. In my opinion, puff pastry beats ordinary pie crust hands down.

The Pepperidge Farm puff pastry is made with shortening. You can get other brands that are made with real butter at twice the price. Although there is no question that the butter brands taste better, for most recipes it won't matter because the flavor will be obscured by the other ingredients.

The Pepperidge Farm puff pastry comes in sheets, bite-size cups and large shells. The sheets can be formed into any shape you like.

Rice

If a recipe calls for long-grain rice, use Basmati rice, preferably from India. It has a nutty flavor that is not duplicated by any other rice. Although purists insist that you use the genuine imported short-grain rice such as the Spanish "Bomba" for paella and the Italian "Arborio" for risotto, when you need short-grain rice, any American brand will work. Jasmine rice goes well with Thai food.

I am partial to wild rice, which is not really rice at all. The wild original comes from a grassy plant that grows in water in the Minnesota-Wisconsin area. It is usually harvested by hand by Native Americans whose ancestors have been harvesting the stuff for centuries. Nowadays, wild rice is cultivated in places like California, Minnesota and Saskatchewan. The natural stuff is quite expensive these days, but the cultivated varieties can be had for as little as $3/lb.

Salt

I use kosher salt exclusively for cooking because it does not contain iodine or other additives that can adulterate your food. I prefer *Diamond* brand, which is available everywhere. By volume, use twice as much Diamond kosher salt as you would regular table salt. Another popular kosher salt brand is Morton. It is 50% denser than Diamond so, if you use it, adjust the amount accordingly. All my recipes that call for salt assume that you are using Diamond kosher salt.

Sour Cream

There is a lot of difference between brands of sour cream. I recommend *Knudsen's*, a Kraft Foods brand, which is available nationally, is carried by most markets and is often available at considerable discount. Many brands have high water content. If you want to get rid of the excess water, set a large sieve on top of a bowl, line it with paper towel, put the sour cream on top of the towel and refrigerate overnight. The excess water will drain into the bowl and can then be discarded. If you are lucky enough to live near a Middle-eastern market, you might be able to find sour cream that has very low water content.

Stock or Broth

You can of course make your own stocks, but good quality stock is available at reasonable cost. However, many brands of stock are too salty, so you have to be careful to buy stocks that are either unsalted or have very little salt. Canned beef broth in particular tends to be too salty. For most recipes, you can use either chicken, veal or beef stock.

Tomatoes, Canned

I strongly recommend that you use imported Italian San Marzano tomatoes that bear the phrase D.O.P. on the can label. That stands for *D*enominazione d' *O*rigine *P*rotetta (roughly, "Protected Designation of Origin"). They are twice as expensive as tomatoes that do not bear this designation, but well worth it, especially for pasta sauces.

Vinegar

Vinegar is an important ingredient in many recipes. If you are using unflavored vinegar, make sure that it is made from wine, not grain.

"Real" balsamic vinegar is made exclusively in the Modena region of Italy and is aged, sometimes over 100 years. As you might guess, it is expensive, as much as $200 for a small bottle, although most of the stuff you find in markets has been aged 10 years and costs $10/bottle. It is almost never used in salad dressings or in cooking, but as a "drizzle" to finish a dish. For cooking and salad dressings, use the inexpensive supermarket brands that are not aged.

There are many other flavored and seasoned types of vinegar, such as sherry vinegar, cider vinegar, rice vinegar, raspberry vinegar, etc. Feel free to experiment.

Wine

There is no reason to spend a lot of money on wine that you use in cooking. On the other hand, steer clear of anything labeled "cooking wine," which is usually disgusting. For most dishes, just use any dry white or red wine that tastes decent when you drink it straight. So-called "Two-buck Chuck" (which now sells for $2.49 in California) is fine. Fortified wines such as port or sherry are a different matter, because the amount of sweetness can vary from very dry to cloyingly sweet. If you are using a fortified wine in a recipe, make sure that your choice fits the dish.

Cookbook Organization

This cookbook is arranged in chapters by type of dish. The chapters are as follows:

1. Introduction
2. Appetizers, Tapas and First Courses
3. Breakfast and Brunch
4. Desserts and Cookies
5. Hors d'oeuvres and Finger-food
6. Main Dishes: Beef
7. Main Dishes: Chicken and Game Hens
8. Main Dishes: Duck and Goose
9. Main Dishes: Lamb
10. Main Dishes: Pork
11. Main Dishes: Seafood
12. Main Dishes: Veal
13. Main Dishes: Vegetarian
14. Salads and Salad Dressings
15. Sauces, Dips, Spreads, Marinades and Rubs
16. Soups
17. Starch Side Dishes
18. Vegetable Side Dishes
19. Sandwiches
20. Miscellaneous

I often found it difficult to assign a recipe to a chapter. Sometimes my decisions were arbitrary. Many hors d'oeuvres can be appetizers. Many appetizers can be main dishes, some side dishes and salads could be served as main dishes, and so forth.

The criteria I used to decide are:

- If you are most likely to serve the dish as something people will probably eat standing up or in front of the TV, I put it in the Hors d'oeuvres chapter.
- If the dish is most likely to be served as the first course to a sit-down meal, I put it in the Appetizer chapter
- If it is a salad, I put it in the Salad chapter, even though it could be served as a main dish.

Within each chapter, the recipes appear in alphabetical order. This is sort of a copout because some recipes start with the main ingredient (e.g., "artichokes") and some start with an adjective (e.g., "roasted"). I tried several different schemes and none of them were very good. Since the longest chapter has only about 20 recipes, I figure you won't be too navigationally challenged.

Out of the 260 recipes in the book, all but 15 of them appear on one page. On those recipe pages that have an inch or more of white space on the bottom, I've ended with the phrase "MY NOTES". This is to encourage you to write in anything you may have done that you particularly like – or want to avoid - the next time you make the dish.

A Few Words About Equipment

There are many references that provide in-depth information about cooking equipment. I have no intention of repeating them, but I would like to give you a few recommendations that I've discovered are particularly useful after more than a half-century of trial-and-error experience.

Baking Pans

Throw away all your old baking pans and replace them with ones made of silicone. This modern miracle material doesn't stick to anything edible. It's available in lots of sizes and shapes. If you ever struggled to remove a Bundt cake from an old-fashioned tube pan, you will think silicone is a gift from the gods. You can also buy silicone in sheets; the most common is sold under the trade name *Silpat*. Cookies and foods that you would otherwise cook on a baking sheet simply will not stick.

Garlic Presses

There is only one I can recommend, the Swiss-made *Susi 3*. It costs around $15, but is worth every penny. A caveat is that you may need a strong grip to press large cloves.

Immersion Blenders

An Immersion Blender is a terrific time-saver for making blended soups and sauces. It is much more convenient than a food processor or regular blender for applications where blending can be done by immersion. Immersion blenders cost from $20 to $200. The cheapest, the *Kalorik* brand, is the best! It is one of the few that lets you detach the blender from the motor so that it can be cleaned in the dishwasher.

Knives

Practically every chef in the world outside of Asia uses forged German or French-made knives. There is nothing wrong with those knives, and I have an extensive collection of them. However, there are a few knives I've found to be particularly useful:

The *Victorinox 4513 6" boning knife* has a thin, flexible blade that is easy to keep sharp. I use it, not only for boning meat and poultry, but for peeling fruit and cutting some vegetables. Less than $20 online.

Martin Yan's all-purpose knife combines the versatility of a French chef's knife and a Chinese cleaver. The knife is now made in China, but it used to be made in Japan. The Japanese-made knife is made of better steel and has a wooden handle that I like, but it is very hard to find. You can use it for everyday tasks as well as for cutting a chicken in half. About $35 online.

A *6" Santoku knife* is my choice for vegetable chopping. The brand I have is "Napastyle," but I don't think it is sold anymore. Any good brand should do you well.

The *Rada R130 grapefruit knife* is the best. $6 on Amazon.com.

Knife Sharpeners

If you want the sharpest possible knives, acquire a set of Japanese waterstones ranging from 800 to 8000 grit. Practice sharpening 4 hours every day for a couple of months, and you will be able to put the finest possible edge on your knives. If you don't feel like expending that effort, buy a *Chef's Choice* Model 220 electric sharpener (About $40 online) and a sharpening steel ($10 - $50). You can also buy sharpening rods instead of steels that are made of ceramic or steel imbedded with diamond dust. These are nice but aren't necessary, since the only function of a steel is to bend the wire edge of a blade so that it is straight. Any piece of hard metal will do that job.

That said, my son gave me a sharpener that I had never seen before called "Edge of Glory." It consists of two opposing carbide sharpening elements set into a 2" diameter plastic housing that has a suction cup on the bottom. The suction cup holds the device securely onto a flat surface. Once secured, all you have to do is draw the knife blade through the carbide sharpening elements. It not only works like a charm, it costs less than $5!

Pots

Any pot will do for boiling or steaming. But for braising, making sauces, etc., I use enameled cast iron pots exclusively. Heat is evenly distributed, temperature is much easier to control, low temperatures maintained and high temperatures used with minimum risk of burning. The downside is that these pots are expensive. On occasion, Costco sells them at a very good price, and, once in a while, they appear as loss leaders in the culinary sections of department stores. These pots last forever, and you might be able to pick them up for next to nothing at a Goodwill or Salvation Army store, or even a garage sale. Some recipes work best with the old-fashioned unfinished cast iron skillets. I got mine at a garage sale for 25 cents.

For cooking pasta, I highly recommend the pasta pot made by Bialetti of Italy. This non-stick pot has a lid that is perforated on one side so that you can drain out the water without dirtying a colander. The hands on the pot are made of a composition material and don't get hot, so no need for hotpads. They retail for around $50, but I bought mine on eBay for $20.

Skillets

The most often used pan is the skillet. You should have an 8" and a 12" skillet, both nonstick. Nonstick pans are not created equal. Get the heaviest pans you can find coated with the latest nonstick technology. Recently Calphalon introduced a new line called "Unison". I bought some and have been extremely pleased. That said, a new generation of ceramic skillets has recently appeared. Some of them are supposed to be very good, but I have not tested any of them and so can't give a recommendation.

Slicers for Vegetables

There are many kinds of equipment for slicing vegetables uniformly. Besides a knife wielded by skilled hands, the most common are a slicing blade mounted in a food processor, a mandoline and a so-called V-slicer. If you can afford it, a mandoline is nice, but my choice is a V-slicer. Made in Europe or Japan, they usually come with several blades, enabling you to cut things such as shoestring or ruffled potatoes, as well as thick or thin slices of almost anything including your fingers. If you do acquire one of these devices, be sure to use the included safety holder. You can get a V-slicer kit for around $30.

I don't like using a food processor to slice vegetables. It goes too fast for me, I don't have any control and sometimes it jams.

Spice Grinders

A spice grinder is a useful tool for many of my recipes. There are several choices: mortar and pestle, manual "twist" spice grinders, dedicated electric grinders and electric blade-type coffee grinders, which is my top choice. They don't clog, are easy to clean and take no more effort than the press of a button. Best of all, they are less than $20. Buy the least expensive one you can find.

Thermometers

Thermometers are important and inexpensive utensils. You'll need one to measure oil temperature for deep frying, one for meat, one for your oven, and one for candy if you are into that. Instant-read thermometers are great. A roast thermometer that you leave stuck into cooking meat that broadcasts the temperature to an external alarmed readout is nice, especially if you are inclined to watch football rather than paying attention to that roast in your oven. If you want the ultimate Father's Day gift, tell your kids to get you a Fluke "Foodpro Plus" thermometer. A professional instrument, it will measure the surface temperature of your food using a non-contact infrared system, read internal temperature using an instant-read probe, and monitor cooking times. This non-frugal item retails for $240, but can be found online at a discount.

Tongs

I find tongs to be an essential kitchen tool. Get the least expensive stainless steel tongs in two or three different lengths. These days you can find them with plastic tips. Don't bother with those – the plastic will chip off. You can also find them with silicone tips. These are good, but expensive, and I don't see the need for them.

Vacuum Food Preservers

A vacuum food preserver is a nice thing to have. You put your food in a plastic bag, and then use a machine to suck out the air and seal the bag. They can be pricey – up to several hundred dollars. However, you can find used ones on eBay for less than $50. Before buying one, check out the product reviews. Some of them don't work very well.

Whisks

There are two types of whisks. Most everyone is familiar with the balloon whisk, but there are also flat whisks that I find are often more versatile and easier to clean. In a pinch, a flat whisk can also serve as a spatula. Of course, the super-frugal use a fork!

Wine Accessories

Although this book doesn't address the subject of wine (maybe a later book?), I couldn't let this section go without saying something about wine accessories. There are three that I recommend:

First is an aerator designed to oxygenate red wine. The best-known brand is called *Vinturi* and it sells for around $20 online and at discount stores. It does the same thing as decanting, but it does it immediately. That is, it lets the wine "breathe" so that it tastes better.

One day, I hope all wine bottles will come with screw tops. Most wine bottles from Australia and New Zealand already do this, but Americans and Europeans are still in the 19th century, believing that tradition matters even if it is not the best. Thus, my second recommendation is an electric corkscrew. If you have ever struggled to remove a cork, those days are over if you use one of these puppies. There are several brands ranging in price from $18 to about $40. I have one of the $18 *Oster* models and am very happy with it. A primary benefit to me is that it works on those stubborn plastic corks that are damn near impossible to remove.

Third is a product called *Private Preserve*, a wine preserver. It is an aerosol canister containing a mixture of nitrogen and argon. You spray it into a partially empty wine bottle, and the gas, which is heavier than air, prevents oxygen from getting at the wine and spoiling it. It is also available from some paint stores under the name *Bloxygen*. It is used to prevent paint from skinning over in a partly empty can. The paint version is generally cheaper than the wine version. Of course, if you never have wine left over, this product is completely useless.

Woks

Unless you have a cooktop with a burner that is specifically designed for cooking with a wok, do not use one. A wok burner provides intense heat on both the bottom and sides. A wok positioned on a standard home cooktop will heat only on the bottom. Instead, use a large skillet. Its flat surface provides an area with maximum exposure to the cooktop.

Wooden Utensils

Throw away your metal and plastic spatulas and large spoons and replace them with wooden ones. I'll bet you didn't know that the word for wooden utensils is "treen." Treen will not scratch the nonstick or enameled surfaces of your skillets and pots, and are poor heat conductors. If you leave one in a pot, it won't burn your hand when you retrieve it. Also, there is something sensory about cooking with wood. I can't define it, but it is there. Get a couple of treen spoons and a couple of flat-bladed spatulas in 10" – 12" lengths. That said, treen is no good for flipping pancakes. For that purpose, get an old-fashioned ultra-thin stainless steel flipping spatula.

Servings, Yield, Prep Time, Cook Time and Measurements

Most recipes include the anticipated number of servings, or, in the case of items like cookies, the yield. Bear in mind that a dish I estimate will serve four might serve only two teen-age boys or as many as eight senior citizens. For this reason, I often cite the number of servings as a range; for example, 4-6 Servings.

I did not include the prep time because it can be misleading. If you can chop food like Martin Yan or Jacques Pepin, prep time may be very low. On the other hand, if you use the Columbus cutting method (first you discover it, then you land on it), prep time may be lengthy. With a few exceptions, all of the recipes in this book have relatively short prep times. If the prep time is lengthy, the recipe mentions it. The recipe will also tell you when some of the prep can be done ahead of time.

You can reduce work time by doing as many prep tasks as possible before you start cooking or even mixing. You may have noticed professional chefs on TV begin a presentation by having everything prepped ahead of time and placed in containers that just have to be dumped into bowl, pot or pan. You should emulate this process. It makes your life so much easier, you won't believe it. Further, it helps you not to forget anything, a particular issue for those of my advanced age.

Most recipes state the cooking times.

All of the measurements in this book are given in the American system; pounds, ounces, cups, Fahrenheit, etc.

What to Have in the Pantry and Where to Get It

If you plan to make more than a few of the recipes in this book, you should have the most common ingredients in your pantry. There is nothing more frustrating than having to run out at the last minute to buy something you know should have had on hand. This section contains my pantry recommendations and where to get them. I've also included recommendations for equipment shopping.

Perhaps I should mention that none of the purveyors that I mention have paid me anything for my recommendations. That is a shame, because, if they had offered to do that, I would have gladly accepted.

Equipment

There are two online stores that I recommend without reservation, *Amazon.com* and *eBay.com*. Both of these websites guarantee your purchases. These multibillion-dollar companies stand behind everything that you buy, so there is virtually no risk in doing business with them.

Although it costs $99/year, Amazon offers a program called *Amazon Prime* that I recommend. If you subscribe to Amazon Prime, most of the things you buy from Amazon.com will be shipped so that you will receive it free of charge within two days of placing your order. (Added benefits include free Kindle books Kindle and streaming movies.)

If you have a Costco in your neighborhood, it is often worth checking out. It generally carries good quality kitchen equipment, and sometimes it has terrific specials. In addition, if you buy something at Costco and don't like it, you can return it for a full refund even if you used it.

Of course, the truly frugal haunt garage sales and Craigslist.

Herbs, Seeds and Spices

My online spice purveyor is Penzeys (penzeys.com). The company also has several stores around the country, so check to see if there is one conveniently located near you. Penzeys carries more than 250 kinds of herbs, spices and mixtures. The quality is extremely high, and the prices are almost always lower than those you will encounter in your local supermarket. You can also buy in quantities that are very inexpensive on a per ounce basis. For example, a small .2 Oz jar of oregano is $2.29 and a 4-Oz bag – 20 times as much - is $7.19! The small jar equivalent in my local market is $3.99.

For peppercorns, I recommend Costco. They sell it in a large container that will probably last you for years. They also sell ground black pepper, but, of course, you always freshly grind your own, don't you? Here are my recommendations:

Dried Herbs

1. Basil
2. Bay leaves
3. Dill
4. Oregano
5. Rosemary, powdered, not leaf
6. Tarragon
7. Thyme.

Ground Spices

1. Cinnamon, preferably Vietnamese Cassia
2. Cayenne pepper or red pepper flakes
3. Cumin
4. Curry powder
5. Garlic powder
6. Hungarian paprika, mild and hot
7. Mustard (Coleman's is my favorite)
8. Nutmeg
9. Spanish smoked paprika (pimenton)
10. White pepper

Seeds

1. Caraway
2. Cloves
3. Cumin
4. Black peppercorns

Grains and Other Dried Foods

Try and find a market that has a wide selection of dried foods sold in bulk. *Whole Foods Markets* and *Sprouts* are chains that have good selections, but there are many other markets just as good or even better. I buy rice, Israeli couscous, regular couscous, nuts, coconut, dried mushrooms and other dried products in bulk and save a ton of money over the pre-packaged stuff. You can save even more on some products by buying in huge quantities; for example, you can't beat the price per pound of a 50-pound sack of rice from Costco. The dried foods that I suggest you have on hand are:

1. Basmati rice
2. Israeli pearl couscous
3. Flour, all-purpose
4. Porcini mushrooms
5. Short-grain rice
6. Thick pasta like penne, ziti or rigatoni
7. Thin pasta like spaghetti, linguini or fettuccini

Nuts

Nuts last practically forever in the freezer, and I recommend that you keep a supply on hand. Although they do not carry every type of nut, Costco has great prices on the ones that it does carry. Otherwise, look in a place that has a large variety of bulk foods. The nuts you should have in your freezer are:

1. Almonds, whole and slivered
2. Pine nuts
3. Walnuts

Vinegars and Oils

You should have a selection of vinegars. The ones I suggest are:

1. Balsamic vinegar, not aged
2. Balsamic vinegar, aged
3. Cider vinegar
4. Raspberry vinegar
5. Red wine vinegar
6. Seasoned rice wine vinegar
7. Sherry vinegar
8. White wine vinegar

You should have three types of oils:

1. EVOO
2. Canola or peanut oil
3. Sesame oil (unless you don't want to make Asian dishes)

I get balsamic vinegar and EVOO from Costco and the other vinegars and oils from my local market.

Tomato Products

There are three types of tomato products you should have:

1. Canned whole tomatoes
2. Tomato purée
3. Tomato paste

For most dishes, I recommend you use Italian San Marzano tomatoes with the initials D.O.P. marked clearly on the can. My favorite brand is LaValle. Other brands you may find locally are Cento, Italbrand, Strianese, Napoli, and Coluccio. In a market, these tomatoes typically sell for around $5 for a 28-Oz can, but you may find them for less online. Be careful if you shop online, because the cans are heavy and the shipping cost can be a killer. Some Costco's carry the Solania brand at around $2.50/ can.

Similarly, buy only imported Italian tomato purée. Good brands are LaValle and Pomi. The latter comes in a box, rather than in a can or jar, and is less expensive to ship, so you might find a good deal online.

Buy any brand of tomato paste you wish. I buy it from Costco in a 6-pack.

Booze and Wine

For cooking purposes, any dry red or white wine will serve you well. There is no need to spend a lot of money on wine that will be cooked. However, if the words "cooking wine" appear on the label, shun it. In short, any wine you can drink without making you grimace will do.

I recommend that you have a few bottles of booze and fortified wines on hand, including:

1. Brandy
2. Dry sherry
3. Sweet Marsala
4. Medium-sweet Port
5. Vodka

If you can find a good deal on a French brandy, get it. It doesn't have to be expensive Cognac or Armagnac, but the less-expensive French products from less well-known regions almost always taste better than domestic brandies.

It isn't advertised, but the only ingredients in non-flavored vodkas are alcohol and water and the taste difference is the water. Therefore, unless you are happy to pay for marketing, buy the least expensive vodka you can find.

Prepared Sauces

Not including such things as ketchup, mustard and mayonnaise that I assume everyone has, there are four types of prepared sauces that you should have on hand:

1. Demi-glace

2. Soy Sauce

3. Tabasco Sauce

4. Worcestershire Sauce

If you do a lot of Asian cooking, you could add Thai or Vietnamese Fish Sauce, Hoisin Sauce and Oyster Sauce to that list.

I recommend the *Demi-glace Gold* brand of demi-glace. Although it is carried in most markets, Amazon sells it at a 35% discount. The other sauces in the list can all be purchased in local markets.

Stocks

You can buy beef, chicken, duck, lamb, veal, and vegetable stocks. However, the only one that I have in my pantry is chicken stock, which will do for almost every dish you would need a stock for. I buy my chicken stock in a 6-pack of quart boxes from Costco. When buying stocks, be careful that they aren't loaded with salt as many of them are, especially the beef stocks. I like to buy stocks in cardboard containers that have been UHT (Ultra-High Temperature) treated. They will last a long time, even after opening.

Making one's own stocks is a hallmark of fine restaurants. It isn't difficult, but it is time-consuming. I say "have at it", if the mood strikes you.

Sweet Stuff

Here is what you need:

1. Granulated white sugar

2. Granulated brown sugar

3. Powdered (confectioner's) sugar

4. Honey

5. Maple Syrup

Please buy real maple syrup. It is more expensive than the phony "maple-flavored" stuff, but well worth it. I get my maple syrup at Costco. No matter where you get it, make sure it is classified "Grade A Dark Amber".

Specialty Foods

The first place I look online for specialty foods is Amazon. The company not only sells stuff directly, but it also represents thousands of smaller companies including specialty food purveyors. For example, I recently planned to make paella and needed chorizo sausage from Spain. Amazon offered nearly a dozen choices! Before they will represent a company, Amazon checks them out, so you can generally trust that you will get what you order. If you don't, then Amazon's guarantee kicks in, and you can you can get your money back without hassle.

If Amazon doesn't have it, then I usually turn to a search engine such as Google or Bing. If you do this and find some stores that appear to carry what you are looking for, don't order anything until you have checked out the website. There are different ways to do this, but the easiest is to install a browser add-on program called WOT, which stands for "Web of Trust." This free program checks out every web site you access by four variables: Trustworthiness, Vendor Reliability, Privacy and Child Safety. If the website is OK, it puts a little green circle next to the search engine listing. If not, the circle is either yellow for questionable or red for don't go near the place. Get this program from mywot.com.

If you are lucky (or unlucky depending on your outlook) enough to live in a big city, there may be many specialty food stores in your local area. I love to shop in these places because you have the opportunity to discuss your potential purchases with people who may know a lot about them. Many offer free tastes, obviously impossible online.

Produce

There are a few produce items that you should keep on hand, including:

1. Carrots
2. Celery
3. Garlic
4. Lemons
5. Onions
6. Parsley
7. Shallots

If you want to buy in large quantities, Costco offers great prices on everything except shallots and parsley, which it does not usually carry. Otherwise, all those items are in your local market. Because garlic lasts a long time stored in a cool dry place, you may want to consider buying it at Costco even though you have to get a large quantity. A whole bag of garlic heads at Costco costs the same as a couple of heads in a market.

Miscellaneous

There are a few other items you need to have in your larder. They are:

1. Bread Crumbs
2. Butter
3. Baking powder
4. Baking soda
5. Cornstarch
6. Salt
7. Vanilla extract

I buy vanilla extract at Costco - price is hard to beat, and the quality is excellent.

The butter should be unsalted and have low water content. My favorite brand is Plugra®. Made in Pennsylvania, it is available nationally and is reasonably priced when compared to the imported brands.

There are a few of types of bread crumbs to consider. *Panko* is a coarse ground product that is great for frying or toppings that are going to be browned under a broiler. Other packaged breadcrumb products are ground fine and are best for mixing with other ingredients. Both kinds come flavored with herbs or unflavored. Matzoh meal and potato flakes are good substitutes for breadcrumbs in some dishes. All are available in your local market. Of course, if you want to make your own bread crumbs by chopping up stale bread in a blender or food processor, be my guest.

As I said earlier, you should always cook with kosher salt. It has no adulterating ingredients such as iodine to spoil the taste of your food. I use Diamond® brand kosher salt that is available everywhere.

Abbreviations and Shorthand Notations

In alphabetical order, the abbreviations and shorthand notations used in this book are as follows:

Butter = Unsalted butter unless otherwise specified

EVOO = Extra Virgin Olive Oil

Cup = Cup or 8 fluid ounces

Flour = All-purpose flour unless otherwise specified

Lb = Pound

Oz = Ounce

Pinch = ⅛ Tsp

Pint = 16 fluid ounces

Quart = 32 Fluid ounces

Salt = Diamond® brand kosher salt unless otherwise specified

Sugar = White granulated sugar unless otherwise specified

Tbs = Tablespoon

Tsp = Teaspoon

Chapter 2: Appetizers, Tapas and First Courses

This chapter contains 14 recipes for first courses or small plates. All of them are quick and easy to prepare. Some of them can be made ahead of time and either served cold or heated just before serving. Most can be made at the last minute.

Asparagus and Artichokes with Lemon Aioli

6 Servings

About This Recipe

This is a simple vegetarian first course that I had at a tapas restaurant in Barcelona. You could serve it hot, but I think it works better served cold or at room temperature. You can of course make your own artichoke hearts, but it is a lot easier to use water-packed hearts that come in jars or frozen ones.

Ingredients

1	Tbs Pistachio nuts, chopped
1	Egg white
½	Cup Water
2	Tbs Breadcrumbs
2	Cloves Garlic, chopped
	Juice of ½ a lemon
	Salt and pepper to taste
¾	Cup EVOO
18	Spears Asparagus, boiled or steamed al dente
9	Artichoke hearts, cut in half lengthwise
	Cherry tomatoes for garnish (optional)
	Chopped chives for garnish (optional)

Procedure

Put the first 7 ingredients in a blender and pulse until smooth. While the blender is running, slowly add the EVOO. The aioli will emulsify. Put 3 artichoke heart halves on each serving plate and top with 3 spears of asparagus. Drizzle aioli on top and garnish with cherry tomatoes and chopped chives.

MY NOTES:

Asparagus Wrapped in Prosciutto

4 Servings

About This Recipe

I adapted this recipe from one created by Chef Charlie Palmer as a brunch dish for the Dry Creek Restaurant in California. His dish was more elaborate and included an egg toast. I've eliminated that and serve the asparagus as a first course.

I recommend that you try and find asparagus with thick stalks because you want the asparagus to retain some crunch and that is hard to do with skinny stalks. 3-4 thick stalks per diner is enough.

Ingredients

12-16	Stalks Fresh asparagus, trimmed
12-16	Slices Prosciutto
1	Shallot, minced
3	Tbs EVOO
1	Tbs Honey
1½	Tbs Sherry vinegar
½	Tbs Dijon mustard
	Salt and pepper to taste
	Shaved Parmagiano Reggiano for garnish

Procedure

Pre-heat oven to 350°. Line a baking sheet with foil and spray it with PAM. Wrap each asparagus stalk with a slice of prosciutto and place on the baking sheet. Bake for 10-12 minutes. Meanwhile place the remaining ingredients in a jar with a tight-fitting lid and shake well to combine.

Take the asparagus out of the oven and allow to cool. Serve at room temperature drizzled with the dressing. Top with shaved Parmagiano Reggiano if desired.

MY NOTES:

Baby Eggplants, North Beach Style

6-12 Servings

About This Recipe

Baby eggplant, 2" - 3" long, don't show up often in markets, but, when they do, be sure to buy them. I recently bought them for $1/dozen, so they are inexpensive. There are lots of things you can do with these babies. I haven't tried it, but I saw one recipe where the eggplants were stuffed with a mixture of goat cheese and chopped sun-dried tomatoes, then drizzled with EVOO and baked. Probably fabulous and hardly any work if you use a pastry bag to inject the stuffing.

This recipe, I am told, is an old North Beach (the original San Francisco Italian district) favorite. I like this recipe because it can be served as a finger-food, as a component of an antipasti, by itself as an appetizer course, as a vegetable side dish or even as a vegetarian main dish. Very versatile and easy to do.

Ingredients

12	Baby Eggplants
	EVOO
	Salt and pepper to taste
1	28-oz can of tomatoes, drained
½	Cup Grated Parmagiano or Pecorino cheese
1	Tbs Dried oregano
1	Cup Water

Procedure

Pre-heat oven to 425°. Cut the eggplants in half lengthwise. You can cut off the stems if you like, but if you intend to serve them as a finger-food, I suggest you leave them on. Make a few score cuts on the freshly cut surfaces. Place the eggplant halves in a baking dish and drizzle them with EVOO. Then sprinkle on salt and grind some pepper over all. Crush the tomatoes with your hands, then put about a teaspoon on each eggplant half. Mix the dried oregano and grated cheese together and sprinkle it over all.

Mix any leftover crushed tomatoes with the water and pour it into the bottom of the baking dish. Cover the dish with foil and bake for 20 minutes. Remove the foil, reduce the oven temperature to 375° and bake until the cheese has browned and the eggplants have started to collapse, about 10 minutes. Serve at once or keep for later. They can be served at room temperature.

You can use the leavings in the baking dish as the basis of a sauce.

MY NOTES:

Bay Scallop Appetizer

4 Servings

About This Recipe

When I was a kid growing up in New England, scallops were cheap, bought mostly by people who couldn't afford "better" seafood. I recall prices in the $.25/Lb range. Now scallops cost $20/Lb in most of the United States and they are almost always frozen. That said, small scallops - the ones we used to call "bay scallops" that came from the waters around Long Island and the Massachusetts Bay - are readily available (frozen of course) at around $7/Lb. They don't come from northern waters, but they taste good if cooked properly.

We used to take these little guys, put a dozen or so in a gratin dish, pour in a lot of melted butter and stick them under the broiler for a few minutes until the tops browned and the butter was bubbling. They were served in the dishes they were cooked in. You can do this if you like, but these days people are leery of that much butter, so this recipe is a compromise.

Scallops contain a ton of water. The secret to cooking them well is to dry them thoroughly and sear them at very high heat for a very short time. Do that and this recipe is foolproof. However, I prefer using clarified butter (See Miscellaneous Chapter) for the sautéing because it won't burn under the high heat needed for this recipe.

Ingredients

2	Tbs EVOO and
2	Tbs Butter or
4	Tbs Clarified butter
1	Lb Bay scallops
3	Cloves Garlic, sliced thin
2	Tbs Lemon juice
2	Tbs White wine
	Salt and pepper to taste
2	Tbs Cold butter
2	Tbs chopped parsley for garnish (optional)

Procedure

Heat the butter and EVOO in a large skillet until very hot. Dry the scallops with paper towels and sauté for 30 seconds without moving the scallops. Flip the scallops and cook an additional 30 seconds. You will probably have to do this in two batches.

Put all the scallops into the pan and add the garlic, wine, lemon juice and parsley. Cook just long enough to heat through. Off heat, enrich with the cold butter, stirring to incorporate. Serve at once. Garnish with chopped parsley if you wish.

MY NOTES:

Clams Casino

4 Servings

About This Recipe

Clams Casino is a classic 100-year old dish attributed to the Little Casino hotel/restaurant in Narragansett, Rhode Island. Since its invention, dozens of variations have been developed. I give you the basics from which you can create your own incredible appetizer.

The three filling ingredients that are a must for this dish are bell peppers, bacon (or pancetta) and garlic. Things you can add include wine, shallots, onions, Worcestershire sauce and Tabasco sauce. Commonly used herbs include oregano, basil and parsley. Grated Parmagiano, bread crumbs, paprika and olive oil or butter are other choices found in many recipes.

Ingredients

24	Fresh hardshell clams or cockles
4	Slices bacon or pancetta
	EVOO
¼	Cup Onions or shallots, minced
¼	Cup Minced green bell pepper
3	Cloves garlic, minced or pressed
1	Cup Fine dry breadcrumbs
	Salt and pepper to taste
1	Tsp Dried oregano
	Chopped parsley for garnish

Procedure

Pre-heat the oven to 350°. Wash the clams, place them on a baking sheet and bake until they open, about 2 minutes. Shuck the clams and discard half the shells. Chop the meat and reserve it. Increase the oven to 450°.

In a large skillet, sauté the bacon or pancetta until the fat is rendered and the bacon pieces are crisp. Reserve the pieces. Pour off some of the fat, leaving about 1 tablespoon. Add a little EVOO to the skillet and sauté the onions, pepper and garlic for about 5 minutes. Allow to cool.

Combine all the ingredients in a bowl and mix well. Spoon into clam shells and place the filled shells on a baking dish filled with rock salt or on top of foil "pillows." Bake 7 minutes. Garnish with chopped parsley and serve immediately with lemon wedges on the side and a bottle of Tabasco sauce for those who like a bit of heat.

MY NOTES:

Cucumber, Fennel and Gravlax

8 Servings

About This Recipe

Sometimes simplest equates to best. If you are looking for a light, cold starter course, stop right here. The dish consists of sliced cucumbers and fennel with a light cream dressing accompanied by a couple of slices of gravlax (See Volume I) or smoked salmon. Couldn't be easier.

This dish came to me by way of the UK, although the gravlax and dill suggest Scandinavia. The English use double (clotted) cream, which is hard to find in America, and, if it can be found, is likely to be very expensive. I find that ordinary supermarket sour cream is almost as good or you can make the mock clotted cream described in the Miscellaneous Chapter.

Ingredients

½	English cucumber or whole seeded American cucumber, thinly sliced
1	Small fennel bulb, cored and thinly sliced
2	Tbs Sour cream, crème fraiche or clotted cream
2	Tbs White wine vinegar or lemon juice
1	Tbs Dijon mustard
	Salt and white pepper to taste
2	Tsp Chopped fresh dill
8	Slices Gravlax or smoked salmon
	Dill sprigs for garnish

Procedure

Mix the cucumber and fennel slices together. Make a dressing by combining the sour cream, vinegar or lemon juice, mustard, chopped dill, salt and white pepper. Plate the cucumber and fennel, spoon a dollop of the dressing on top and garnish with dill sprigs. Put a slice of gravlax or smoked salmon on the plate, arranged attractively.

MY NOTES:

Filipino Chicken Wings

6-12 Servings

About This Recipe

I adapted this recipe from Mario Batali. He calls it adobo, but I think my Filipino sister-in-law would probably object to that moniker. To resolve this conundrum, I looked it up and learned that Filipino adobo is any sauce made with vinegar and seasonings, and there are a thousand variations on that theme

Mario uses palm sugar vinegar and coconut balsamic vinegar. These may not be easy to find in your local market, but my Filipino neighbor told me I could use rice vinegar, red or white wine vinegar or cider vinegar with good results.

In any event, this is a great dish for a Superbowl party, but you need to serve it with plenty of napkins.

Ingredients

3   Lbs Chicken wings
4   Cups Canola or peanut oil

ADOBO SAUCE

3   Tbs Vinegar (see description)
2   Tbs Fish sauce
2   Tbs Soy sauce
2   Serrano chilis, chopped
3   Tbs Brown sugar
¼   Cup Chopped cilantro
1   Bunch Scallions, chopped

Procedure

Heat the oil in a deep pot or deep fat fryer to 365°. Fry the wings in several batches until golden.

Mix together all the rest of the ingredients except the scallions. Place the wings in a serving dish and pour over the sauce. Sprinkle with chopped scallions.

MY NOTES:

Garlic Calamari Rings

4-6 Servings

About This Recipe

This is an incredibly simple dish to prepare. Serve it on small plates with lemon wedges or put it all in an appropriate serving dish and serve it as an hors d'oeuvres. In that case, squeeze lemon juice over the dish and accompany it with toothpicks for stabbing. It also works as a tapas along with a glass of very dry sherry.

Ingredients

1	Tbs EVOO
2	Tbs Butter
1	Tbs Garlic, pressed or minced
1	Lb Calamari rings
1	Tsp Brandy
	Salt and pepper to taste
1	Tsp Parsley, chopped
	Lemon wedges

Procedure

Heat the butter and EVOO in a skillet. Add the garlic and cook 30 seconds until fragrant. Add the calamari and cook 1-2 minutes until rings are opaque. Season with salt and pepper and add the chopped parsley. Serve at once with lemon wedges on the side.

MY NOTES:

Grilled Shishito or Padron

About This Recipe

I've been to Japan nearly 40 times, and became well-acquainted with its cuisine. Shishito (accent on the first syllable) is a small pepper with a unique flavor. It is normally not hot, but once in a while you might encounter one that is. A related pepper is the padron, which comes from Spain. In truth, Columbus brought the padron to Iberia from the New World, and many years later, the Portuguese brought the padron to Japan, where it was hybridized into a different shape.

Shishito are used as everything from a garnish to a street food in Japan, whereas padron are most commonly encountered in tapas. You will find the shishito in Asian markets, particularly those that cater to Japanese or Korean ethnicities. You may find padron in Latin markets or stores catering to Spanish cuisine. Trust me, they are worth seeking out.

The European way of preparing padron is to grill or pan-fry them in EVOO until slightly charred, then serve them sprinkled with a fancy salt and drizzled with lemon juice.

In Japan, shishito are often skewered and grilled, turning and brushing every 30 seconds with a mixture of soy sauce and sake until slightly charred and blistered. They are also fried tempura-style, or served with a sprinkling of togarashi, a mixture of several spices that you can buy in an Asian market or order online.

MY NOTES:

Pintxos with Peppers, Anchovies and Garlic

About This Recipe

In the Basque country of Iberia, tapas are very popular. Many of them are called "Pintxos" (pronounced pinchös) which refers to the toothpicks that are used to hold the tapas together. Pintxos are almost always assembled on top of slices of bread. I find that a crusty artisan sourdough baguette cut on the bias into oval-shaped slices is perfect for this application.

This recipe is so simple, it is almost embarrassing. Take a slice of bread, put a piece of oil-packed roasted pepper on it, shiny side up, lay an oil-packed anchovy on top of the pepper and a slice of garlic on top of the anchovy. Secure it all with a toothpick and you are done in less than 30 seconds!

You are eating raw garlic and anchovies, which may be off-putting, especially on a first date, so this recipe might be more appropriate for a stag or hen party.

MY NOTES:

Roasted Peppers Stuffed with Frying Cheese

8 Servings

About This Recipe

There is a group of cheeses that can be subjected to high heat without melting, so-called frying cheeses. Most of them come from the eastern Mediterranean from countries such as Greece, Lebanon and Turkey. Queso Blanco from Latin America also fits the description. The Greek cheeses have names such as Halloumi, Yanni, Kasseri, Kefalotiri and Kefolograviera. Kasseri and Queso Blanco are easy to find in America, but you will probably have to get the others from a specialty purveyor.

This easy recipe is a great start to a Mediterranean-style meal. Cooking takes a while, but the prep time is only 10 minutes, and you can make the dish ahead of time. Essentially, you roast some bell peppers, fill them with a mixture of couscous, frying cheese, mushrooms and parsley, and then bake them again.

I got the idea for this dish from the Philadelphia restaurant in East Jerusalem where it was served as one of many Mezze dishes. (Mezze is a collection of small plate dishes, similar to an Italian antipasti.) My recipe isn't exactly the same, but close enough I think. The waiter told me that the cheese was Halloumi, which comes from the Island of Crete.

Ingredients

4	Large Red bell peppers
2	Tbs EVOO
	Salt and pepper to taste
1	12-oz Jar of small marinated mushrooms, drained
2	Oz couscous
½	Cup Hot vegetable or chicken stock
10	Oz Frying cheese, cut into small cubes
1	Tbs Chopped parsley
2	Cloves Garlic, minced

Procedure

Pre-heat the oven to 400°. Cut the peppers in half through the stem and remove the seeds and membranes. Season the peppers with salt and pepper and drizzle with EVOO. Bake for 20 minutes.

Put the couscous in a bowl and pour over the hot stock. Leave for 5 minutes to absorb the liquid, then add the cheese, mushrooms and parsley. Season with a bit more salt and pepper, mix well and spoon into the pepper halves. Return to the oven and bake 15 minutes, stuffing side up.

MY NOTES:

Shrimp with Sherry Sauce

4 Servings

About This Recipe

This is another tapas recipe that came from the "Tapa Tapa" restaurant in Barcelona. It must have had 300 tapas on the menu when I was there about 20 years ago and is one of the largest restaurants I've ever seen. I thought the food was terrific, but the Trip Advisor website gives it lousy marks today, so maybe it has gone downhill since I was there. The menu that is published online is a mere shadow of the extensive menu that used to be. Nevertheless, I had this tapas there and liked it enough to get the recipe. The dish is no longer on the menu, so don't bother to look it up on their website. Like most tapas recipes, it cooks in minutes.

Ingredients

1	Lb Medium shrimp
1	Tbs EVOO
1	Tbs Onion, chopped fine Mushrooms, whole or cut depending on size
1	Clove Garlic, minced
3	Tbs Dry sherry like Fino or Amontillado
1	Tbs Tomato sauce
1	Tbs Heavy cream
¼	Tsp Dried thyme
1	Salt and pepper to taste
	Chopped parsley for garnish

Procedure

In a large skillet, sauté the onion and garlic in the EVOO for 2-3 minutes. Add the shrimp and sauté 30 seconds on each side. Add the remaining ingredients, stir to combine and cook just long enough to heat everything through. Serve at once garnished with chopped parsley.

MY NOTES:

Spanish Tortilla

6 Servings

About This Recipe

Let me say at the outset, that this recipe has exactly zero in common with a Mexican tortilla. It is a potato and onion pie that uses the same ingredients as potato kugel! It takes a bit of time to prepare, but is easy to do. It can be made well ahead of time and served room temperature. In Spain, almost every tapas bars has these tortillas on the counter.

Although the tortilla is often served plain, you can add garlic, chopped herbs or even vegetables. You could add chilis or red pepper flakes to the mix to give the dish some heat.

Ingredients

1	Lb Russet potatoes, peeled and thinly sliced
1	Medium onion, peeled and thinly sliced
7	Tbs EVOO
	Salt and pepper to taste
4	Eggs
1	Tbs Milk or water
	Coarse ground black pepper (optional)
	Chopped garlic (optional)
	Chopped herbs (optional)

Procedure

Keep the potato slices in water until you are ready to cook with them so that they do not turn brown. Just before cooking, dry the slices with paper towels.

Heat 6 Tbs EVOO in a medium skillet or pot. Add a bit of salt and pepper and cook the onions and potatoes until the potatoes are soft, about 15 minutes. Drain the potatoes and onions in a colander and discard the oil. Allow to cool.

Beat the eggs and milk or water with a pinch of salt and pepper. Add the potatoes and onions to the eggs. Stir well and allow to sit for a minute or two.

Heat 1 Tbs EVOO in an 8" skillet, preferably non-stick. Add the potato-egg mixture, pressing it down in the skillet. Cook 1 - 2 minutes on medium heat, then turn down the heat to low and cook 10 - 20 minutes until the eggs are firmly set. The amount of time will depend on the initial temperature of the potato-egg mixture.

Put a plate over the pan and flip it so that the tortilla is now resting on the plate upside down. Slide the tortilla back into the pan and cook for a couple of minutes to brown the top (which is now down in the pan). Do your plate-flipping trick once again. Allow to cool to room temperature, slice into wedges and serve.

MY NOTES:

Tempura

About This Recipe

The secret to tempura is to minimize the development of gluten in the batter. Gluten makes a batter bread-like causing it to absorb some of the oil in which it is cooked. By keeping the effect of gluten to a minimum, well-made tempura has a lacy coating that is virtually oil free. To do that, don't over-mix the batter and keep it as cold as possible. Another secret is to eat it right out of the fryer. The longer you wait from cooking to eating, the more the coating deteriorates. That said, you will find that that the process for making great tempura in your home kitchen is both fast and easy.

In Japan there are "tempura-ya" restaurants that serve nothing but tempura. Patrons sit at a bar behind which stands the tempura chef with containers of hot oil, raw foods, batter and dredging flour. You order the vegetables or seafood that you want by pointing. The chef immediately dredges it in flour, dips it in the batter, then into the fryer. Two minutes later, he serves you the pieces you ordered which you eat as soon it has cooled enough to devour.

The tempura is usually accompanied by "ponzu" dipping sauce into which you mix grated ginger and/or daikon (Japanese radish) to the degree you desire. Ponzu sauce can be purchased in any market that carries Asian food. You can use regular radishes if you can't find daikon, but look for mild ones.

If you follow this recipe, you will make tempura that will compete with the best Japanese restaurants in Tokyo.

Ingredients

	Canola or peanut oil for frying
1½	Cups Cake flour
1½	Cups Rice flour
2	Eggs
1½	Cups Very cold seltzer or club soda
½	Cup Vodka (optional)
	Seafood including shrimp, calamari, chunks of fish, etc.
	Veggies including sweet potatoes, stringbeans onion rings, zucchini, broccoli,
	Mushrooms, peppers, etc.

Procedure

In a heavy pot, heat 1-2" of oil to a temperature of 375° using a deep-fry thermometer. If you like the flavor of sesame oil, add 1/4 cup of it to the oil. Put the seltzer and vodka (if using) in the freezer.

Mix together the cake and rice flours. Take 1/3 of the mixture and spread it on a plate for dredging.

To make the batter, mix together the eggs, seltzer and vodka. If you don't use the vodka, increase the amount of seltzer to 2 cups. Take half that mixture and combine it with half the

(Recipe continues on next page)

flour mixture in a separate glass bowl. Stir to combine, but - and this is important - do not mix more than a few seconds. Otherwise the gluten will develop. The mix should be lumpy. Place that bowl in a larger bowl that is lined with ice.

Reserve the rest of the flour mixture and the egg mixture for the next batch of batter. Put the egg mixture in the fridge to keep it cold.

Set out the plate of dredging flour and the batter in its ice bath next to your hot oil.

Using tongs or chopsticks, dredge a piece of seafood or veggie in the flour mix, then dip it in the batter, making sure that it is coated all over. Immediately place it in the hot oil and cook about 2 minutes. While the food is frying, dip your fingers in the batter and drizzle a little on top of the frying food. This process is called "hana o sakaseru". It will give you those lacy crispy tendrils that you find on well-made tempura. When you take the cooked food out of the oil, let it drain for a minute on paper towels.

When you run out of batter, make a new batch by mixing up the remainder of the egg and flour mixtures.

I like to have two pots of oil going. One for seafood and one for veggies. If you have only one pot, cook the veggies first and the seafood afterward, so that the seafood flavor does not taint the veggies.

You may have noticed that the shrimp tempura you get in restaurants is often straight rather than curved. Here is how to get that effect: Peel and devein the shrimp. On the curved side, make a small slit on the inner curve in the middle using a sharp knife, being careful not to cut too deep. Then pull the shrimp, gently, in effect stretching it until it is flat.

You can keep the tempura warm in a 200° oven for a short while, but it won't be as good as it is right out of the pot.

Grate some daikon and ginger. Serve them in little piles next to individual dipping cups of ponzu sauce, allowing your guests to mix their own dip as they wish.

MY NOTES:

Chapter 3: Breakfast and Brunch

In Volume I, I presented only 5 recipes in this Chapter and felt that I short-changed my readers. Here are 10 more recipes, all of them easy to prepare and, in my not-so-humble opinion, delicious.

All-in-one Breakfast

4 Servings

About This Recipe

A typical American breakfast might include scrambled eggs, home fries and bacon with each ingredient cooked separately. This twist combines all three ingredients. Doesn't taste all that much different, but makes for an interesting conversation piece.

The bacon and potatoes can be prepared ahead of time. The final cooking is done in the oven, so you don't have to stand over the stove to make scrambled eggs at the last minute.

Ingredients

8	Slices Thick-cut bacon, coarsely chopped
2	Lbs boiling potatoes, cut into bite-size chunks
1	Onion, coarsely chopped (optional)
8	Eggs
½	Cup Water, milk or half-and-half
	Salt and pepper to taste
2	Tbs Butter
2	Tbs Chopped chives

Procedure

Pre-heat oven to 350°. In a 12" skillet, cook the bacon until the fat is rendered and the bacon pieces are crisp. Reserve the bacon in a bowl. Add the onions and potatoes to the skillet and cook, stirring frequently until the potatoes can be easily pierced by a fork. Add the potatoes and onions to the bacon and discard the remaining bacon fat.

In a separate bowl, beat the eggs with the water or milk, salt and pepper. Add the butter to the skillet and when it is melted and the pan thoroughly coated, add the egg mixture. Cook about 30 seconds until the bottom of the eggs is just set. Add the potatoes and bacon mixture in an even layer on top of the eggs. Bake 15 minutes, cut into quarters and serve.

MY NOTES:

Baked Apple Puff

4 Servings

About This recipe

This is basically a pancake that is puffed up with meringue and coated with sliced apples. Prep time is about 10 minutes and cooking time no more than 15 minutes. An excellent brunch dish.

You have lots of opportunity to vary the flavor profile. You could use a different type of juice or a different type of fruit - peaches or pears come to mind. You could add a bit of ground cloves and/or nutmeg. If you do have evaporated milk, use it. It has a lower water and fat content than either cream or half-and-half.

Ingredients

½   Cup Heavy cream, half-and-half or evaporated milk

⅓   Cup Flour

½   Tsp Baking powder

1   Pinch Salt

2   Tbs Sugar

3   Eggs, separated

2   Tbs Orange juice

½   Tsp Ground Cinnamon

1   Tbs Butter

1   Cooking apple, peeled, cored, quartered and thinly sliced

1   Tbs Cinnamon sugar

Procedure

Pre-heat oven to 375°. Place a 10" - 12" ovenproof skillet in the oven to get hot.

Mix together the milk, flour, baking powder, salt, 1 Tbs sugar, egg yolks, orange juice and cinnamon. You can do this in a blender if you wish.

Beat the egg whites with 1 Tbs sugar until stiff peaks form. Add the milk mixture and fold it into the egg whites.

Drop the butter into the hot pan and smear it around to coat. Pour in the batter. Place the apple slices all around the batter, slightly overlapping the slices to make a pleasing pattern. Sprinkle with cinnamon-sugar and bake 10-15 minutes until set and golden. Serve immediately.

MY NOTES:

Blintz Pie with Blueberry Sauce

8 Servings

About This Recipe

I stole this recipe from Ina Garten (known on TV as the "Barefoot Contessa"). I did not believe it would work, but it does, and it makes for a terrific brunch main course dish. I use the word "pie" to indicate that it is not the usual blintz recipe.

This is basically a giant blintz, made in a baking dish. Pour some crepe batter in the dish and bake it. Top with a cheese filling and cover with the remaining crepe batter. Bake once again and it is done. Amazing.

I included Ina's very simple blueberry sauce accompaniment. You can use any kind of fruit sauce you like, or, if you want to be more traditional, serve the dish with sour cream and whole berries.

Ingredients

CREPE BATTER

1¼	Cups Milk
2	Tbs Sour cream
4	Tbs Melted butter
1	Tsp Vanilla extract
1⅓	Cups flour
2	Tbs Sugar
1	Tbs Baking powder

FILLING

24	Oz Ricotta cheese
8	Oz Mascarpone
⅓	Cup Sugar
1	Tsp Salt
	Juice of a lemon
½	Tsp Vanilla extract

SAUCE

¾	Cup Orange juice
⅔	Cup Sugar
2	Quarts Blueberries
	Grated zest of half a lemon
	Juice of half a lemon

(Recipe continues on next page)

Procedure

Pre-heat oven to 350°. Put all the ingredients for the crepe batter in the food processor and process until well combined. Pour the batter into a 4-cup measuring cup. Pour half the batter into a 9 x 13 baking dish and bake for 10 minutes.

Mix all the filling ingredients together until well combined. Remove the crepe from the oven and allow to cool slightly. Add the filling mix, smoothing it with a spatula to cover the crepe evenly. Pour the remaining batter on top of the filling, being careful to cover the filling evenly. Put the pan in the oven and bake 35 - 40 minutes.

Allow the blintz to rest for 10 minutes. Cut into 8 squares and serve.

To make the sauce, put the orange juice sugar and cornstarch in a sauce pan and cook until the mix is transparent and thickened, about 5 minutes. Add the berries, stir well and cook until a few berries pop, about 5 minutes. Transfer to a serving boat or pitcher. Cut the pie into 8 pieces and serve with the sauce on the side.

MY NOTES:

Cardamom French Toast

2 Servings

About This Recipe

After saffron, cardamom is the world's most expensive spice. Like saffron, you don't need much of it to make an impact. This French toast recipe is flavored with cardamom which imparts a unique flavor profile to an otherwise ordinary dish. The batter also includes orange zest, sugar and vanilla to make it even more interesting. This recipe comes from Aida Mollenkamp from her Cooking Channel TV show.

Aida prefers to use brioche for the bread. While that is fine, I like stale challah better.

You could use any kind of suitable topping you like (or none at all), but give the macerated berry recipe in the Miscellaneous chapter a try.

Ingredients

1	Cup Milk
4	Eggs
1	Tsp Vanilla extract
1	Tbs Light brown sugar
	Grated zest of an orange
1	Tsp Ground cardamom
1	Tsp Salt
8	Slices of your favorite French toast bread, brioche or challah
	Butter for frying

Procedure

In a large baking dish, whisk together all the ingredients except the bread and butter. Soak the bread in the mixture about 2 minutes per side. Fry on a hot buttered griddle or skillet about 2 minutes per side. Serve at once.

MY NOTES:

German Pancakes

2 Servings

About This Recipe

A German pancake, also known as a Dutch pancake, is sort of a hybrid between a crêpe and a popover. One variation is provided in Volume I where the pancake is coated with apples. This recipe is more basic. It is consists of eggs, milk, flour and butter with optional flavorings or sweeteners added. It can be served plain or with a topping. My favorite topping is fresh lemon juice and powdered sugar.

Instead of frying it like a regular pancake or crêpe, A German pancake is baked. It takes 5 minutes to make the batter and 12-20 minutes to bake, depending on your oven.

The size of the pancake depends on the dish or pan you use. You can make a big one in a large Pyrex baking dish and then cut it up into serving size pieces. Or you can make individual ones in gratin dishes. This recipe will serve 2 hungry people.

Ingredients

BASIC PANCAKE

3	Eggs
½	Cup Milk or half-and-half
½	Cup Flour
¼	Tsp Salt
2	Tbs Melted butter

TOPPING SUGGESTIONS

Cinnamon sugar

Lemon juice (serve lemon wedges on the side)

Powdered Sugar

Fresh fruit

Fruit compotes

Maple syrup or honey

Procedure

Pre-heat the oven to 400° - 425°. Butter the bottoms of the pan(s) or dishes that you will be using and place in the oven while it is heating. Using a hand or stationary electric mixer, beat together the batter ingredients one at a time, starting with the eggs. Add flavoring agents if using. Pour the batter into the hot pan(s) and bake 12 - 20 minutes until the pancakes are puffed up and golden. Remove from the oven. The pancake will soon deflate. Lay on your choice of topping and serve at once.

MY NOTES:

Matzoh Brie

2 Servings

About This Recipe

I debated with myself about including this recipe because it is more of a peasant food than a gourmet dish, but taste won out. Basically, matzoh brie (pronounced "bry") consists of pieces of matzoh crackers mixed into scrambled eggs. It is a distinctly Jewish dish hailing from Eastern Europe. It is a great breakfast dish, especially when accompanied by ham, sausage or bacon - I know, that ain't kosher, but it tastes sooooo good!

Just as some people like their scrambled eggs very dry and some like them creamy, you have the same option with this dish. Personally, I prefer the eggs creamy and the matzoh crunchy, but you can adjust the recipe to meet your own requirements. Some people like to cook it long enough so that a crust forms. Whichever way you go, this is an inexpensive, easy-to-prepare breakfast dish that will appeal to anyone who likes eggs. This recipe serves 2 people, and can easily be expanded to serve a crowd.

A word about matzoh. Several kinds are available. The most commonly sold in the US come in a box containing about a dozen pieces that measure about 6" x 6". I use one piece per egg. It comes in several varieties including plain unsalted, plain salted, egg, and seasoned. I prefer to use the plain salted matzoh, but feel free to try any or all of them. It doesn't matter if the matzoh is marked "Kosher for Passover" or not. The taste is the same.

Some people like to flavor matzoh brie. Cinnamon is common, but you can try other spices such as ground cloves, nutmeg, black or white pepper, etc. I like it plain, but the dish is often served with sour cream and/or berry jam as toppings.

Ingredients

4	Eggs
½	Cup milk
	Salt to taste
	Cinnamon or other spices to taste (optional)
4	6" x 6" Pieces of matzoh
2	Tbs Butter (or more if you like)
	Sour cream and/or jam for topping (optional)

Procedure

Whisk the eggs, milk, salt and spices together in a large bowl until frothy. Add the matzoh, broken into small pieces, and stir to coat. Allow the matzoh to soak in the egg mixture for about 5 minutes more or less depending on how crunchy you want the finished dish to be.

Melt the butter in a large skillet on medium heat. When the pan is hot, dump in the matzoh/egg mixture and fry it, stirring constantly until cooked to the desired doneness. Serve at once with sour cream and jam on the side if you wish.

Omelet Soufflé

2 Servings

About This Recipe

If you have not seen Julia Child or Jacques Pepin make omelets, you have truly missed a treat. They do them in less than a minute in the classic French way, and they are perfect every time. If you wish make about 1000 of them, you may achieve that level of proficiency, but, if you don't want to do that, make this foolproof recipe and you will be amazed at how good it is. The secrets are 1) to whip and add the egg whites as you would in a soufflé; and 2) to bake it in the oven like a pizza pie which makes it a no-brainer to stuff and flip. Admittedly, this recipe takes longer than the less than a minute that Julia would spend, but I believe you will think it is worth it.

There are two steps to the recipe. The first is to make the filling which can be anything you want. Chopped veggies such as onions, shallots, garlic, peppers, tomatoes, mushrooms, etc. all work. Chopped ham, precooked bacon or sausage are great if you want meat in your filling. The only caveat is not to use anything that has a high water content. Sauté onions, shallots or mushrooms first to cook all the water out of them. Seed and drain tomatoes. You get the idea. Adding a dash of vinegar to your filling mix is something you should try. Balsamic vinegar or any wine vinegar or flavored vinegar are all reasonable choices.

Chopped fresh herbs are always great additions to omelets. My favorites are chives, tarragon, basil and Italian parsley, but you can use whatever you like. Cheese is a favored filling ingredient. Grated Reggiano is universal, but almost any cheese will do nicely including crumbled blue cheese or feta.

You will need a quality nonstick, ovenproof skillet. If the omelet sticks to the pan, it will be visually ruined although it will taste the same as a visually perfect dish. The diameter of the pan will determine how thick the omelet is. For a 2-egg omelet, I like an 8" pan. For 4 eggs, either a 10" or 12" will work.

Ingredients

    Filling ingredients (See above)

4	Eggs, separated
1	Tbs Melted butter
¼	Tsp Salt
¼	Tsp Cream of tartar
1	Tbs butter

Procedure

Pre-heat the oven to 375°.

Get your filling ingredients ready. If some are to be cooked, do it now. Shred or grate cheese if using, chop veggies and/or meat, etc. Bacon needs to be pre-cooked.

(Recipe continues on next page)

Separate the eggs. In one bowl, beat the whites with a pinch of cream of tartar to the stiff peak stage. In another bowl, beat the egg yolks together with a bit of salt and a tablespoon of melted butter. Fold the yolk mixture into the egg whites until the mix is a uniform color.

Melt a tablespoon of butter in the skillet over medium heat. Pour in the egg mixture and spread it out with a spatula until the skillet is covered evenly. Then turn off the heat. Sprinkle the top with your filling ingredients as you would if you were making pizza. Put the pan in the oven for 5 minutes. The top should be set but still tender.

Take the skillet out of the oven, run a spatula around the edges and slide the omelet onto a cutting board or other flat surface. Wait 30 seconds (this wait period is important) and, using two spatulas, fold the omelet in half. Cut into the size pieces that you want and serve at once.

MY NOTES:

Omelet Stuffed Bread

1 Serving

About This Recipe

I got the idea for this dish from a Food Network show in which Giada Delaurentiis made something similar with an Italian slant. If you like the idea of eating olive oil, lemon and parmagiano for breakfast, by all means look up Giada's recipe. However, with all due respect to the Italian culinary tradition, nobody makes better breakfasts than Americans.

To make this dish, you need a great artisan loaf of bread or large rolls. Personally, I like sourdough, but you can use anything you like. I recommend that you use those small round loaves that some restaurants use for serving chowder. In any case, you cut off the top of the bread, scoop out the insides, fill it with your favorite omelet mix, and bake it. It's even better if you chop up the bread top and the removed guts and stir into the mix. My personal favorite is a Denver omelet, the recipe I've presented here, but feel free to use whatever flavor ingredients that you like.

I would give serious consideration to serving this dish at brunch along with broiled tomatoes and a tequila sunrise or two.

Ingredients

1	Sourdough "bowl" loaf
	Melted butter
2	Eggs
¼	Cup Milk or water
	Salt and pepper to taste
2	Oz Chopped ham
½	Bell pepper, red or green, chopped
¼	Small onion, chopped
¼	Cup Shredded cheddar cheese

Procedure

Pre-heat the oven to 350°. Slice off the top of the bread and dig out the insides with your hands. Coarsely chop up the top and insides. Brush the interior of the bread with melted butter and put in the oven to toast for 10 minutes.

Whisk together all the omelet ingredients and stir in the chopped pieces of bread. Bake in the oven for 45 minutes or until eggs are set and the top is lightly browned. Drizzle melted butter over all and serve at once.

MY NOTES:

Schnecken

Yields 12 Schnecken

About This Recipe

A long time ago, some enterprising Eastern Europeans created a breakfast bun coated with caramel and filled with nuts, cinnamon and raisins. The buns were rolled in a coil shape, and so the inventors named them "schnecken", the German word for snails. Today the original (immortalized in the *Settlement Cookbook*) has evolved into pastries variously called sticky buns, pecan rolls, cinnamon rolls or morning buns.

Recently, I was in a Starbucks that had nice-looking schnecken in its pastry case. The price for one was $3.49. Highway robbery in my opinion ($4 for a cup of coffee is too). I got to thinking that there must be an easy way to make these rolls that tasted great and cost far less. I researched the subject and found a recipe that relied on pre-made puff pastry dough that completely eliminates the need to make a yeast dough from scratch - no rising, punching, kneading. Besides, I am a sucker for puff pastry.

This recipe is almost identical to the one I uncovered in my research, but there are variations you might like to try. You could use walnuts instead of pecans. You could use another dried fruit (chopped small) instead of raisins - I think dates would be a good choice. You could add a bit of maple syrup or honey to the sugar/butter mixture or use an exotic sugar like demerara or muscovado. Let me know if you find a combination that you think works particularly well. In any event, the cost of these schnecken will be about $1 each, less than 30% what Starbucks charges.

You can freeze the schnecken and bake them as needed. Just add 5 - 10 minutes to the baking time if frozen to start with.

Ingredients

2	Sheets of puff pastry
6	Oz Butter at room temperature
⅓	Cup Light brown sugar
½	Cup Toasted pecans, coarsely chopped
2	Tbs Melted butter
⅔	Cup Light brown sugar
1	Tsp Ground cinnamon
1	Cup Raisins (optional)

Procedure

Defrost puff pastry sheets overnight in the refrigerator. Pre-heat oven to 400°.

Cream together the brown sugar and butter using a hand or stationary electric mixer. Grease a 12-cup muffin tin (preferably non-stick) and drop a Tbs of the sugar butter mixture in each cup. Distribute the chopped pecans evenly in each cup.

(Recipe continues on next page)

Flour a flat surface large enough to hold a full sheet of the puff pastry. Unfold the pastry and press it out flat. Brush the pastry on one side with the melted butter leaving a 1" unbuttered border all the way around the sheet.

Make the filling by combining the 2/3 cup sugar with the cinnamon and raisins. Spread half the filling over the buttered surface of the puff pastry sheet. Roll the sheet tightly like a jelly roll. Slice 1/2" from each end of the roll and discard. Cut the roll into six equal size pieces and put each piece in a muffin cup so that the swirl can be seen. Repeat this process with the second pastry sheet.

Bake 30 minutes. On a flat surface, set out a piece of parchment paper slightly larger than the muffin pan. When the baking is done (should be dark brown on the top and firm to the touch), take the muffin tin out of the oven and allow to cool for 5 minutes. Put the parchment paper on top of the muffin pan and invert it. The schnecken should settle on the paper where they can finish cooling. If a schnecken does not fall out, ease it out gently with a spoon.

MY NOTES:

Shirred Eggs with Mushrooms, Ham and Cheese

4 Servings

About This Recipe

Shirred (baked) eggs were once a common menu item at American restaurants. I think they went out of favor because they take more effort than the usual fried or scrambled preparations. In this recipe, I make them with ham (or Canadian bacon), cheese (Parmagiano or Emmenthaler are good choices) and mushrooms.

To make this dish, you will need to use rectangular or oval gratin dishes just large enough to hold 2 eggs side by side. I like to make this dish under the broiler, but you have to keep your eye on it to ensure that it doesn't burn or overcook. If you don't want to do that, bake in a pre-heated 375° oven for 10-15 minutes.

Ingredients

1	Tbs Butter
½	Lb Mushrooms, coarsely chopped
	Salt to taste
2	Cloves Garlic, Minced or pressed
2	Tbs Marsala or Madeira
½	Cup Heavy cream
4	Slices Ham or Canadian bacon
8	Eggs
2	Tbs Mixed chopped herbs such as parsley, thyme, tarragon or rosemary
2	Tbs Grated cheese such as Parmagiano Reggiano or Emmenthaler
	Salt and pepper to taste
4	Tbs Heavy cream
4	Tbs Butter

Procedure

Sauté the mushrooms in 1 Tbs butter until they have given up their water, about 3-5 minutes. Add a bit of salt and the garlic and sauté a minute more. Add the wine and cook until most of it has evaporated. Add cream and cook until the cream has thickened. Set mushroom mixture aside.

Grease the gratin dishes with butter and line each dish with the ham. It is OK if the ham goes up the sides of the dish. Spoon the mushroom mixture on top of the ham. Carefully break two eggs into each dish. Then top the eggs with salt and pepper, the cheese, the chopped herbs, 1 Tbs of cream and 1 Tbs of butter. Place the gratin dishes on top of a baking sheet and place under the broiler about 6" from the heating element. Broil until the eggs are just set, about 5-6 minutes. Remove from the oven. The eggs will continue to cook and should be perfect when you serve them.

Chapter 4: Desserts and Pastries

Here are 13 recipes for desserts and pastries. I am not much of a baker because I don't like to measure ingredients, so all of these recipes are easy to make.

Bananas Foster

6 Servings

About This Recipe

Bananas Foster was created by the famous New Orleans restaurant, *Brennan's*, in 1951. It is named for Richard Foster, a close friend of one of the owners. In the 60 plus years since it was invented, there have been many variations on the theme, but its basics consist of a sauce made from butter, flavorings, brown sugar and rum. The bananas are peeled, cut in half lengthwise and cooked briefly in the sauce. The rum is added at the last minute and flambéed. The bananas are then served with vanilla ice cream.

Brennan's makes the dish at tableside. If you have an appropriate portable cooktop, you can do the same and impress the hell out of your guests

Although Brennan's uses only cinnamon, other flavorings you can try include allspice, nutmeg, vanilla extract, pumpkin spice and banana liqueur.

Ingredients

4	Oz Butter
1½	Cups Dark brown sugar
½	Tsp Salt
	Flavoring agents to taste (see above)
6	Under-ripe bananas, peeled and halved
¾	Cup Meyers or other dark rum

Procedure

In a large skillet, melt the butter. Add the sugar and salt and stir until dissolved. Add whatever flavoring agents you like and cook for a couple of minutes. Add the bananas, spoon the sauce over them and cook no more than 5 minutes. Add the rum and flambé it to get rid of the alcohol. Serve at once with the ice cream.

MY NOTES:

Chocolate Hazelnut Tart in Filo Cups

6 Servings

About This Recipe

This is an easy to make impressive dessert. Using a cupcake or muffin pan as a mold, you make cups out of filo dough and fill them with a chocolate-hazelnut concoction. You could use a different type of nut and you can use any kind of chocolate that you like from white to dark. You can buy pre-made filo dough in any market. It comes as a stack of paper-thin sheets. I never counted the number of sheets, but there are a lot of them, so if you mess up some, don't worry, there will be plenty to work with. The recipe calls for Nutella, which is a sort of peanut butter made from hazelnuts and is available in most markets.

A word about hazelnuts: The term "hazelnut" is used interchangeably with the words "filbert" and "cobnut". In truth, hazelnuts are round and filberts are oval, but they taste alike, so it doesn't matter which you buy. A bit of trivia: If you order a martini in Minnesota, it comes with a filbert instead of an olive!

Ingredients

1	Package of filo dough, defrosted
½	Stick Melted butter
½	Cup Hazelnuts, shelled and coarsely chopped
12	Oz Chocolate (any kind), coarsely chopped
¾	Cup Heavy cream
1	Jar of Nutella
	Mint leaves for garnish (optional)
	Shaved chocolate for garnish (optional)

Procedure

Pre-heat oven to 375°. Place a sheet of filo dough on a damp dish towel (to prevent the dough from drying out) and brush with melted butter. Set the sheet aside, and repeat with three more sheets of dough, stacking them up as you go. Cut the stacked dough sheets into six equal pieces about 5" x 5" each, and place each piece into a muffin cup, pressing it against the sides. Bake for 9 minutes or until the dough is golden and crisp. Set the cups aside to cool.

Melt the chocolate in a pan together with 1/4 cup of cream. Whisk until smooth. Place the nuts in a large bowl and pour the melted chocolate over them. Stir to evenly coat the nuts. Separately, beat 1/2 cup of cream to stiff peaks and carefully fold it into the nut-chocolate mixture. Chill this mix for 1-8 hours in the refrigerator.

Just before serving, place a heaping teaspoon of Nutella into the bottom of each filo cup, and fill with the chocolate cream. Garnish with mint leaves and shaved chocolate.

MY NOTES:

Chocolate Mousse

8 Servings

About This Recipe

A mousse is defined as a "prepared food that incorporates bubbles to give it a light and airy texture." There are many different ways to make a mousse. Some produce a very dense product and some are like eating flavored air.

I tried several different recipes before settling on the one here, the basics of which I stole from Gordon Ramsey, known on TV as the "Angry Chef." He claims that it can be made in 4 minutes. Maybe he can do it that fast, but it will take the rest of us 15 minutes or thereabouts.

Gordon suggests using amaretto as a flavoring agent, but I like Meyers rum better. Or you could use a fruit brandy such as framboise, or, if you want a minty flavor, crème de menthe. If you are going to serve it to children, you may want to leave out the booze altogether. You can also vary the flavor by using different types of chocolate. I've suggested using bittersweet, but the choice is yours. The key thing is to use good-quality chocolate. The cheap stuff just doesn't melt right. The recipe calls for sweetening the meringue with superfine sugar. You can buy it, but, you can also make it by grinding regular sugar in a blender or food processor. You can dress up the mousse by garnishing with mint leaves, shaved chocolate, chopped pistachios, chocolate jimmies or even M&Ms.

Ingredients

8	Oz Bittersweet chocolate, chopped
2½	Cups Heavy cream
½	Cup Superfine sugar
2	Egg whites
1	Tbs Booze (optional)
	Garnishes as described above

Procedure

To prep for this recipe, you will need an electric hand beater, a metal bowl set in a larger bowl that has been filled with ice water, a bowl for whipping the egg whites and a double boiler or pot for making ganache.

First make the ganache. Heat half the cream in the top of a double boiler or pot, but do not let it boil. Add the chocolate, a little at a time and stir to mix thoroughly. Immediately pour this mixture into the metal bowl in the ice water bath, add the rest of the cream and the booze and beat it to stiff peaks.

In a separate bowl, beat the egg whites with the sugar to make a stiff meringue. This can be done before you make the ganache. Add the chocolate mixture to the egg whites and fold it in. Spoon into serving dishes, garnish if desired and refrigerate until you are ready to serve.

MY NOTES:

Chocolate Truffles

Yields 24 Truffles

About This Recipe

A chocolate truffle is nothing more than ganache, which is nothing more than a mixture of cream and chocolate. To make truffles, ganache is rolled into little balls and then dusted with a coating, traditionally cocoa powder. You can use any kind of chocolate you like: milk, semi-sweet, bittersweet, white, dark, light, sugarless, etc. or a combination of different types. You can add butter to the ganache for extra richness. You can add flavoring ingredients such as booze, aged balsamic vinegar, vanilla or almond extract, cinnamon, cardamom, coffee or even sea salt, Good booze choices include Grand Marnier, Cognac, Myers rum and fruit brandies such as Framboise or Kirsch. You can roll the ganache balls in cocoa powder, finely chopped nuts, toasted coconut, powdered sugar or anything else that hits your fancy. It's fun to make them with several different coatings.

Rolling out the truffle balls and coating them with your hands is a messy proposition. I recommend that you use non-powdered disposable latex gloves.

It goes without saying that the finished product will reflect the quality of the cream and chocolate, so use the best you can afford.

Ingredients

½	Lb	Your favorite chocolate
½	Cup	Heavy cream
2	Tbs	Butter, cut into small pieces
		Flavoring agents, your choice
2	Tbs	Booze (optional), or
3	Tbs	Aged balsamic vinegar, or
3	Tbs	Strong coffee
1	Tsp	Vanilla or almond extract
1	Tsp	Ground cinnamon or cardamom
½	Cup	Powdered sugar, cocoa powder, toasted coconut shreds or finely chopped nuts for coating the truffles

Procedure

Heat the cream on the stovetop or in the microwave to just below the boiling point. Add the butter if using and melt it into the cream.

Chop the chocolate up into small pieces. (Unnecessary if you are using chocolate bits.) and place it in a large bowl. Pour the cream over the chocolate and stir until the chocolate is melted and the mixture is smooth and uniform. If the chocolate doesn't melt enough, nuke it for a few seconds until it does. Add your choice of flavoring ingredients and stir to combine thoroughly. Cover the bowl with plastic wrap and refrigerate it for at least 2 hours until the ganache is set firm. Overnight is fine.

(Recipe continues on next page)

Put your coatings in shallow dishes. Using a melon baller, teaspoon measure, small ice cream scoop or other suitable device, scoop out some ganache and roll it around with your hands until a ball is formed. Roll the ball in a coating. Place the ball on the baking sheet. Repeat until all the ganache is used up, then place the baking sheet in the refrigerator and chill the ganache balls for at least an hour.

Store the finished truffles in the refrigerator for up to two weeks or in the freezer for up to three months. Serve them at room temperature.

MY NOTES:

Classic French Apple Tart

6 Servings

About This Recipe

On my first trip to Paris in 1972, I had apple tart for dessert and fell in love. Years later, I learned that it is one of the simplest to make, yet most elegant desserts there is on this earth. If you look up recipes, most will start by telling you how to make the pastry crust. Ignore this advice. Instead, go to your local market and buy a sheet of frozen puff pastry. It is more delicious that any pie crust you can make yourself - I guarantee it.

The remainder of the recipe consists of placing apple slices on top of the puff pastry crust, sprinkling with sugar, dotting with butter, baking and glazing. The classic French glaze is made from apricot jam, but you can use any glaze material that you like. Honey works quite well as do other flavors of jams and jellies.

Whipped cream is a standard accompaniment, but créme fraiche or ice cream are excellent too.

You can use pears, peaches or other fruits instead of apples. Just make sure that they aren't too soft and/or juicy or your tart will turn out soggy. I prefer pippin apples, but granny smiths, golden delicious, honey crisps, fujis, macoums are good too. The apple you use should be crisp and a bit on the tart side. I can't tell you how many apples you will need because they come in such a large size range. Buy extra and put the ones you don't use in your kid's lunchbox.

You can make this tart in any size. Round, square, oblong, oval, whatever you like. You can make it big or small for individual servings. Very flexible indeed.

Ingredients

1	10" x 15" Sheet of puff pastry, thawed
4-8	Apples, peeled, halved, cored and sliced thin
½	Cup Sugar
1	Cup Apricot preserves
2	Tbs Calvados, Applejack, apple cider or apple juice

Procedure

Pre-heat oven to 400°. Line a baking tray large enough to hold a puff pastry sheet with parchment paper. Set the pastry sheet on top of the paper.

Cover the pastry with overlapping apple slices in a pattern that you find appealing. Sprinkle the sugar over the apple slices and dot with the butter cubes. Bake 20 - 30 minutes until the edges of the apples and the pastry sheet are dark-tinged.

While the tart is baking, melt the apricot jam or jelly and the calvados or apple juice together in a small pan. If you used jam, push the mixture through a sieve to strain out any solids. When the tart is done baking, brush the top with the glaze using a pastry or paint brush. Put the tart back into the oven until the glaze is slightly charred, about 2-4 minutes.

Serve warm or at room temperature.

Floating Island

6 Servings

About This Recipe

Floating Island, also known as *Oeufs a la Neige* ("Snow eggs") in French and *Iles Flottantes* ("Floating Islands") in Italian, is a classic dessert that has been around for a long time. It was popular in the US 30+ years ago and is still found on many fine restaurant menus in the UK and France. It is one of my all-time favorites.

The dish consists of a base of crème anglaise topped with unbaked soft meringues. In the French style, the meringues are shaped into "eggs", hence the word oeufs in the name. There are a number of ways to go about making this dish. I've given you a simple way to make the crème anglaise in the Sauce Chapter, so here is a recipe for making the meringues that I think is the simplest and produces excellent results.

In this recipe the meringues are poached in boiling water. Many recipes don't poach the meringues, but, unless you are using pasteurized eggs, poaching is the smart way to go.

You can serve your floating island without embellishment, but you can dress it up with berries, chopped nuts (pistachios are especially good), mint leaves, candied pecans, maraschino cherries, orange zest or a dozen other toppings. It is also common to drizzle chocolate or caramel over the dish.

Ingredients

8	Egg whites at room temperature
½	Tsp Cream of tartar
1	Cup Sugar
1	Tsp Vanilla extract
	Crème anglaise
	Embellishments such as mint, berries, cookies, etc.

Procedure

Beat the egg whites with the cream of tartar using a hand or stand mixer to the soft peak stage. Add the sugar and beat until stiff peaks are formed. Fold in the vanilla extract.

While beating the eggs, heat a shallow pot of water to the simmer stage. When the beating is finished, using two large spoons, form egg-shaped mounds of meringue and drop them into the simmering water. Poach them for 2-3 minutes, turning them once, then remove them and set on paper towels to drain the excess water. Chill them in the fridge.

To serve, put a layer of cold crème anglaise on a plate or shallow bowl. Top with 2-3 meringues, embellish if you wish and serve.

MY NOTES:

Home-made Baked Donuts

Yields 12 Medium Donuts

About This Recipe

To make this recipe, you will need donut pans. These come in several sizes that will make from six large donuts up to 18 small ones. You can buy them non-stick or made out of silicone that won't stick to anything.

I saw a famous TV chef make baked donuts on her show. I tried her recipe, but the results were more like hockey pucks than donuts. I experimented and came up with my own formula, presented here.

You have a lot of latitude in preparing the batter for these donuts. You can use brown sugar instead of white sugar or a combination of both. Add more eggs for a more custard-like interior. Use buttermilk instead of sour cream. Use a mix of whole wheat and regular flour. Use whatever spices you like or none at all.

You can coat these donuts with any topping or glaze that will stick. Cinnamon sugar, powdered sugar, chocolate, vanilla glaze, etc. Top your icing with sprinkles, chopped nuts or toasted coconut shreds. If you are just going to dust the donuts with powdered sugar, use non-melting sugar (also known as "sucre neige"). It won't melt and disappear like regular powdered sugar. You can find it in gourmet stores or online.

The recipe presented here is an amalgam of several other variants. Use it as is or as a point of departure. It is very difficult to go wrong.

Ingredients

1	Cups Flour
¾	Cups Sugar
1	Tsp Baking powder
½	Tsp Baking soda
1	Tsp Ground cinnamon (optional)
½	Tsp Ground nutmeg (optional)
½	Tsp Salt
2	Eggs
⅔	Cup Sour cream
2	Tbs Melted butter
1	Tsp Vanilla extract (optional)

CINNAMON SUGAR TOPPING

½	Cup Sugar
2	Tbs Cinnamon
½	Stick Melted butter

(Recipe continues on next page)

VANILLA GLAZE

½ Stick Butter
1½ Cups Powdered sugar
2 Tsp Vanilla extract
3 Tbs Evaporated milk

CHOCOLATE GLAZE

4 Oz Semi-sweet chocolate
2 Tbs Butter
1 Cup Powdered sugar
1 Tsp Vanilla extract
4 Tbs Evaporated milk

LEMON GLAZE

2 Tbs Lemon juice
1½ Cups Powdered sugar

Procedure

Pre-heat oven to 350°. Spray the donut pans with non-stick baking spray. Sift together all the dry ingredients into a large bowl. In a separate bowl, beat together all the wet ingredients. Pour the wet into the dry and mix well to make a smooth batter. Pour the batter into the donut pans, about ⅔ - ¾ full. Bake 15-20 minutes until golden. Allow to cool for a few minutes and then knock the donuts out of the pan. After they are cool enough to handle, apply topping or glaze.

For a cinnamon sugar topping, first mix the cinnamon and sugar together until a uniform color. Brush the donuts with melted butter, then dip the donuts into the cinnamon sugar and roll around until evenly coated.

To make the vanilla glaze, melt all the ingredients together in a small pot. If it is too thick, add a bit more evaporated milk. Pour the glaze into a shallow plate and dip the donuts into it to coat. Add sprinkle if desired while still wet, and allow the glaze to set.

To make the chocolate glaze, heat everything together and follow the instructions for the vanilla glaze.

To make the lemon glaze, mix together the lemon juice and powdered sugar and dip the donuts into the mixture.

MY NOTES:

Melons Macerated in Wine

4 Servings

About This Recipe

This is a quick and easy dessert recipe. You marinate cubes or balls of melon in wine and serve them topped with mascarpone or whipped cream. You can use almost any kind of melon for this dish except watermelon. You could also use a sweet wine such as Port, Madeira or Manischewitz. If money is no object, use a dessert wine such as a German Beerenauslese, a French Sauternes or an Ice Wine from British Columbia.

A note on storing melons. They should be stored at room temperature, but chilled just before eating them or when cut. If the melon is hard, put it in a paper bag with a few holes cut into it. It will soften more rapidly in the bag, but sweetness will not improve.

Melons develop sweetness only on the vine. Once picked, melons will soften but won't get any sweeter. Determining if a melon is sweet is often a tough proposition. A few melons, such as cantaloupe, have an aroma if ripe. Smell the melon from the stem end. If it smells sweet, it will be sweet. Unfortunately, many melon varieties have no smell at all. You can try shaking the melon. If you can hear the seeds rattling around, there is a good chance that the melon is ripe. A third test is to press the flower end of the melon. If it is hard with no give, it is probably not ripe. If it gives slightly, it may be ripe. If it gives a lot, it might be rotten. Good luck!

Ingredients

1   Cup wine
3   Tbs Sugar
1   Melon, cubed or balled
      Zest strips from 1 lemon
      Mascarpone or whipped cream

Procedure

Put the wine in a pot, add the sugar and zest and bring to the simmer. Stir until all the sugar is dissolved. Allow to cool. Discard the zest.

Cut the melon into 3/4" cubes or make melon balls with a melon baller tool. Immerse the melon in the wine and allow to macerate at least 1 hour. Serve the melon topped with mascarpone (see recipe in Miscellaneous chapter) or whipped cream.

MY NOTES:

No-Bake Cheesecake

6 Servings

About This Recipe

I like cheesecakes, but they are a pain to make and you can buy very good ones already made at very reasonable prices. This recipe is not only easy and fast, there is a lot you can do to alter the flavor profile. I've suggested using berries, but you can use many kinds of fruit. Peaches and mangos are a couple that come to mind. You can also use different toppings. I've suggested using chocolate ganache, but you could use, for example, ice cream sprinkles.

You can use an electric hand or standing beater, but I find that a food processor does the best job of blending the fruit.

The original recipe called for making a bottom crust out of crushed Oreo cookies mixed with butter, but I think a crust is unnecessary and makes for more work. However, feel free to make a crust if you don't mind spending the extra time.

Ingredients

8	Oz	Cream cheese at room temperature
6	Oz	Mascarpone at room temperature
1	Cup	Frozen strawberries, blueberries or raspberries
⅓	Cup	Condensed milk
1	Tsp	Vanilla extract
½	Tsp	Salt

TOPPING

1½	Tbs	Heavy cream
4	Oz	Bittersweet chocolate, chopped
		Fresh mint leaves for garnish (optional)
		Whipped cream for garnish (optional)
		Chopped pistachios for garnish (optional)

Procedure

In a large bowl, beat or process the cream cheese, mascarpone and fruit until well blended. Add the condensed milk, vanilla and salt and mix or process until very smooth. Distribute the cheesecake into 6 cups of at least 4-ounce capacity. Put the cups in the fridge and chill at least 2 hours.

In a small saucepan, heat the cream, but don't let it boil. Off-heat, stir in the chocolate and stir until it is melted and evenly combined with the cream. Allow to cool and spoon over the cheesecakes. Chill at least 30 minutes before serving. Garnish with mint leaves and a dollop of whipped cream and/or a sprinkle of chopped pistachios if desired.

Puff Pastry Berry Tart

6 Servings

About This Recipe

Three of my very favorite things to eat are puff pastry, whipped cream and berries, so I decided to make a quick and easy dessert that combined all three. I use store-bought frozen puff pastry shells and fill them with a mixture of berries and whipped cream. To make it more interesting (to adults), I like to macerate the berries in a bit of booze like Grand Marnier. Yum.

Instead of whipped cream, you can use crème fraiche or mascarpone. Any of these choices can be sweetened if you wish. If you would like a bit of crunch, throw some slivered almonds, chopped unsalted macadamias, pistachios or even some chocolate bits into the filling. Dress it up with a sprig of mint.

Ingredients

1   Box of 6 Puff pastry shells

    Mixed berries

    Grand Marnier or other macerating liquor

    Whipped cream, crème fraiche or mascarpone

Procedure

Defrost the shells and bake them about 15 minutes in a pre-heated 400° oven until golden. Allow to cool.

While the puff pastry is baking, clean the berries and macerate them in your choice of booze. Fold the berries into the whipped cream and spoon the mixture into the pastry shells. Serve at once.

MY NOTES:

Roasted or Sautéed Fruit

4-6 Servings

About This Recipe

The idea here is to cook fruit with honey by roasting or sautéing it and serving it either warm or cold for dessert. The cooking process causes the fruit sugars to caramelize, intensifying the flavor.

Pineapple is an excellent fruit for this recipe, but other fruits such as peaches, pears or mangos are good choices. I like to sprinkle chopped nuts over the fruit. Almonds, walnuts, pecans or hazelnuts are nice, but my favorite is pistachios. Make sure that the nuts are unsalted.

If you want a topping, you have many choices. Whipped cream, yogurt, crème fraiche (see Volume I to make your own) real clotted cream, mock clotted cream (see Miscellaneous chapter) ice cream, sherbet, sorbet or gelato will all serve the purpose. The dish looks good if you serve it in clear glass parfait goblets.

Ingredients

2	Lbs Fruit, peeled and cut into large cubes
2	Tbs Butter
3	Tbs Honey
½	Cup Orange juice (optional)
	Chopped nuts (optional)
	Topping (optional)

Procedure

For the roasting method, pre-heat oven to 450°. Mix the honey and orange juice together, and in a large bowl, macerate the fruit cubes in this mixture for at least 15 minutes. Remove the fruit and place it in a single layer on a baking sheet lined with parchment paper or Silpat. Roast for 10-15 minutes or until the fruit caramelizes slightly. Allow to cool a little and return it to the bowl with the honey/orange juice marinade. Mix well and serve.

For the sauté method, melt the butter in a large skillet and cook it until it begins to brown, then add the fruit and honey and cook until the fruit begins to caramelize, about 5-10 minutes. Add orange juice if desired and cook until the juice is reduced a bit. Serve hot, warm or cold.

MY NOTES:

Sabayon, Zabaglione, Custard or Whatever

4-8 Servings

About This Recipe

In France it is called "Sabayon", in Italy, "Zabaglione", in the UK, it is "Custard". A rose by any other name, etc., etc. Traditionally, this dish involved standing over a pan set into a double boiler and whisking by hand for 10 to 15 minutes. Maximum tedium, it is why it ain't too popular in American restaurants or home kitchens. I substitute an electric hand beater for the whisk and get the same results in about one-third the time!

There are only three ingredients to this dish: egg yolks, sugar and a flavoring liquid. Traditionally, a sweet wine such as Marsala was used, but anything will work so long as it is wet and you like it. Strong coffee, for example works very well.

Sabayon can be served by itself, either plain or topped with a bit of whipped cream, or used as a topping for fruits such as strawberries or raspberries. It can be served either hot or cold. If you don't beat it too much, it will be a thick liquid that can be drunk out of a cup. If you beat it a lot, it will be a firm custard. No matter how you fix it, it makes a great finish to a great meal.

If you like crème brulée, you can sprinkle brown sugar on top of the sabayon and put it under the broiler for a minute or use a torch to caramelize the sugar. If you use the broiler, keep an eye on it, because the sugar can burn very quickly.

Ingredients

⅔ Cup Wine, coffee or other flavoring liquid

⅓ Cup Sugar

6 Egg yolks

Procedure

Set a pot of water to the boil and put it on a low simmer. You will need a bowl that will sit on top of the pot, close to, but not touching the hot water. In that bowl, combine the sugar and liquid, and then add the egg yolks. Place the bowl on top of the pot and beat the contents with an electric hand beater until the desired consistency is reached.

If you want it cold, chill in the refrigerator for at least 1 hour, or serve it hot right away.

MY NOTES:

St. Clement's Pie

8 Servings

About This Recipe

When I lived in London, I ran into this dessert at a no-name restaurant. Apparently, it was acquired from a purveyor, not made at the restaurant, so I couldn't get the recipe there. I looked it up and found that it is very simple to make and tastes pretty darn good.

This pie is named after Pope Clement, who is the patron saint of blacksmiths. (Of course you knew that.) He is celebrated on St. Clement's Day, November 23rd, and this pie is traditionally served on that day. After I learned this piece of trivia, I queried some British friends about it. None of them had ever heard of St. Clement's Day, or St. Clement for that matter, so there you go.

The original that I had used a crust made from corn flakes, but I recommend using a store-bought pie crust that comes in an aluminum baking pan for the least amount of fuss. You could also make a puff pastry crust by rolling out a frozen puff pastry sheet and cutting it to size. Or, if you are a proud baker, make your own damn piecrust.

The pie filling is essentially a citrus-flavored custard, similar to that found in key lime pie. It is embarrassingly simple to make.

Ingredients

1	Pie crust
1	Whole Egg
4	Egg yolks
1	14-oz can of condensed milk
	Zest and juice of 3 lemons
	Zest and juice of 2 oranges
1	Cup Heavy cream
½	Cup Powdered sugar

Procedure

Prepare your pie crust according to package directions or your own recipe. Pre-bake the crust according to package directions.

Pre-heat oven to 350°. With an electric beater, whip the egg and yolks in a large bowl until pale and frothy. Beat in the condensed milk and the citrus juices and zests. Reserve a little zest to use a garnish. Pour the mix into the piecrust and bake 20 minutes. Allow to cool and then refrigerate.

Just before serving, whip the cream with the powdered sugar to stiff peaks. Layer the whipped cream over the pie and sprinkle with left over zest.

MY NOTES:

Chapter 5: Hors d'oeuvres and Finger-foods

This chapter contains 14 recipes that can be eaten standing up, although many of them can be served as a first course at a sit-down meal, and some can be adapted for a main course. Make a few of them for a fabulous Superbowl party or when next you entertain the President.

Angels on Horseback

Yields 24 Angels

About This Recipe

This recipe has its genesis in the UK where I once lived. The original recipe used oysters and bacon, but I think my version, which uses scallops and prosciutto is much better. By the way, there is another dish called "Devils on Horseback" which is often confused with this one. The Devils dish uses a fruit like a date or prune in place of the seafood. You can make it if you want, but it doesn't do much for me.

You can also make this dish with bacon instead of prosciutto. If you do, partially pre-cook the bacon first because it takes much longer than the scallops to cook.

Ingredients

24   Bite-size pieces of scallop or Bay scallops
12   Slices of prosciutto
      Lemon juice

Procedure

Cut the prosciutto slices sized to wrap around the scallops Wrap the prosciutto around each scallop and secure it with a toothpick. Put the pieces on a baking sheet set about 6" under the oven broiler. Broil about 3 minutes on one side, then flip them and broil the other side for 3 minutes. Just before serving, drizzle the angels with fresh lemon juice. Serve warm or at room temperature.

MY NOTES:

Bacon-wrapped, Cheese-stuffed Dates

Yields 24 pieces

About This Recipe

I got this when I lived in the Palm Springs area, which has a sizable date growing industry.

The cheese is an important component. Blue cheeses such as stilton, gorgonzola, or Roquefort are good choices. Goat cheese, either flavored or unflavored, is also excellent.

I recommend using the medjool date variety.

Ingredients

24   Medjool dates, pitted

8   Oz soft cheese

12   Slices of bacon, cut in half

Procedure

Pre-heat the oven to 400°. Stuff the dates with the cheese, wrap them with a strip of bacon and secure with a wooden (not plastic) toothpick. Place the dates on a grate over a drip pan and bake them for 15 minutes, turning once during the cooking. Drain on paper towels. The bacon should be crisp, so add more cooking time if necessary.

MY NOTES:

Bagel Chips

Yields 36 Chips

About This Recipe

You may have had bagel chips out of a bag that you bought in the supermarket. They were pretty good, I'm sure, but these are even better, because you can flavor them whichever way you want and you can use any kind of bagel.

The process involves tossing the bagel slices in a mixture of EVOO or butter and herbs or spices and then baking them for as long as it takes for them to get crisp. You can use a low temperature or high temperature oven. Try it both ways and see what results you like best.

The tough part of this recipe is slicing the bagels so that the slices are only ⅛" thick. This is going to take some practice and maybe a few bleeding knuckles before you get it right. Here are some suggestions:

1. Try cutting with the bagel partially frozen.

2. Use an electric knife

3. Instead of trying to cut circles, cut perpendicular to the center. The pieces will be small but big enough if you use large bagels.

Ingredients

6	Bagels, any kind
¼	Cup EVOO or melted butter
	Herb blend such as Italian seasoning
	Garlic powder or onion powder or both
	Superfine salt

Procedure

For low temperature method, pre-heat oven to 250°. For high temperature method, to 375°.

Slice the bagels ⅛" thick. Put the EVOO and herbs or spices in a large bowl and whisk to combine. Dump in the bagel slices and flip them around with your hands until they are evenly coated.

Put the slices on baking sheets in a single layer. Sprinkle with a bit more salt. Bake 10 - 15 minutes for high temperature oven or 45 minutes in the low temperature oven, turning every so often to ensure that they cook evenly. Remove from the oven and allow to cool. The chips will keep up to two weeks in a covered jar.

MY NOTES:

Brined Garlic Shrimp

Yields 40-50 Shrimp

About This Recipe

Most people don't think about brining shrimp - after all they are raised in salt water. But, trust me, it is a good thing to do because the shrimp won't shrink like they usually do. They will stay nice and plump and brining adds only 15 minutes to the recipe timing.

The other unique thing about this recipe is that the shrimp are cooked with the shells on because they contribute a lot of flavor. Your guests will have to peel the shrimp before devouring them. C'est la vie.

Ingredients

1	Quart Cold water
¼	Cup Salt
2	Lbs Large shrimp (20-25 per Lb), shell on
2	Tbs Canola or peanut oil
4	Tbs Melted butter
6	Cloves Garlic, pressed or minced
1	Tsp Seasonings such as cumin, dried rosemary, curry powder or herbes de Provence,

Procedure

Mix the water and salt together in a 2-quart container and add the shrimp. Allow to sit for 15 minutes. Drain the shrimp and dry them with paper towels.

Heat the butter and oil in a large skillet or sauté pan, add the garlic and seasonings and cook 1 minute. Add the shrimp in a single layer. Cook 45 seconds, flip them and cook another 45 seconds. Remove to a serving platter. Repeat the cooking process until all the shrimp have been cooked. You can serve these shrimp hot, room temperature or cold as you prefer. Don't forget the napkins and someplace to discard the shells.

MY NOTES:

Bruschetta with Prosciutto and Other Stuff

Yields 12-24 pieces

About This Recipe

You have probably had something called bruschetta as an appetizer in a restaurant. Usually, it is toasted bread topped with chopped tomatoes and maybe a few herbs. Real bruschetta (the ch is pronounced like a 'k') is a Tuscan dish associated with celebrating the olive harvest. The key ingredients are bread and olive oil, but garlic is common as well.

In this version, I use prosciutto (which comes from Parma, not Tuscany) and give you the opportunity to add other stuff like herbs and cheese. It is an easy to prepare great-tasting appetizer that allows you to exercise a bit of creativity.

The quality of the bread and the olive oil are crucial to the success of this dish. I like to use a crusty artisan sourdough, but Italian breads like Ciabatta will do nicely. I like to serve larger pieces than can be cut from a baguette. This is also the time to break out that fancy EVOO you have been saving for a special occasion.

If you use cheese, grated Parmagiano, Pecorino or Romano are good choices. Shredded mozzarella, asiago or gruyère are also very good. If you use herbs, you will probably want one of them to be basil.

Ingredients

BASIC RECIPE

1	Loaf artisan bread, sliced and cut into serving size pieces
	EVOO
	Raw peeled garlic cloves
	Sliced prosciutto
	Grated or shredded cheese (optional)
	Chopped shallots or onions (optional)
	Chopped fresh herbs (optional)
	Freshly grated black pepper

Procedure

Paint the bread pieces on one side with EVOO. Grill them, oiled side down for a couple of minutes until they start to brown and/or show grill marks.

Remove the bread from the grill and paint the ungrilled side with EVOO.

Off heat, grilled side up, place a slice of prosciutto on each piece and top with a mixture of cheese, herbs and onions or shallots as you wish. Put the bruschetta back on the grill and cook 2 minutes until the bottoms are slightly brown and/or show grill marks.

Just before serving, drizzle a little bit of a great EVOO over each piece.

MY NOTES:

Caviar and Cucumbers

About This Recipe

In Volume I, I said that none of my recipes contained caviar because it didn't meet my definition of "frugal." I changed my mind. There are in fact, several varieties of caviar that are not very expensive. However, the caviar business is a bit confusing. In the US, by law, if it is called "caviar" it must come from sturgeon. Any other type of fish eggs has to be identified by the name of the fish; e.g., salmon or lumpfish.

I'll bet you didn't know that the United States once produced 90% of the world's caviar. Unfortunately, the sturgeon were fished out, and the business was taken over by the countries surrounding the Caspian Sea where several varieties of sturgeon are indigenous. That said, the American caviar industry is beginning to come back. Three varieties of caviar-bearing sturgeon are being farmed in Missouri, Georgia and California. The product is still expensive, although much less expensive than the stuff from the Caspian. Prices will undoubtedly come down as stocks rise and more companies get into the business.

If you can't afford sturgeon caviar, you can buy, at reasonable prices, caviar from bowfin, salmon, whitefish, trout, lumpfish and capelin. Consider that Caspian Sea sturgeon caviar can cost up to $150/oz, American sturgeon caviar up to $20/oz and American caviar from non-sturgeon varieties around $1 - $5/oz. A serving is defined as ½-ounce, so the cost per person can be reasonable if not entirely frugal.

There is essentially nothing to this recipe. Take a thin slice of cucumber, put a dollop of sour cream or crème fraiche (see recipe in Volume I) on it, and then a ½-Tsp of caviar on top of that. If you wish, you can serve it with some finely chopped shallots, dill sprigs and/or lemon wedges (to squeeze lemon juice on top) on the side.

Although this dish does not require utensils, if you serve caviar with spoons, make sure that the spoons are not stainless steel. Something in the steel reacts with the caviar and makes it taste metallic. Ceramic or plastic spoons are safest.

MY NOTES:

Ceviche

Yields 16-32 pieces

About This Recipe

Ceviche originated in Mexico, Central or South America. Nobody knows for sure, but today it is popular everywhere in Latin America and the Caribbean. Ceviche is seafood "cooked" in an acid, usually lime, lemon or grapefruit juice. The acid does indeed change the structure of the fish, but it does not kill bacteria, so you must be certain to use only very fresh seafood. Seafood that has been frozen as soon as it is caught and just defrosted is OK.

There is a wide variety under the ceviche banner. Ecuadorian ceviche is often made with shrimp and ketchup in addition to the lime juice and served with corn nuts. In Chile, ceviche is made with Chilean sea bass, grapefruit juice and cilantro. In Peru, ceviche is garnished with thinly sliced onions and chili peppers. In the Bahamas, ceviche is made with conch, lime juice and very hot chilis.

Only a true ceviche lover would dare try tiger's milk (leche de tigre), which is the leftover ceviche marinade served in a small glass. Brightly colored from spicy chili peppers, and sometimes mixed with vodka, tiger's milk is considered a great cure for hangovers.

I like ceviche served as an hors d'oeuvres. I like to put out a bowl of the stuff and have people help themselves using toothpicks to spear the pieces they want. I also like to use a mix of shellfish and regular fish, so everyone can choose his or her favorites. I like to use bay scallops, calamari rings, conch, snapper, sea bass, rockfish and tilapia. This recipe is basic, and you are welcome to try any of the infinite variations that exist or maybe you will invent a new one.

Ingredients

1	Lb Seafood, cut into bite-size pieces
	Juice of 2-3 limes
	Juice of 1-2 Lemons
1	Small red onion, finely chopped
2	Tbs Chopped cilantro
1	Serrano pepper
½	Cucumber, peeled, seeded and diced
	Salt and white pepper to taste

Procedure

Combine everything in a bowl and allow to sit for 30 minutes up to 4 hours maximum. Serve with toothpicks.

MY NOTES:

Cheese Crisps (Fricos)

Yields 16 Fricos

About This Recipe

Fricos is the name given to this dish in a fancy Italian restaurant or the area around Venice from whence they came. Us boorish Americans call them cheese crisps. If you like *Cheez-its* or *Goldfish* crackers, you will go nuts over this dish.

You can make fricos with one ingredient, grated cheese. Or you can make it more interesting with the addition of flavorings. Some of the flavoring agents that I've tried are cumin, fennel or dill seed, lemon zest, chopped fresh basil, chives or dill. They are all good.

Traditionally, fricos are made with Parmagiano Reggiano cheese, but you can use any hard, grated cheese that you like. Asiago, aged cheddar, Manchego are good choices.

The trick to making these crisps is to not let them stick to the pan. The most surefire way of defeating this problem is to cook them on a Silpat sheet. Failing that, try parchment paper or non-stick spray on a new aluminum throwaway pan.

Each cup of grated cheese makes about 16 2½" diameter crisps. You don't have to make them round, however. Sometimes they are made larger and, while still soft, wrapped around a shape to make them come out, for example, like little cups or tubes. You can also make them in shapes by using cookie cutters to define them. You are limited only by your imagination.

The recipe mentions flour, which is optional. Some chefs think it improves the texture of the final product. Try it with and without and see which you like best. It is a matter of personal preference.

Ingredients

1   Cup Finely grated hard cheese
¼   Cup flour (optional)
      Flavoring agents, your choice

Procedure

Pre-heat oven to 375°. Mix the grated cheese together with the flour (if using) and your flavoring agents. On a baking sheet lined with Silpat, drop heaping tablespoonfuls of your mixture onto the Silpat and press down lightly to form disk shapes. Bake 5-7 minutes. The edges should be brown. Allow to cool and carefully remove the fricos with a spatula and set on a paper towel to absorb excess fat. Eat immediately or keep them for up to 3 days.

MY NOTES:

International Chips

Yields 96 Chips

About This Recipe

I call these my "International Chips" because you can give them a flavor profile to remind you of any one of a hundred different countries. If you like chips 'n dip, try this easy and delicious recipe. You take a soft flatbread such as tortillas (flour or corn), lavosh, or split pita, brush it with EVOO flavored with garlic and herbs or spices, sprinkle with grated, crumbled or shredded cheese, cut it into chip size pieces and bake it for a few minutes until crispy. Couldn't be any simpler. By the way, Wikipedia lists 75 different kinds of flatbread from all over the world, so no matter where you shop, you will find something to fit the bill. Speaking of tortillas, the range available today is huge. You can get whole wheat, gluten-free, low-fat, etc. in many sizes including large "wraps." The only caveat is not to use cheese that has a high water content because the chips won't crisp.

To make them Italian, use oregano and shredded or grated Parmagiano Reggiano; Greek, try rosemary, lemon, salt and feta; Mexican, cumin and shredded cheddar; and on and on. Even plain old salt and pepper tastes good!

Serve these chips plain or with an appropriate dip. Aioli (Italian), raita (Indian), tzatziki (Greece), green or red salsa (Mexico), blue cheese dressing (America) - the choice is endless.

Ingredients

	EVOO
	Chopped garlic
	Dried herbs or spices
12	7" Tortillas, or
6	7" Pitas or naans, split, or any other soft flatbread
	Cheese, shredded, grated or crumbled as appropriate for type

Procedure

Pre-heat oven to 375°. In a large skillet, heat some EVOO with some chopped garlic and cook until the garlic starts to turn brown. Remove and discard the garlic bits. Add the herbs and spices and cook for 1 minute to infuse the flavor. Let the EVOO cool off a bit.

Brush each side of the bread with the flavored EVOO. Stack up the breads and slice them into pieces the size you prefer. I like to do them about 1½" wide and 3" long. This will make about 8 pieces per bread. Place the pieces on baking sheets, sprinkle with the cheese and bake them for about 12 minutes or until crisp.

MY NOTES:

James Beard's Onion Sandwiches

Yields 72-96 Sandwiches

About This Recipe

FYI, James Beard is known as the "Dean of American Cookery". I debated (with myself) about whether to include this recipe in my book since it is (was?) so well-known. I decided to do it because I thought it might be a generational thing, and today's generation needs to know it. For those of you under the age of 50 who might not know better, this recipe won just about every culinary award on this planet. Unbelievably easy to make (your kids can do it), it is incredibly delicious. However, it is human nature for memories to fade. Maybe I can bring a good one back.

There are only five ingredients in this recipe. No cooking necessary. You can get fussy about the bread you use, but, with all deference to the foodies out there, you can use Wonder Bread with excellent results!

Ingredients

1   Loaf of white bread, challah or brioche, sliced
1   Cup Mayonnaise
6   Small mild onions, sliced paper-thin
    Salt to taste
1   Bunch parsley, chopped fine

Procedure

Using a 1½" - 2" round cookie cutter or an equivalent diameter shot glass, cut rounds out of the bread slices. Spread mayonnaise thinly on one side of each slice. On half the slices, the bottoms, place some onion and sprinkle with salt. Top the sandwiches with the other pieces and press together. Spread mayonnaise on the edges of the sandwiches and roll them in the chopped parsley. Refrigerate for at least 1 hour. Serve.

One variation is to butter the inside bread surfaces rather than spreading mayonnaise on them. Another variant uses a fancy salt like fleur de sel.

MY NOTES:

Mini Quiches

Yields 24 Quiches

About This Recipe

I know that real men don't eat quiche. However, accompanied by a stiff drink, I think that most men will like these one-bite hors d'oeuvres. Quiches (if you are French, or frittatas if you are Italian) are nothing more than baked scrambled eggs, or, to be more couth, baked omelets. Basically, you prep as you would for scrambled eggs and add whatever flavoring ingredients you like. For example, if you want it to taste like a Denver omelet, add a bit of ham, pepper and cheese.

You will need a mini-muffin tin which has 24 cups, preferably non-stick. Most ovens will hold two of these pans, so you can make 48 of these at once if you double the recipe. You can make them ahead of time and serve them at room temperature.

Ingredients

4	Eggs
¼	Cup Milk
	Salt and pepper to taste
2	Oz Finely chopped ham or pancetta
¼	Cup Grated cheese such as Parmagiano or Emmenthaler
1	Tbs Chopped fresh herbs such as parsley, basil, chives or tarragon

Procedure

Pre-heat the oven to 375° Spray the muffin cups with non-stick spray. Put all the ingredients in a bowl in a bowl and beat with a whisk or an electric beater. Ladle the mix into the mini muffin cups, filling them about ¾ full. Bake 8-10 minutes or until the eggs are well set. When cool enough to handle, pop them out of the cups and set them on a rack to finish cooling.

MY NOTES:

Nuts to You

Yields 3 Cups of Nuts

About This Recipe

The idea is to jazz up ordinary nuts with a spicy coating. You can use any kind of nut that you like, but make sure that you buy them unsalted. Depending on the type of nut, you may get them whole, halved or sliced. These nuts will keep for a couple of weeks at room temperature or for months in the freezer.

Ingredients

¼	Cup Melted butter
1	Tbs Vanilla extract
¼	Cup Sugar
1	Tsp salt
¾	Tsp Ground cinnamon
¾	Tsp Ground allspice
¼	Tsp Ground cardamom
¼	Tsp Cayenne (optional)
3	Cups Unsalted nuts

Procedure

Pre-heat oven to 325°. Whisk all the ingredients except the nuts together until foamy. Stir in nuts to coat. Spread the nuts on a nonstick or parchment lined baking sheet. Bake 15 minutes. Turn off the oven. Toss the nuts and return the baking sheet to the oven for 10 minutes. Allow to cool before serving.

MY NOTES:

Onion Apple Bites

Yields 32 Bites

About This Recipe

Although the cooking for this recipe takes more than an hour, the prep time is only about 10 minutes if you use pre-made frozen puff pastry. The combination of apple and onion may sound weird, but the onion is caramelized and thus quite sweet. Trust me, the combination works.

The original recipe for this dish called for melting cheese on top. I think this detracts from the dish, so I've left it out, but, if you think you would like it, use it.

You can make these ahead of time up to the point of baking and freeze them.

Ingredients

3   Tbs Butter
1   Lb Onions, thinly sliced
     Salt and pepper to taste
2   Cooking apples, peeled, cored and thinly sliced
1   Sheet puff pastry, defrosted

Procedure

Sauté the onions in the butter with salt and pepper for about 5 minutes. Add the apples and stir to coat. Cook the mixture for about 30 minutes over medium heat or until the onions are well-caramelized. Set aside to cool.

Pre-heat oven to 375°. Cut a puff pastry sheet into 16 squares and then halve each square diagonally to make 32 triangles.

Place a teaspoonful of apple-onion mix on each triangle and set them on 1 or more baking sheets. Bake 15 - 20 minutes until the pastry is golden. Serve hot.

MY NOTES:

Stuffed Mushrooms

Yields 24 pieces

About This Recipe

Stuffed mushrooms are a caterer's staple. This is because they are cheap, easy to make and everybody likes them. This variation fits the genre. You simply remove the stems from mushrooms, fill the cavities with a stuffing mix and bake them. The options for the stuffing are endless. I've provided one suggestion, but feel free to invent your own. The only caveat is to get mushrooms that are large enough to hold the stuffing.

Some other things you might consider putting in your stuffing are shallots, pine nuts, olives, sausage meat, prosciutto, ham, crabmeat and a soft cheese like goat cheese or even cream cheese.

Ingredients

24   Button mushrooms, 2 – 2.5" in diameter
½   Cup Roasted red peppers, finely chopped
½   Cup Seasoned bread crumbs
½   Cup Grated Parmagiano Reggiano or Pecorino
3   Cloves garlic, minced
2   Tbs Finely chopped basil leaves
      Salt and pepper to taste
2   Tbs EVOO

Procedure

Pre-heat oven to 400°. Clean the mushrooms and remove the stems. Mix the remaining ingredients together to make a stuffing. The mix should be damp, so add more EVOO if needed. Stuff the mushrooms and set out on a baking sheet. Bake for 25 minutes or until lightly browned. Allow to cool and serve at room temperature.

MY NOTES:

Chapter 6: Main Dishes: Beef

There is nothing more American than beef. Here are 16 recipes guaranteed to please the beef eater. Most of these recipes use inexpensive cuts, so there is no reason not to enjoy great beef dishes often.

Beef Braised in Red Wine

6-8 Servings

About This Recipe

Volume I included Marcella Hazan's recipe for veal braised in white wine. This recipe is similar in that a chunk of beef is braised in red wine. If you like pot roast, try this recipe, a departure from the usual. You will need a full bottle of a hearty red wine. It does not have to be expensive. I don't like to use brisket for this dish. It works better with a thicker cut such as chuck, bottom round or rump roast.

I like to serve this roast with roasted red potatoes and a green vegetable like stringbeans or peas.

Ingredients

3	Lbs Beef roast suitable for braising
	Salt and pepper to taste
¼	Lb Pancetta or blanched bacon, small dice
2	Medium onions, medium dice
2	Medium carrots. Peeled and diced
2	Stalks celery, diced
1	Tbs Tomato paste
3	Cloves garlic, pressed or minced
1	Bottle Red wine
1	14-oz can of tomatoes
1	Tbs Chopped fresh oregano or rosemary

Procedure

Trim excess fat from the meat, but keep some on. Pat the roast dry and sprinkle it with salt and pepper. In a Dutch oven on medium-low heat put about ¼ cup of water and then sauté the diced pancetta or bacon until it is crispy. Reserve.

Brown the roast on all sides in the Dutch oven over medium-high heat. If there is not enough fat from the pancetta, add a little oil. Reserve the meat.

(Recipe continues on next page)

Add the onions, carrots, celery and garlic to the pot. Sprinkle with salt and pepper. Sauté about 3 minutes. Add the tomato paste and stir. Cook 1 minute and add the tomatoes with their juice, the pancetta, the chopped herbs and the red wine. Stir and place the roast on top of the vegetables. Cover the pot and braise for about 3 hours, turning the roast once or twice.

Remove the roast and tent it with foil to keep it warm. With an immersion blender, purée the contents of the pot. If desired, you can strain the liquid, but I don't think it is necessary. Bring the sauce to a boil and reduce the sauce to the consistency you like. Adjust seasoning.

Cut the meat into 1/2" thick slices and pour the sauce over them. Sprinkle with the chopped herbs. Serve at once or reheat later on.

MY NOTES:

Beef Stroganoff in One Pan Revised

2 Servings

About This Recipe

In Volume I, I presented a recipe for Beef Stroganoff in one pan which I stole from *America's Test Kitchen*. Since then, I've made it a few times, experimented, and, I think, have improved upon the original. While the original recipe served four, this one serves two, but it can easily be expanded to serve many more.

This recipe takes 15 minutes less than the Volume I version which you can use to enjoy an additional cocktail.

Ingredients

10	Oz Tri-tip steak
	Salt and pepper to taste
1	Tbs Garlic-infused EVOO
1	Small onion, finely chopped
6	Oz mushrooms, any kind
2	Tbs Flour
2	Cups Chicken or veal stock
¼	Cup cognac or dry sherry
	Thyme sprigs or ½ Tsp dried thyme
1	Tbs Worcestershire sauce
8	Oz Manischewitz broad noodles or other pasta
½	Cup Sour cream at room temperature
1	Tbs Fresh thyme or ½ Tsp dried thyme
	Juice of 1 lemon
2	Tbs Chopped parsley

Procedure

Pound the steak to a uniform ¾" thickness. Slice it cross-grain into 1/4" thick pieces. Partially freezing the meat can make it easier to slice.

Sprinkle the meat on both sides with salt and pepper. In a large skillet over high heat, sauté it in the garlic-infused EVOO, about 30 seconds per side, working in batches if necessary. Reserve the meat.

Add the onion and mushrooms to the pan, sprinkle with salt and cook 8 minutes, stirring often. Add the flour and stir to coat evenly. Add the thyme, stock, cognac or sherry and Worcestershire sauce. Bring to a boil, add the meat, cover and simmer 15 minutes. Uncover and add the noodles. If using the recommended noodles, cook 8 minutes. Otherwise cook up to 12 minutes depending on the pasta you are using.

Remove the thyme sprigs and correct the seasoning. Off-heat, stir in the sour cream and lemon juice. Sprinkle with the chopped parsley and serve in the skillet.

Braised Beef Cheeks

6-8 Servings

About This Recipe

Talk about frugal, it is hard to find a cut of beef cheaper than cheeks. I've seen it as low as $1.50/lb. If your local market doesn't carry it or won't order it, look for it in a Latino market. Although cheeks are a tough cut, when cooked for a long time, they turn into one of the most mouth-watering meats you have ever had

Ingredients

4	12-oz Beef cheeks
	Salt and pepper to taste
	EVOO for sautéing
1	Medium Onion, finely chopped
1	Medium Carrot, finely chopped
1	Stalk Celery, finely chopped
3	Cloves Garlic, minced or pressed
1	Tsp Cocoa powder (optional)
2	Cups Red wine or 1 cup red wine and 1 cup Port
1	28-oz Can of tomatoes with their juice
½	Tbs Salt
1	Tsp Ground black pepper
1	Tsp Spanish smoked paprika (optional)
1	Tsp Dried thyme (optional)
½	Tbs Dried oregano (optional)
2	Bay leaves (optional)

Procedure

Cut the cheeks in half. Dry them with paper towels and sprinkle with salt and pepper. Heat a large Dutch oven to medium-high. Coat the bottom with EVOO and sear the cheeks on both sides until very brown, working in batches. Reserve the meat. Pour off the fat, add a bit more EVOO and cook the vegetables over medium heat for 10-15 minutes until they begin to caramelize. Stir in the cocoa powder if using, then deglaze the pot with the wine. Cook over high heat until the liquid is reduced by half. Return the cheeks to the pot add the tomatoes, crushing them with your hands or with a wooden spatula. Add the salt and pepper and any herbs you wish. Bring to a boil, reduce to a simmer, cover and braise for 3 hours, either on top of the stove or in a pre-heated 300° oven. If there is not enough liquid in the pot, add a little stock (any kind). During the cooking, check every hour and add stock if needed.

You can serve it immediately, but better, let it cool and refrigerate it. The next day, scoop off any congealed fat. Remove the meat and reduce the liquid until you get it the way you like it, or thicken it with a corn starch slurry.

Bruce Aidell's Steak with Pepper Sauce

2-4 Servings

About This Recipe

I stole this recipe from Bruce Aidell. He is the person who popularized chicken-based sausages when much of America was going freaky over cholesterol. Unknown to many, Bruce likes all kinds of meat, a subject that he has written about extensively in his cookbooks.

This recipe creates a grilling rub and a sauce based on the pequillo, a pepper from Spain that you buy in a jar already roasted and packed in water, brine or oil. It takes about 25 minutes to make the sauce, about the same time it takes to grill a thick steak and let it rest. I like to make this dish with a large thick cut of meat and then to slice it to expose more surface area to the sauce. Sirloin or tri-tip are cuts that work well with this recipe.

You can substitute roasted red bell peppers for the pequillo, but the sauce will have a slightly different taste. The original; recipe calls for fresh sage, but I think oregano works better. It also calls for capers, but I think they can be left out, so I made them optional.

Ingredients

2	Tsp Paprika
1	Tsp Dark brown sugar
2	Tsp Salt
1	Tsp Ground black pepper
1½	Lbs Your favorite steak
¼	Cup EVOO
3	Cloves Garlic, thinly sliced
2	Medium shallots, thinly sliced
1	Tbs Drained capers (optional)
1	Tsp Chopped fresh sage or oregano
8	Pequillo peppers (or regular roasted bell peppers), drained, seeded and chopped
1	Tsp Dijon mustard
½	Tsp Worcestershire sauce

Procedure

Make a rub by combining the paprika, sugar, salt and pepper. Rub it over the meat and let stand a few minutes while your grill heats up. Grill the steak to 125° for medium-rare, then let it stand for 10 minutes before slicing.

To make the sauce, sauté the garlic, shallots and capers in the EVOO for about 3 minutes. Stir in the herbs and cook 1 minute. Add the pequillos, mustard and Worcestershire sauce and cook over moderate heat for 15 minutes. Spoon over the slices of steak.

MY NOTES:

Catalan Beef Stew

6-8 Servings

About This Recipe

Italian food gets most of the culinary press in North America, but I think that Spanish food is right up there with Italian and deserves to be on a lot more menus. Like the Italians, there is a lot of emphasis on simplicity and hearty flavor profiles. Spanish cuisine also has a Moorish influence (the Moors ran Spain for 700 years). Since the Moroccans know a thing or two about food, this is a very good thing. I think you will agree that this might be the best beef stew you have ever tasted.

I had a beef stew in Barcelona, the capitol of Catalonia, and loved it. However, I was not able to get the recipe. When I got home, I went searching on the Internet and found a recipe from the *Epicurious* website that comes close to what I had in Spain. I made a few minor changes that I think make life simpler and don't markedly change the result.

You can use whatever cut of beef you like, but Epicurious suggests using boneless English-cut (parallel to the bone) shortribs. This turns out to be an excellent suggestion. Shortribs have a lot of collagen-rich tissue that, when slow-cooked, produces a silky sauce and melt-in-your-mouth meat. In addition, shortribs can be inexpensive, although some upscale markets often charge a lot for them. They are popular in Mexican and Korean cuisine, so if you have a Korean or Latino market in your neighborhood, they may be cheap. When I tested this recipe, my local supermarket charged $9/lb for scrawny shortribs, but my local Mexican market charged $4/lb for big meaty ones.

Unlike most stew recipes that call for browning the meat first, this recipe relies on oven browning to do that job. It turns out that meat brought to a temperature of 300° or more will brown if cooked long enough. This phenomenon is called the "maillard reaction." If you are curious, look it up on Wikipedia.

This recipe calls for the addition of a "picada" at the end. A picada is a Catalan flavoring and thickening agent made (usually) with nuts, bread, parsley and garlic. It has nothing to do with the Mexican "piquante" or the Italian "piccata". Picada is a term also used in South American cuisine, but it is not the same as Catalonian.

As with other stews, I'm happy with a green salad and a terrific bread for sopping up the juices. If you insist on a starch accompaniment, I'd go for a rice pilaf, broad noodles or Moroccan or Israeli couscous.

By the way, the Catalonians call this dish "Estofado de Ternera", which translates to "beef stew." Fancy that.

Ingredients

2	Tbs EVOO
2	Large Onions, finely chopped
½	Tsp Salt
½	Tsp Sugar
2	Tbs Tomato paste

(Recipe continues on next page)

1	Tsp Smoked Spanish paprika or more to taste
2	Bay leaves
1½	Cups Water
1½	Cups White wine
1	Sprig Fresh or ½ Tsp dried thyme
¼	Tsp Ground cinnamon
2½	Lbs Boneless shortribs, trimmed of fat and silverskin
½	Lb Mushrooms, cut into bite-size pieces
1	Tsp Sherry vinegar

PICADA

¼	Cup Blanched almonds, hazelnuts or pine nuts
2	Tbs EVOO
1	Large Slice of rustic bread, crust removed, cubed
2	Cloves Garlic, peeled
3	Tbs Parsley, finely chopped

Procedure

Pre-heat oven to 300°. In a large Dutch oven, heat the EVOO to the shimmering stage and add the onions, sugar and salt. Cook, stirring often, until the onions are caramelized and dark brown in color, about 30 - 40 minutes. Add the tomato paste, paprika and bay leaves. Cook, stirring often, for a couple of minutes.

Add the wine, water, thyme and cinnamon and deglaze the pot. Sprinkle the meat with salt and pepper and add to the pot. Bring the liquid to the simmer and place the pot in the oven uncovered. After 1 hour stir the pot and return it to the oven. Cook for an additional hour and a half. Keep an eye on the pot. If it looks like too much liquid has evaporated, add more water.

The original recipe called for oyster mushrooms, but I prefer regular button mushrooms or cèpes. Sauté the mushrooms in a little EVOO in the skillet until they give off their moisture, 5-7 minutes. Reserve the mushrooms.

Meanwhile, make the picada. In a skillet, brown the nuts in a little EVOO until golden. Transfer them to a food processor. In the same skillet, toast the bread cubes until golden, and add them to the food processor. Toss in the garlic cloves and process until the mixture is finely ground. Remove the mixture to a bowl and stir in the chopped parsley.

Take the stew out of the oven. Remove and discard the bay leaves and thyme sprigs. Stir in the picada, mushrooms and vinegar. Adjust seasoning. If you don't have any sherry vinegar lying around, you can add a little dry sherry and a little white wine vinegar. Results will be similar.

MY NOTES:

Churrasco

2-4 Servings

About This Recipe

To my ears, Brazilian Portuguese is one of the world's most beautiful languages - for sure, the sexiest. You have to admit that the name of this dish just flows off the tongue and fits right in to a dialog of sweet nothings. Over the last 15 years or so, Brazilian grilled meat restaurants have spread all over North America. One of the variations always served at these places is churrasco, which is nothing more than marinated grilled steak served with chimichurri sauce (See Volume I).

I've suggested flank steak because the Brazilian version generally uses a thin steak, but you can use any kind of steak you like. The marinade variations are endless, as are the formulas for the sauce, so feel free to experiment. Basically, you can't go wrong.

There are some Argentines who will claim that this recipe is theirs. Pay them no heed.

Ingredients

1	Small Onion, finely chopped
6	Cloves Garlic, pressed or minced
2	Tbs EVOO
1	Tbs Red wine vinegar
1	Tbs Lemon juice
1	Tbs Fresh oregano, chopped or ½ Tbs dried
	Salt and pepper to taste
1½	Lbs Flank steak

Procedure

Place all the ingredients except the steak in a jar and shake it fiercely to combine. Place the steak in a Ziploc bag, add the marinade, seal the bag, squish it around to make sure that the steak is completely coated and refrigerate it overnight. If you can, turn it over a couple of times during the marinating process.

Allow the steak to come to room temperature. Grill the steak to your liking, let it rest 10 minutes, slice it cross grain and serve it with the chimichurri sauce on the side.

MY NOTES:

Filet of Beef, Low Temperature Method

12-20 Servings

About This Recipe

The faster meat cooks, the larger the temperature gradient between the outside and the center. Have you ever wondered how restaurants can serve some cuts of beef like prime rib and tenderloin where the outside is well-browned and the meat is uniformly pink throughout? The answer is to cook it a low temperature.

A whole beef tenderloin weighs 4 - 5 pounds and will serve 12 - 20 people. The problem with the whole piece is that it is thick on one end and thin on the other. Thus, if you do a whole piece, you need to fold the thin end back so that the thickness is relatively uniform. Ideally, you would buy just the center cut, also known as the chateaubriand, but that is likely to be very expensive.

The filet is, of course, the most expensive cut of beef. However, you can save a lot of money if you buy the whole tenderloin untrimmed and do the trimming yourself. You can find YouTube videos online that will show you how to do that. It isn't complicated.

When I researched this recipe, I found quite a variation in oven temperature and length of cooking time. Recommended temperatures varied from 225° to 275°. Some chefs recommend a last minute browning under the broiler, some don't. You decide.

Ingredients

1	Beef tenderloin
1	Tbs Salt (more if needed)
2	Tbs EVOO
2	Tsp Coarsely ground black pepper (more if needed)
1	Bunch Fresh thyme

Procedure

Pre-heat the oven to 275°.Tie the meat every two inches. Do this even if the thickness of the piece you are using is uniform. Generously salt the meat all over and let it sit on a baking sheet or shallow baking pan for 30 minutes.

Coat the meat all over with EVOO and the black pepper. Cover the meat with the thyme sprigs. Tie the sprigs onto the meat if necessary to hold them in place. Brush a little more oil over the top of the thyme.

Roast for 60 - 90 minutes until an instant read thermometer registers 125° for medium-rare.

Remove the roast from the oven, tent with foil and allow to rest for 30 minutes. Slice the meat 1/2" thick and serve at once with your choice of sauce (or not) on the side.

MY NOTES:

Individual Beef Wellingtons

2 Servings

About This Recipe

The origins are controversial. Some say it was developed for the Duke of Wellington - the one who bested Napoleon. Others claim it was invented in New Zealand in the early 1960s and named after the city of Wellington. Regardless of the truth, it first appeared in a published work in 1966. The inventor of the dish coated a whole beef tenderloin with paté de foie gras and a mushroom duxelle and wrapped it in a puff pastry shell before baking it. Sometimes black truffles were added to the duxelle, making the dish one of the least frugal recipes ever, especially since the tenderloin is the most expensive cut of a bovine. I suppose that is why one rarely encounters Beef Wellington these days. However, it is a fantastic dish that doesn't deserve to be shunned.

In this recipe, I attempt to do something similar to the classic dish, but make it more affordable and easier to make, but, if you happen to have some paté de foie gras and black truffles laying around, by all means use them.

I suggest that you use filet mignon steaks that weigh 4-6 oz each. At this writing, you can get them for around $12/pound, so one of them will cost $3 - $4. Not cheap, but not a killer for a special occasion. Beef Wellington is traditionally served with a sauce. You can use any of the meat-friendly sauces in this book or Volume I.

Ingredients

2	4-6 Oz Thick filet mignon steaks
1	Tbs EVOO
½	Lb Mushrooms, chopped fine
2	Shallots, chopped fine
	Salt and pepper to taste
2	Tbs Brandy
1	Sheet Frozen puff pastry dough, defrosted
	Egg yolk wash

Procedure

Pre-heat oven to 425°.In a large skillet, sear the steaks on top and bottom in EVOO. Set the steaks aside. In the same pan, add the mushrooms and shallots, season to taste and cook until the liquid is gone and the mix is browned. Deglaze the pan with brandy and cook until the liquid has evaporated. Allow to cool.

Roll out the sheet of puff pastry on a floured surface to a thickness of around ⅛". Cut the sheet into pieces large enough to wrap around a steak. Place a spoonful of mushroom-shallot mix in the middle of the pastry and top with a steak. Top the steak with another spoonful of the mix. Pull the pastry over the meat and press the edges together to seal. Cut off any excess pastry and/or tuck it under. Paint the pastry with an egg yolk wash and bake for 25 minutes. Take the meat out when it registers 125° on an instant read thermometer (for medium rare). Allow to sit for 10 minutes before serving.

La Genovese

6-8 Servings

About This Recipe

La Genovese, also known as beef and onion ragu, is a classic Neapolitan pasta dish. The meaty flavor of this dish derives from the onions that contain a compound known as MMP, which, if heated correctly creates a flavor like beef broth! In Naples, the meat is taken out of the sauce and either served as a second course or saved for another meal. I like my pasta meat sauces meaty, so I leave the meat in.

Ingredients

2	Lbs Chuck roast
2	Tbs Salt
2	Tsp Ground black pepper
1	Tbs EVOO or lard
4	Oz Salami, pancetta, prosciutto or a combination, diced
1	Carrot, diced
1	Stalk Celery, diced
2	Tbs Tomato paste
2	Cups Water
3	Lbs Onions, chopped fine
1	Cup Red or white wine
2	Tbs Fresh marjoram or oregano, chopped
1	Lb Thick cooked pasta like ziti or rigatoni
2	Tbs Grated Parmagiano Reggiano

Procedure

Cut the meat into 4 chunks, weighing about ½ pound each. Remove any hard fat and gristle. Coat the meat with salt and pepper and let stand for at least 30 minutes. Put the pancetta, salami or prosciutto in the food processor and process to a paste. Add the carrot and celery and process 30 seconds.

Pre-heat the oven to 300°. In a large Dutch oven, coat the bottom with lard or EVOO and add the contents of the food processor. Stir well and cook about 5 minutes until the paste has begun to brown. Add tomato paste and cook 1 - 2 minutes. Add 2 cups of water and deglaze the pot. Add the chopped onions and bring to a boil. Add ½ the wine and a tablespoon of chopped marjoram or oregano. Submerge the beef pieces in the pot. Transfer the pot to a 300° oven, uncovered, and bake 2½ hours.

Remove the pot from the oven and transfer to the stove top. Take out the meat and shred it using a couple of forks. Reduce the sauce over medium heat for about 10 minutes. Return the shredded beef to the pot and add ½ cup of wine and another tablespoon of chopped marjoram or oregano. Adjust seasoning to taste, and cook for a few minutes to burn off the alcohol. Add the drained pasta and grated cheese. Stir and serve at once.

Marinated Tri-Tip Roast

4-6 Servings

About This Recipe

A few years ago, almost nobody had heard of Tri-Tip. Today it is very popular on the West Coast and has migrated to the East coast where it is sometimes known as "Newport steak." The cut, which comes from the bottom of the sirloin, is popular in Europe where it has a variety of unpronounceable names, and in South America, especially Brazil and Argentina.

The Tri-Tip is a single muscle weighing 1½ - 2½ pounds. It can be sliced into steaks or cooked as a roast. It has a very low fat content, so works best when it has been marinated and cooked rare or medium-rare. It does not take well to long slow cooking. The taste is superb, as good as a New York steak, and a lot less expensive.

This recipe uses a lime juice based marinade. The acid in the juice will partially cook the meat, so it needs relatively little cooking time. You can cook this roast in a high-temperature oven or on a covered grill. You want the temperature to be at least 500°. I prefer doing this on an outdoor grill, because at that high temperature, there is likely to be a lot of smoke, which will make your significant other very angry.

Serve this roast like you would a boneless prime rib roast. It doesn't need a gravy or a sauce, but anything that goes with roast beef will work. Same with side dishes.

Ingredients

1	Head Garlic
1	Jalapeno pepper
2	Cups Warm water
1	Tsp Salt
1	Tbs Lime juice
1	1½ – 2½ Lb Tri-tip roast

Procedure

Break up the head of garlic and peel all the cloves. Put everything except the meat into a blender or food processor and blend for 15 seconds. Put the mixture into a sealable baggie and add the meat. Smush it around until the meat is uniformly coated with the marinade. Marinate in the refrigerator overnight.

Heat a covered grill or oven to 500°. Place the roast on a foil-lined roasting pan, fat side up. Roast 20 v- 40 minutes depending on size and desired doneness. For medium rare, the internal temperature should be 125° measured on an instant-read thermometer. Let the roast stand for 15 minutes before carving.

MY NOTES:

Michael Jordan's 23 Delmonico Steak

4 Servings

About This Recipe

Michael Jordan once lent his name to a restaurant called 23 in Chicago. One of its signature dishes was "Delmonico Steak". Although 23 used ribeye, you can use whatever cut you wish. New York, filet mignon and tri-tip are all good choices. The thing that makes this steak special is the sauce which is based on balsamic vinegar.

You can grill the steak, but consider making it the restaurant way by searing first and then finishing the cooking in the oven. To do that, pre-heat the oven to 450° - 500°. Put an ovenproof skillet large enough to hold the steak in the oven and heat it for 5 minutes. A cast iron skillet is ideal for this application. Season the steak with salt and pepper. Move the skillet to the stove top. With the heat on high, sear the steak 30 - 60 seconds on each side, then move the steak into the oven and cook it 2 minutes on each side for medium rare (assuming the steak is about 1.5" thick). Remove to a plate, tent with foil and allow to rest 10 minutes before serving.

This is a very hearty dish that calls for sides like mushrooms, onions and roasted potatoes. The mushroom ragoût recipe in the vegetable chapter is a perfect accompaniment. Maybe warm up with something like a Caprese salad.

Ingredients

1	Tbs EVOO
¼	Cup Ginger, minced
¼	Cup Carrots, finely chopped
¼	Cup Shallots, finely chopped
¼	Cup Celery, finely chopped
½	Cup Balsamic vinegar
1	Cup Beef or chicken stock
4	Steaks
	Salt and pepper to taste

Procedure

Heat the EVOO in a skillet and add the vegetables. Cook them until they are well caramelized, 15 minutes or so. Stir in the balsamic vinegar. Bring to a boil and reduce by half. Add the stock, return to the boil and reduce by half again. Transfer to a gravy boat.

Dust the steaks with salt and pepper. Grill them the way you like them or do what many restaurants do; that is, sear them on both sides in a skillet and finish cooking them in the oven as described in the intro.

MY NOTES:

Oxtails, Caribbean-Style

6 Servings

About This Recipe

Oxtails are one of my favorites. This dish comes from Sarah Kirnon, chef-owner of Miss Ollie's in Oakland, California. She specializes in soul food with a distinctly contemporary influence. This dish is one of her restaurant's staples.

This recipe calls for cassareep, a thick bitter liquid made from cassava root. If you don't live near a market that sells Caribbean food, you can get it online for about $5/bottle. The original recipe calls for habañeros, the world's hottest chili peppers. If you aren't into heat, omit them or substitute a less aggressive chili such as jalapeño.

In the Caribbean, you would probably accompany a dish like this with rice, but baked or mashed sweet potatoes work well too.

Ingredients

6	Large Oxtail sections
1	Large Onion, coarsely chopped
	Salt and pepper to taste
1	Bunch Fresh thyme
1	Tbs Whole cloves
5	Bay leaves
3	Cinnamon sticks
1	Cup Cassareep
2	Habañero chilis
	Zest strips from half an orange
½	Tsp Ground nutmeg
	Brown sugar (optional)

Procedure

Put the oxtails and the onion in a Dutch oven, add water to cover and salt and pepper to taste. Bring to a boil, reduce heat and simmer 40 minutes, skimming off any scum that forms.

In a piece of cheesecloth, tie up the thyme, cloves, bay leaves and cinnamon and add to the pot. Add the remaining ingredients except the sugar. Cover pot and simmer about 2 hours. Reserve oxtails. Skim off the fat and discard the cheesecloth, orange peel and chilis.

Bring to a boil and reduce the sauce until it reaches the consistency you want. Taste and add brown sugar if you wish. Return oxtails to the pot and heat through before serving.

MY NOTES:

Sherry's Brisket Pot Roast

12-20 Servings

About This Recipe

My wife Sherry makes the world's best beef brisket pot roast. After much pleading, she has agreed to share her recipe with my readers. There are two secrets to her recipe. The first is to coat the meat with a layer of ground ginger. The second is to cook it literally smothered in aromatic vegetables.

Brisket comes in two forms, so-called "single" and "double" The double brisket is two layers of meat separated by a thick layer of fat. Single brisket is the bottom layer. Unfortunately, double brisket is hard to find these days. This is not a deal-breaker, but, if you can find a double brisket or a single one with the fat left on, your brisket will be better than without it. Of course, if you are lucky enough to buy from a real butcher, you can get it any way you want. Briskets weigh anywhere from 3 to 12 pounds.

Warning: This recipe requires a fair amount of work. Sherry makes it only twice a year for holidays, and every time she makes it, she says never again. I'll let you be the judge.

Sherry likes to serve this with a green vegetable such as stringbeans.

Ingredients

6	Lbs Beef brisket
	Salt and pepper to taste
½	Cup Ground ginger
4	Large Onions, coarsely chopped
6	Large Carrots. Coarsely chopped
1	Head Celery, coarsely chopped
1	Head Garlic, cloves left unpeeled and smashed
1	Lb Flavorful mushrooms, fresh or reconstituted, coarsely chopped
1	Bunch Curly parsley, coarsely chopped
¼	Cup Canola or peanut oil
½	Bottle Manischewitz wine
2	Cups Water or stock
2	Tbs Kitchen Bouquet seasoning sauce
3	Lbs Boiling potatoes, cut in large chunks or left whole if small
6	Large Carrots, peeled and cut into 2"-3" lengths

Procedure

Pre-heat oven to 375°. Sprinkle with meat with salt and pepper on both sides, then apply a layer of ground ginger, completely coating the meat.

(Recipe continues on next page)

In a roasting pan large enough to hold the brisket flat and at least 3" deep, add the oil and smear it around to coat the bottom of the pan. Add the smashed garlic cloves and cook on high heat for 1 minute to infuse the oil. Mix the chopped vegetables and herbs together in a large bowl. Put half the vegetables in the bottom of the pan. Lay the brisket on top of the vegetables and spread the rest over the top of the meat. Mix together the water or stock, wine and Kitchen Bouquet and pour it into the pan. Cover the pan and roast until the meat can be easily pierced with a carving fork, about 4 hours.

Take the roast out of the oven and allow it to cool to room temperature, then refrigerate it overnight. Be careful taking it out of the onions as there will be quite a bit of liquid that has been given off by the vegetables.

The next day, pre-heat the oven again to 375°. Remove the meat from the roasting pan, scraping off the vegetables. Carve the meat while it is cold into cross-grain slices about 1/4" - ⅜" thick (It is easier to cut thin slices when cold.) Keep the slices in the carving order to make a nice presentation when you serve. The fat will have congealed in the refrigerator making it easy to remove if you wish.

Put the roasting pan on the stove top and bring the contents to a boil. Pour the contents through a sieve set over a large bowl, retaining the liquid. Press the vegetables with the back of a large spoon to extract as much liquid as possible. That liquid is your gravy. Skim off the fat if you wish. You can thicken the gravy with a cornstarch slurry if you wish.

Here are two alternative gravies: 1. Purée the vegetables and roasting liquid with an immersion blender or food processor, which will make a thick, flavorful gravy. Try a little and see if you like it. If you do, then you can purée the rest. 2. Don't do anything extra. Just serve the sliced meat with the pan juices and vegetables spooned over it.

MY NOTES:

Spanish Steak Stir-Fry

2 Servings

About This Recipe

This recipe can be made in less than half an hour. The idea is to take some thinly sliced steak, marry it with peppers and finish it off with some Spanish seasonings. You can use whatever combination of peppers appeals to you. Hot ones, mild ones, the choice is up to you.

This recipe suggest three types of peppers, two of which come in cans or jars. Fresh red bell peppers, piquillo peppers from Spain (or Peru) and peppadews from South Africa. If you can't find the latter two in your local market, try Amazon or other online sources. Or just use regular roasted peppers that come in a jar. I warn you that there is a wide variation in the prices of piquillos and peppadews but they all taste pretty much the same. Look for the good deals.

You can use any kind of steak you like, but I suggest flank steak. It is relatively inexpensive and lends itself to thin slices. If you don't want to use steak, you can substitute chicken or pork.

You could serve this over rice, or over Israeli pearl couscous.

Ingredients

1	Flank Steak or tri-tip, 8-10 oz, sliced ¼" thick cross-grain
	Salt and pepper to taste
	EVOO
½	Medium Onion, Coarsely chopped
2	Cloves Garlic, peeled and thinly sliced
1	Red bell pepper, seeded and cut into strips
4	Oz Piquillo peppers, drained and diced
4	Oz Peppadews, chopped
2	Tbs Sherry vinegar
1	Tsp Spanish smoked paprika (pimenton)

Procedure

Sprinkle the meat with salt and pepper. In a large skillet, sauté the steak in batches in EVOO about 30 seconds per side. Reserve steak.

Add onions, scallions, bell pepper and garlic to pan and sauté about 3 minutes. Add piquillos, peppadews, paprika and sherry vinegar to pan along with a little of the piquillo or peppadew liquid. Cook until liquid thickens, about 4 minutes. Return meat to pan and heat through. Serve immediately.

MY NOTES:

Sukiyaki

4 Servings

About This Recipe

Sukiyaki (pronounced more like ski-ya-ki) is one of my favorite dishes. It is one of the Japanese dishes that appeals to the American palate. The Japanese have many variations, but there are a few constants, which I have incorporated in this recipe. If you ever get to Japan, don't miss eating at a sukiyaki restaurant. Typically, these are tiny places that serve only sukiyaki plus beer, sake and booze. A lady sits at your table (or on the floor) and creates the dish on your table as the evening wears on. She also pours your sake or other drink. God forbid that you should lift a finger to do anything other than chew, swallow, and belch!

When the Japanese eat sukiyaki, it is accompanied by a bowl containing a beaten raw egg. One picks up the food with chopsticks and dips it into the raw egg before eating. Frankly, I find this practice unappealing, but if you are into authenticity, try it. Although sukiyaki can be cooked all at once and served in a bowl, it is more fun if you cook the ingredients as the meal progresses. To that end, layout the raw ingredients on a large platter. The cooking can be done on a pan set on a hot plate or in an electric skillet which will be more convenient in most American kitchens. Whichever you choose, the heat needs to be adjustable so that you can maintain a good cooking temperature.

The choice of ingredients is up to you, but the basics are thinly sliced steak and sukiyaki sauce. A first-class meal will use wagyu or matsuzaka beef that has been sliced almost paper thin - very expensive in America. I recommend that you use a tender steak of your choice, partially freeze it and then slice it cross-grain as thin as you can get it, but if you are able to find a well-equipped butcher, he can slice it very thin by machine. Ribeye is probably the best choice. The choice of vegetables and noodles is up to you. I've given you some commonly used items, and you can choose the ones you want. At the end of the meal, you are likely to have broth left over in the cooking pan. The Japanese often finish a sukiyaki meal with precooked udon noodles added to the broth.

Appearance is all important to the Japanese. If you go online and Google sukiyaki, you will find lots of pictures and videos that show you how to cut the various veggies, some of them quite decorative.

In any event, sukiyaki is not difficult to prepare, and the ingredients are readily available in most markets. Go for it. You will be glad you did, especially if you accompany the dish with lots of hot sake! By the way, "suki" means fondness and "yaki" means cooked. You get the idea.

(Recipe continues on next page)

Ingredients

SAUCE

½   Cup Mirin or ½ tsp sugar dissolved in ½ cup sherry
     Salt and pepper
½   Cup Sake
⅓   Cup Soy sauce
1   Tbs Garlic, minced
¼   Cup Sugar

INGREDIENTS PLATTER

Beef, sliced very thin, cut in manageable pieces
Napa cabbage (hakusa) leaves, white part only
Shiitake mushrooms, whole or sliced, stems removed
Enoki mushrooms
Scallions, cut on the bias in pieces 2" long
Onions, sliced
Carrots, thinly sliced on the bias
Celery, thinly sliced on the bias
Bamboo shoots
Japanese radish (daikon) cut on the bias
Shiritaki (cellophane) noodles or bean-thread noodles soaked in hot water and drained
Udon noodles, precooked (optional)

Procedure

Put all the sauce ingredients in a pot and bring to a boil. Boil a couple of minutes to get rid of the alcohol. Transfer sauce to a pitcher.

Arrange the main ingredients attractively on a large platter.

Get your cookpot hot and pour in some sauce. Add the ingredients a little at a time, and cook them as long as you like. After a while, you'll figure out just how long you like them cooked, although, after a few sakes, you may not care.

At the end, add the precooked udon to the pot, heat through and eat, slurping noisily and belching to indicate your satisfaction with the meal.

MY NOTES:

Thai Beef and Peppers Stir-fry

4 Servings

About This Recipe

My Thai friend tells me this recipe is not authentic, but it does have those well-known Thai flavors. It is fast and easy to fix, no more than 20 minutes start to finish. I don't recall the genesis of this recipe, but I made it a few times and changed things each time, for the better I hope, so it is (sort of) my invention.

You can add heat or not. If you want heat, you can use hot chilis, red pepper flakes, cayenne, Tabasco sauce or sriracha. Doesn't matter much.

A word or two about the noodles. I recommend rinsing them to get rid of some of the surface starch. This will help prevent them from becoming gluey in the final product. Further, when you add the noodles, use only half at first and add more only if you think the dish needs more.

Ingredients

8	Oz Rice noodles
½	Cup Soy sauce
3	Tbs Rice wine or dry sherry
2	Tbs Cornstarch
2	Tbs Brown sugar
1	Tbs Fresh ginger, minced
2	Cloves Garlic, pressed or minced
1	Tsp Thai red curry paste (more if desired)
½	Tbs Thai fish sauce
½	Tbs Lime juice
1	Lb flank steak, cut cross-grain
2	Tbs Canola or peanut oil
1	Onion, sliced
1	Red bell pepper, seeded and sliced into rings
	Hot stuff (optional)
	Thai basil leaves for garnish
	Cilantro leaves for garnish

Procedure

Make the noodles according to package directions. When they are cooked, drain and rinse them. Reserve the noodles in a warm oven if needed.

Mix the next 9 ingredients together. Put about half the mixture in a bowl and add the meat. Stir to coat the meat evenly.

(Recipe continues on next page)

In a large skillet, heat 1 Tbs of oil and add the onions. Cook one minute and add the bell peppers and hot peppers if using. Cook for another minute and reserve the vegetables. Add the remaining Tbs of oil to the pan, crank up the heat and stir fry the meat, about 30 seconds per side. You want the meat to be evenly browned. Add the remaining marinade and the vegetables. Turn down the heat and allow the dish to simmer a couple of minutes. Add half the noodles and toss. Add more noodles if desired and toss again. If the sauce is too thick, add a bit of hot water or stock

Put the contents of the skillet in a serving bowl. Squeeze lime juice over all and garnish with Thai basil and coriander leaves.

MY NOTES:

Chapter 7: Main Dishes: Chicken and Game Hen

No protein is more flexible than chicken. Here are 14 chicken recipes that run a broad gamut of flavors and cooking styles. There are several recipes calling for chicken thighs, the cut I like best, especially for braised recipes.

Best Chicken Stew

6-8 Servings

About This Recipe

I just happened to be watching the *America's Test Kitchen* TV show recently, and this dish was prepared by one of the cooks. It was so different than any other chicken stew recipe that I've ever seen, I decided to try it. I now agree that the adjective "Best" fits.

This recipe is one of those rare cases where I could not think of a way to improve it. So this is the recipe that is in the TV show verbatim.

The aim of this dish was to create a chicken stew that had many of the characteristics that one normally associates with beef stew. The use of flavoring ingredients like the bacon, anchovy paste and soy sauce contributes to that, but using the chicken wings is nothing short of genius. The wings add collagen which imparts a silky texture to the sauce and flavor from the browned skin. The cook also claimed that cooking the stew in the oven uncovered created a "crust" and fond that contributes to a meaty flavor. Sounds weird, but it works!

Ingredients

2	Lbs Boneless, skinless chicken thighs trimmed of excess fat and cut in half crosswise
	Salt and pepper to taste
2	Slices Bacon, chopped
1	Lb Chicken wings, halved at joint
1	Medium onion, finely chopped
1	Stalk Celery, finely chopped
2	Cloves Garlic, minced or pressed
2	Tsp Anchovy paste
1	Tsp Minced fresh thyme
5	Cups Chicken stock
1	Cup White wine
1	Tbs Soy sauce
3	Tbs Butter, cut into pieces
⅓	Cup flour

(Recipe continues on next page)

1	Lb Small boiling potatoes, unpeeled and halved or quartered depending on size
4	Medium Carrots, peeled and cut into ½" pieces
2	Tbs White wine
2	Tbs Chopped parsley

Procedure

Pre-heat the oven to 325° and position the rack in the next-to-lowest slot.

Place the chicken thighs on a baking sheet, sprinkle them with salt and pepper on both sides, cover with plastic wrap and set them aside.

In a large Dutch oven, brown the bacon pieces over medium heat, stirring occasionally, until the fat is rendered and the bacon bits are crispy, about 6 - 8 minutes. Transfer the bits to a bowl and set aside, leaving the bacon fat in the pot. Add the chicken wings and brown them well on both sides. This should take 10 - 12 minutes. Add the wings to the bacon bowl.

Add onion, celery, garlic, thyme and anchovy paste to the Dutch oven and cook 2 - 4 minutes until a dark fond forms on the bottom. Increase heat to high and add broth, wine and soy sauce. Deglaze the pot and bring to a boil. Boil 12 - 15 minutes until the liquid has evaporated. Add butter and stir until it is melted. Sprinkle in the flour and stir to combine with the vegetables.

Gradually whisk in the remaining four cups of chicken broth. Add the bacon and wings, potatoes and carrots. Bring to a simmer and transfer the pot, uncovered to the oven. Cook 30 minutes, stirring once during that period.

Remove the pot from the oven. With a wooden or plastic spoon scrape the fond that has accumulated on the sides of the pot into the stew. Add the thighs and bring the pot to the boil. Immediately transfer the pot to the oven and cook, uncovered, for 45 minutes.

Remove the pot from the oven. Discard the wings. Add a couple of Tbs of white wine and the chopped parsley. Adjust seasoning to taste.

MY NOTES:

Braised Herbed Chicken Thighs

2-4 Servings

About This Recipe

This is another easy and delicious method for cooking chicken. This recipe comes from Nestlé, the giant Swiss food company. I have no idea why they would promote this because I don't see any Nestlé products in it, but ours not to reason why.

You could serve this with pasta, rice or potatoes, but I like it with Israeli couscous, flavored to match. A green salad will finish off the meal.

Ingredients

4	Chicken thighs, bone-in, skin on or off as you prefer
½	Cup Flour for dredging
2	Tbs EVOO
6	Medium Shallots, coarsely chopped
4	Cloves Garlic, pressed or minced
¼	Cup Chicken stock
2	Tbs Balsamic vinegar
1½	Cups Chicken stock
1	Tsp Dried thyme
1	Tsp Dried basil
1	Tsp Dried marjoram
	Salt and pepper to taste

Procedure

Heat the EVOO in a large sauté pan or Dutch oven. Dredge the thighs in flour and brown them on both sides, about 2-4 minutes per side. Reserve the chicken. Wipe out the pot, add a little more EVOO and sauté the shallots until they begin to brown. Add the garlic and cook 1 minute. Deglaze the pan with 1/4 cup chicken stock and the vinegar. Boil until the liquid is reduced by half, about 2-3 minutes. Add the remaining ingredients and the chicken. Bring to a boil and simmer, covered, for 20-30 minutes. Serve at once.

MY NOTES:

Catalan Chicken Picada

4 Servings

About This Recipe

I happened across this recipe on both the Food & Wine and Epicurious web sites. It looked interesting, so I tried it. I'm glad I did. It is uniquely delicious. Picada is a finishing sauce that contains bread and almonds, and has nothing in common with the Italian "piccata." As you read the recipe, you will probably think it is not going to work, but, trust me, it does. Among other things, it contains chocolate. You might think this makes it tastes like a Mexican molé, but it does not.

The F&W recipe calls for using whole chicken legs, but I think the drumsticks are more trouble than they are worth, so I recommend using only thighs. In Spain, this dish would be served by itself, and what we think of as side dishes would be separate courses. If you want to serve it with something, I'd suggest couscous with vegetables.

Ingredients

4	Large Chicken thighs, skin on
	Salt and pepper to taste
2½	Tbs EVOO
1	Medium Onion, finely chopped
1	14-oz can of tomatoes, drained and chopped
1½	Cups Chicken stock
¼	Cup Dry sherry
1	Bay leaf
1	3" strip of orange peel
½	Tsp Chopped fresh thyme

PICADA

1	Large slice of coarse bread, crust removed and cut into cubes
¼	Cup Slivered almonds
	3 Cloves garlic, chopped
1	Oz Bittersweet chocolate, chopped
¼	Cup Chopped parsley
¼	Tsp Ground cinnamon
1	Pinch Saffron threads
1	Pinch Aniseed
1	Pinch Ground cloves

(Recipe continues on next page)

Procedure

In a Dutch oven or heavy-bottomed pot, heat 2 Tbs of EVOO. Dry the chicken pieces with paper towels, sprinkle with salt and pepper and brown them on both sides about 4 minutes for each side. Reserve the chicken.

Add the onion and cook until softened, about 5 minutes. Add the tomatoes and cook an additional 5 minutes. Add the stock, sherry, bay leaf, orange peel and thyme. Bring to a boil. Add the chicken, bring to the simmer and braise over low heat for 30 minutes.

While the chicken is cooking, make the picada. Toast the bread and almonds on a baking sheet in the oven for about 8 minutes. Sauté the garlic in ½ Tbs of EVOO in a small skillet until golden, about 3 minutes.

Put all the ingredients for the picada in a food processor and process to a paste. Stir it into the sauce and simmer for 15 minutes. Discard the orange peel and bay leaf and serve.

MY NOTES:

Chicken and Mushrooms

4 Servings

About This Recipe

If you Google "chicken and mushrooms" you will find dozens of recipes. Some use whole cut up chickens, some chicken breasts, some whole pieces, some chunks of meat. This one, my personal favorite, uses bone-in chicken thighs which I feel offers the most flavor with little danger of drying out like breast meat tends to do.

You have your choice of mushrooms. Regular white buttons, criminis, oysters, morels, porcinis, shiitakes, etc. They all work. Combining two or three types makes the dish more interesting. You could also add an ounce of reconstituted, chopped dried porcinis. That will give the dish an earthy flavor that you won't get from fresh mushrooms.

In researching this recipe, I found a variation that uses balsamic vinegar instead of sherry. I haven't tried it, but it sounds like a good idea.

If you want a smooth sauce, remove the mushrooms and chicken and strain the liquid through a sieve. Discard the solids and return the liquid to the pot before adding the thickener.

You could serve this dish with spaetzle, making it reminiscent of old-fashioned chicken and dumplings. For that matter, make some old-fashioned American dumplings if you have the time and inclination!

Ingredients

8	Bone-in, skin-on Chicken thighs
	Salt and pepper to taste
2	Tbs EVOO
2	Tbs Butter
1	Onion, thinly sliced
12	Oz Fresh mushrooms, cut into bite-size pieces
6	Cloves Garlic, peeled and smashed
1	Tsp Dried thyme or 6 sprigs fresh thyme
2	Bay leaves
¼	Cup Dry sherry or white vermouth
1	Cup Chicken stock
1	Cup White wine
	Flour/butter roux or cornstarch slurry
1-2	Tbs Butter for enrichment (optional)
2	Tbs Chopped parsley for garnish

(Recipe continues on next page)

Procedure

Pre-heat oven to 325°. Trim the thighs of excess fat and skin and dry them with paper towels. Sprinkle liberally with salt and pepper.

Heat the oil and butter in a Dutch oven until the fat shimmers and brown the thighs on all sides, working in two batches. This will take about 4 minutes per side. Set the thighs aside and, if there is a lot of fat in the pan, pour off all but a tablespoon.

Add the sliced onion and mushrooms and cook 5-7 minutes. Add the garlic cloves, bay leaves and thyme and cook 2 minutes. Deglaze the pan with the sherry or vermouth and cook until almost all the liquid is gone. Add the chicken stock, white wine, 1 Tsp salt and ½ Tsp pepper and bring to a boil. Add the thighs, cover the pot and place it in the pre-heated oven for half an hour. (The internal temperature of the chicken thighs should be at least 160°.) At the end of that time, remove the pot and lower the oven temperature to 200°. Remove the chicken and the mushrooms, place them in a container and into the oven to keep warm.

To finish the sauce, thicken the pot liquid with either a roux made of 1 Tbs softened butter and 1 Tbs flour or a cornstarch slurry made from 1 Tbs water mixed with 1 Tbs cornstarch. After adding the thickener, bring to the simmer, stirring constantly. Add more roux or slurry if the sauce is not as thick as you want. Adjust seasoning to taste. If you wish, swirl in a tablespoon or two of cold butter off-heat to enrich the sauce.

Plate two thighs and some mushrooms per person and pour over some sauce. Sprinkle with chopped parsley. Serve remaining sauce on the side.

MY NOTES:

Chicken Cacciatore II

4- 6 Servings

About This Recipe

I put a recipe for chicken cacciatore in Volume I. I made it the other day for the first time in several years, and (surprise) thought it could be better. After a couple of trials, I came up with this one, which I think is a big improvement.

The trick to either recipe is to do a thorough job browning the chicken pieces, which should be darker than just golden. This process can be more time-consuming than you think, especially if you have to do the browning in batches. The recipe calls for chicken thighs, but you can use any parts of the chicken that you prefer.

You can use any kind of mushroom. For max flavor, use porcinis, either raw or reconstituted. You can also use a green bell pepper instead of a red one, but, of course, the taste is different. My wife likes the dish with black olives in it. Not my choice, but maybe you will agree with her.

You can make the dish well ahead of time, and heat it up before serving. You may even find that it tastes better eaten the next day! I like to serve this dish over a thick pasta. Pappardella, ziti or mostaccioli are good choices.

Ingredients

8	Chicken thighs, bone-in, skin-on
	Salt and pepper to taste
	Flour for dredging
2	Tbs EVOO
1	Onion, coarsely chopped
1	Head Garlic, cloves peeled and coarsely chopped
1	Red bell pepper, coarsely chopped
4	Oz Mushrooms, coarsely chopped
2	Cups Red wine
1	28-oz can of tomatoes
2	Tbs tomato paste
1	Tbs Dried oregano
1	Tsp Dried thyme
1	Cup Chicken stock
1	Cup Pitted and halved black olives (optional)
1	Tbs Chopped Italian parsley for garnish

(Recipe continues on next page)

Procedure

Rinse and dry the chicken pieces with paper towels. Sprinkle on both sides with salt and pepper and dredge in flour, shaking off the excess. In a Dutch oven or deep sauté pan, brown the chicken pieces on both sides, in batches if the pan can't hold them all at once. Reserve the chicken.

In the same pan, add the chopped onion, garlic, bell pepper, and mushrooms. Cook for 10 minutes over medium heat, stirring occasionally. Add the wine and cook over high heat until the liquid has reduced by two-thirds. Add the can of tomatoes with juice, tomato paste, and dried herbs and cook for five minutes.

Return the chicken to the pot and bury the pieces in the sauce. If there is not enough liquid to cover the chicken pieces, add a little chicken stock. Bring to the simmer, cover and cook 20 minutes.

With a slotted spoon, scoop out the chicken and vegetables, leaving the sauce in the pan. Bring the sauce to a boil and cook until it is reduced and is thick enough to coat the back of a spoon. Return the chicken and vegetables (including the olives if using) to the pan and heat everything through. Serve immediately, or make it ahead of time and heat before serving.

MY NOTES:

Chicken Paprikash

4-6 Servings

About This Recipe

This is a simple dish, and the secret to making it delicious is in the paprika(s) that you use. The stuff you buy in an average market is OK if it isn't too old, but, if you can get your hands on some really great paprikas, the dish will come alive. The best paprikas come from Spain (where it is called "pimenton") and Hungary. The heat evinced by paprikas ranges from very sweet to very hot. Adjust the quantities of each to suit your heat preference.

Since this dish is essentially a stew, I recommend that you use only dark meat, either just thighs or whole hindquarters. I would serve this dish with broad noodles such as pappardella or dumplings/spaetzle which are traditional in Hungary.

Ingredients

8	Chicken thighs or 4 hindquarters
	Salt and paprika to coat chicken
1	Tbs Butter
1	Tbs EVOO
2	Medium onions, diced medium
6	Cloves Garlic, pressed or minced
3	Tbs Paprika, mixed to desired heat
3	Tbs Brandy
1	Tbs Tomato paste
1-2	Cups chicken stock
½	Cup Sour cream
	Chopped parsley for garnish

Procedure

Season the chicken pieces all over with salt and paprika. Allow to sit for an hour to overnight in the fridge.

In a Dutch oven, brown the chicken pieces in EVOO and butter over medium-high heat. Reserve the chicken. Add onions and sauté them for 10-15 minutes. Add garlic and cook 1 minute more. Add 3 Tbs of paprika that you have mixed to taste, stir and deglaze the pan with the brandy. Whisk in the tomato paste and chicken stock. Return the chicken to the pan, bring the liquid to a boil, cover the pot, turn down the heat and simmer for 45 minutes. If you need more liquid, add more chicken stock. Remove and reserve the chicken, crank up the heat and reduce the liquid until it thickens slightly. Correct the seasoning and stir in the sour cream. Pour the sauce over the chicken, sprinkle with chopped parsley and serve immediately.

MY NOTES:

Chicken Thigh Escalopes

2-4 Servings

About This Recipe

An escalope is just a piece of meat, pounded thin. It used to be called a paillard, but I'm told that word is now considered passé in France where it originated. Please let me know when you have figured out why the French do what they do. In any event, most recipes for chicken paillards/escalopes call for chicken breasts, but I think you will find that the thighs taste better and aren't as dry. Feel free to substitute breasts for the thighs in this recipe if the mood strikes you.

I like to serve these thighs with a salad made from tangy greens such as escarole or arugula. I looked this up online and found that Mario Batali apparently agrees with me. He serves his with an arugula salad made with a dressing that contains orange juice, black olives and sun-dried tomatoes. Sounds interesting, but I haven't tried it. I think roasted fingerling potatoes that have been flavored with the same marinade used for the escalopes are a good accompaniment.

The thighs are first marinated overnight in a dressing made with chopped fresh herbs, an acid and EVOO. You can experiment with different herb combinations and different acids to get different flavor profiles.

When was the last time you made a French recipe in less than 10 minutes? That is all this one takes.

Ingredients

½   Cup Mixed fresh herbs (parsley, thyme, basil, etc.)
½   Cup EVOO
½   Cup Acid (vinegar, lemon juice, cider, etc.)
4   Boneless, skin-on Chicken thighs
     Salt and pepper to taste

Procedure

Pound the thighs to a thickness of about ¼".

Mix the herbs, acid and EVOO together. Dredge the thighs in the mixture and put them in a plastic bag. Refrigerate overnight.

Grease a hot skillet or griddle with EVOO and grill the thighs for a couple of minutes on each side.

MY NOTES:

Chicken Vesuvio with Potatoes and Artichoke Hearts

4-6 Servings

About This Recipe

This dish comes not from Italy, but from Chicago, where it is the signature dish of many restaurants. There are as many variations on the theme as there are restaurants that make it, but it ain't Chicken Vesuvio if it doesn't contain chicken, potatoes and garlic.

Although you could use any chicken parts you like for this dish, the thighs stand up to braising better than the other parts, so that is what this recipe calls for. This is a one pot meal since it contains both potatoes and a vegetable. Although the recipe calls for artichoke hearts, you could use any veggie you like or none at all.

A variation on this dish that I like better involves dirtying another pan and starting much earlier. Instead of browning the potatoes and cooking them with the chicken, roast them separately and add them to the chicken at the last minute.

Ingredients

8	Chicken thighs, skin-on, bone-in
	Salt and pepper to taste
	EVOO
1½	Lbs Boiling potatoes, whole if small
1	Head Garlic, cloves peeled and coarsely chopped
1	Cup White wine
1	Cup Chicken stock
½	Tbs Dried oregano
8	Artichoke hearts, frozen or water-packed, cut in half lengthwise
2	Tbs Butter
2	Tbs Chopped parsley for garnish

Procedure

Season the chicken thighs with salt and pepper. In a Dutch oven, brown the chicken in a little EVOO until it is golden brown all over. Don't crowd the pan. Do it in batches if necessary. Reserve the chicken.

In the same pot, add the potatoes and cook until browned, about 10 minutes. Add the garlic and cook 30 seconds. Deglaze the pot with the wine and then add the stock, oregano and thyme. Return the chicken to the pot, bring to a boil and simmer 20 minutes. Add the artichoke hearts and cook an additional 3-5 minutes. Transfer the chicken, potatoes and artichoke hearts to a serving platter. Enrich the sauce with the butter and pour it over the chicken platter. Garnish with chopped parsley if you wish.

MY NOTES:

Chicken with 40 Cloves of Garlic

6-8 Servings

About This Recipe

Chicken with 40 Cloves of Garlic is thought (by most food writers) to be a classic French recipe, some 500 years old, but there is evidence that suggests it may have originated in Catalonia. No matter, it deserves to have lasted this long.

The classic French recipe calls for leaving the garlic cloves in their skins, but I like them peeled because it makes life easier. You can simplify the task of peeling the cloves if you have one of those rubber tubes for peeling garlic. They will peel 5 -10 cloves at once and you don't have to get your hands messy. You can also blanch the cloves in boiling water and the skins will peel off easily. You can buy garlic cloves already peeled, but they are usually coated with citric acid as a preservative and that changes the flavor. Not necessarily worse, but different.

Ingredients

12	Chicken thighs, bone-in, skin-on
	Salt and pepper to taste
2	Tbs EVOO
2	Tbs Butter
3	Heads Garlic, cloves separated and peeled
⅔	Cup Brandy
1½	Cups White wine
1	Tbs dried thyme or 6 Fresh thyme sprigs
1	Tbs Cornstarch mixed with 1 Tbs cold water
¼	Cup Heavy cream or coconut milk
1	Tbs Brandy
2	Tbs Chopped herbs for garnish

Procedure

Dry the chicken thighs in paper towels. Dust them with salt and pepper and brown them in the EVOO in a Dutch oven, working in batches, 3-5 minutes per side. Reserve the chicken.

Add the butter to the pot and let it melt. Add the garlic cloves and cook, stirring every couple of minutes for 5-10 minutes until they just begin to brown. Add the wine and brandy, deglaze the pot, bring to a boil and simmer for a few minutes. Add the thyme and stir. Add the chicken with any accumulated juices, cover the pot and simmer for 30 minutes. Remove the chicken to a serving platter and cover with foil to keep warm. Remove the thyme sprigs and discard them.

Make a slurry with 1 Tbs cornstarch combined with 1 Tbs water and add to the pot. Stir until the sauce has thickened. If not thick enough for your taste add more slurry. Add the cream or coconut milk and 1 Tbs brandy. Cook for 3 minutes and adjust seasoning to taste.

Pour the sauce with the garlic over the chicken and garnish with chopped herbs as desired. Serve at once.

Cider-braised Chicken Legs

4 Servings

About This Recipe

This recipe, based on one provided by Lisa Abraham, food writer for the Akron Beacon Journal, is simple. You first brown the chicken legs, then braise them in cider and stock that has been flavored with onions, garlic, mustard and apples. The original recipe called for sage as the primary seasoning, but I prefer thyme. The flavor will also change as a function of the variety of apple. Try a sweet apple and then a tart one and see which you prefer.

This recipe will work for pork chops or pork loin although you may need to adjust the quantity of the braising liquid. You could serve this dish with spaetzle or a small pasta such as orzo or Israeli pearl couscous.

Ingredients

4	Chicken quarters (legs with thighs attached)
	Salt and pepper to taste
2	Tbs EVOO
1	Medium onion, finely chopped
2	Cloves Garlic, pressed or minced
2	Apples, peeled, cored and cut into six segments each
1	Tsp Dried thyme
1½	Cups Apple cider
¼	Cup Dijon mustard (optional)
½	Cup Chicken stock
¼	Cup Heavy cream (optional)

Procedure

Dry the chicken quarters with paper towels. In a Dutch oven, brown them in the EVOO on both sides in batches, about 5-6 minutes per side. Try and get them very dark. Reserve chicken. Drain off all but a tablespoon of fat. Add onions and sauté 15 minutes. Add apples and garlic and cook for 5 minutes. Stir in the flour. Add cider, mustard, stock and thyme. Bring to a boil, scraping to deglaze the pan. Add back the chicken quarters together with any juices that may have collected. Cover the Dutch oven and braise for 45 minutes (in a 325° oven or on top of the stove set to simmer) until chicken has reached an internal temperature of 160°. Add the cream if using and heat through.

If you think the sauce is too thin, remove the chicken to a warm oven and boil the sauce until it is reduced and the thickness is what you want. You can also thicken it with a cornstarch slurry if you are in a hurry.

MY NOTES:

Moroccan Chicken Tagine

4-6 Servings

About This Recipe

The word "tagine" refers to a slow-cooked stew made in a conical ceramic cooker of the same name. The good news is that you can make tagines in any sort of pot. Maybe it won't impress your guests so much, but it will taste the same. You don't even need to use chicken for this dish. Rabbit and pork, for example, will work well, although Moslems aren't supposed to eat them. It can also be made with lamb or goat, but needs to be cooked longer.

It looks like a lot of ingredients, but most of them are spices. It is actually an easy dish to make, and one that I think you will come back to often. Traditionally, the dish would be served over couscous flavored with lemon and parsley with toasted pine nuts. The recipe lists preserved lemon as an option. You can buy preserved lemons in a Middle-eastern market or you can make them yourself using the recipe in the Miscellaneous Chapter. I also listed harissa in the recipe, a North African chili paste that is very hot. Many markets carry it. You can use red pepper flakes or cayenne instead if you want heat. If you do use harissa, be careful.

Ingredients

2	Tbs EVOO
8	Chicken thighs, bone-in, skin-on
1	Onion, thinly sliced
6	Cloves Garlic, pressed or minced
	2" piece fresh ginger, peeled and minced
1	Tsp Ground cinnamon
1	Tsp Ground coriander
1	Tsp Sweet paprika
½	Tsp Ground black pepper
2	Cardamom pods, crushed or 1 Tsp seeds
1	Tsp Harissa or ½ tsp red pepper flakes (optional)
1	Tsp Salt
12	Dried apricots, halved (optional)
12	Medjool dates, pitted and halved (optional)
1	Medium Carrot, peeled and large diced
2	Cups Chicken stock
¼	Cup Italian parsley, chopped
1	Cup Moroccan or Greek green olives, pitted and halved
	Preserved lemon (optional)
2	Tbs Chopped fresh coriander for garnish

(Recipe continues on next page)

Procedure

In a tagine or other suitable stewing pot, heat the EVOO and brown the chicken thighs on both sides, working in batches if necessary. Reserve the chicken and drain off most of the fat from the pot.

Add the onion and sauté until golden, 5 - 7 minutes. Add the garlic and ginger and cook an additional 2 minutes. Add all the spices and stir to combine. Add the apricots, dates, parsley and chicken stock. Return the chicken to the pot. Bring to the boil, reduce heat to low, cover and simmer 30 - 40 minutes. At the last minute, add the olives and preserved lemon if using.

Place chicken on a bed of couscous and pour over the pan sauce. Garnish with chopped cilantro.

MY NOTES:

Saffron Chicken Breasts in Cream Sauce

4 Servings

About This Recipe

This is another of the pounded chicken breast recipes like those I put into Volume I. I can never get enough of these because they are inexpensive, fast and versatile. In addition, you can use pork or veal in place of the chicken if you want. The recipe calls for saffron, but, if you are on the cheap, use a bit of turmeric instead.

I'd serve this with a green veggie like buttered peas or stringbeans and a rice pilaf.

Ingredients

4	Chicken breasts, boneless and skinless
	Salt and pepper to taste
	EVOO
2	Large Shallots, thinly sliced
4	Cloves Garlic, pressed or minced
½	Cup White wine
1½	Cups Chicken stock
1	Pinch Saffron threads, or 1 Tsp Turmeric
½	Cup Heavy cream
	Chopped parsley for garnish

Procedure

Pound the chicken breasts to ⅛" – ¼" thick. Brown well on both sides in a little EVOO. Reserve the breasts in a warm oven pre-heated to 200°.

Add the shallots and garlic to the pan and cook about 5 minutes. Deglaze with the wine and then pour in the chicken stock. Add the saffron or turmeric and a bit more salt and pepper. Bring to a boil and cook until the liquid is reduced by half. Add the cream, stir and heat to just below the boiling point. Adjust seasoning. Pour the sauce over the chicken breasts and sprinkle with chopped parsley.

MY NOTES:

Sweet and Sour Glazed Game Hen

1-2 Servings

About This Recipe

This is a very easy to prepare dish. Prep time is 5 minutes, but it needs to cook about an hour. There is enough sauce in this recipe to do 4 whole game hens, so if you want less, make less. The sauce will freeze well, so I suggest you make the full recipe and save any extra for another time.

Game hens weigh from about 14 ounces to 1½ pounds. The small ones will feed 1 person, the larger will serve 2 people (not including teenage boys).

Ingredients

½	Cup Chinese Sweet and Sour Sauce (Duk Sauce)
¼	Cup Dijon mustard
6	Cloves Garlic, pressed or minced
¼	Cup Ketchup
¼	Cup Soy sauce
1	Tbs Honey
4	Cornish game hens, split

Procedure

Pre-heat the oven to 375°. Mix all the glaze ingredients together. Dry the birds with paper towels and coat them with the glaze mixture. Let them sit for 30 minutes, then put them in a greased roasting pan and roast for 45 minutes to an hour. During the cooking, brush with more glaze every 15 minutes. If the glaze has not caramelized well, turn up the heat to 425° and roast another 10 minutes, but be careful that the glaze does not burn.

MY NOTES:

Tandoori Chicken

4 Servings

About this Recipe

Since this dish is served in 9 out of 10 Indian restaurants, I hesitated to put it in this cookbook, but then I thought about it and decided to include it because it is so easy to make at home.

A "tandoor" is a deep clay oven. A charcoal fire set in the bottom makes the internal temperature very hot, around 700°- 900°. Traditionally, marinated pieces of chicken or lamb are threaded on very long skewers then placed vertically in the tandoor, which cooks them quickly because of the intense heat. Indian naan bread is made by forming dough into patties and slapping the patties on the tandoor's side. I am not recommending that you acquire a tandoor to get exactly the restaurant product, but this recipe will get you close enough to impress your guests.

To simulate the results you get from cooking in a tandoor, first broil the chicken until it starts to blacken and then finish by baking. You can also do it on a grill by cooking first over direct heat and then moving it to indirect heat. The differentiator here is the marinade which is a combination of yogurt, lemon juice and spices. Here you have several choices. You can make the marinade yourself from scratch, or you can buy a pre-made spice mix. If you do that, I recommend the brands *Sharwood's* or *Patak's* which are available in many markets and online. These off-the-shelf preparations are available as pastes or as dry spice powders.

A typical tandoori spice mix (technically a "masala") uses 15 - 20 ingredients, many of which need to be toasted as seeds and then ground to a powder. This is too much work for me, but if you are interested in the classical approach, I recommend you Google the name Aarti Sequeira, and look up her traditional Tandoori Chicken recipe.

In an Indian restaurant, they serve both the breasts and legs. Often, the skins are removed. I like to use only the legs and I leave the skin on. I think the breasts come out too dry and I think the skin adds flavor, but you can go either way. When you get tandoori chicken in a restaurant, it is usually a bright red color that is achieved with red food dye that adds nothing to the taste. Add a couple of drops of the stuff to your marinade if you wish.

Serve your tandoori chicken with basmati rice, an Indian vegetable dish, raita, naan bread and some chutney for dipping. You can buy frozen naan that just needs to be heated and pre-made chutneys in jars or make it from the recipe in the Sauce Chapter.

Ingredients

4   Leg/thigh quarters, skin-on
1   Cup Plain yogurt
     Salt
½   Cup Lemon juice
     Sharwood's or Patak's Tandoori marinade or paste

(Recipe continues on next page)

Procedure

Slash the chicken pieces in several places to allow the marinade to penetrate. 5-6 cuts on each side will do the trick. Rub the pieces well with salt and then with the lemon juice. Set the chicken aside for 30 minutes.

Rub the spice blend or paste into the chicken pieces, working it into the slashes and under the skin. Set aside again for another 30 minutes.

Mix the yogurt together with 2 Tbs of the spice mix or paste. Coat the chicken pieces with the mixture, again working it into the slashes and under the skin. You should have a little of the yogurt mixture left over. Save it for basting. Set the pieces aside for an hour up to overnight in the refrigerator.

Set the chicken pieces (on a rack over a foil-lined pan to catch the drippings) under the broiler and cook until the outside is slightly charred. Flip the chicken pieces and repeat. Turn the oven to 350°, and bake until an instant-read thermometer registers 160°. If you like you can bake first, then broil to get the char. During the cooking, baste once or twice with the leftover marinade.

You can make the dish ahead of time and heat it up before serving - that is what most restaurants do.

MY NOTES:

Chapter 8: Main Dishes: Duck and Game Birds

Here are 8 recipes. In this volume I try to give some attention to uncommon birds like pheasant and squab. Dare to be different.

Asian Quail

4-8 Servings

About This Recipe

Quail are delicious. One bird makes for a great first course, two for a main course. If you buy them cleaned, they typically run around 4 oz. If you get them at a regular market, you will very likely pay through the nose for them, maybe as much as $8 each. If you have an Asian market nearby, they will be much cheaper, around $4 each. However, if you buy them online in quantity, you can get them for $2 each! I suggest that you get together with a couple of friends and buy a box of 50. They will keep frozen for months.

Although quail can be cooked whole, they are often cooked with the rib cage removed. Once you get the hang of it, it takes no more than 2 minutes to debone a quail. If you go online, you will find several videos that show you how to do it, including one from Jacques Pepin. If you don't want to debone the quail, you can just split it in half lengthwise and roast it in a 375° oven for 15 minutes, followed by 10 minutes at 425°. If you do debone your quail, you can stuff it with a dressing. Google "quail stuffing" and you will find dozens of suitable recipes.

This recipe is from Chef Jean-Georges Vongerichten. Unlike many of his recipes, this one is très simple. Jean-Georges serves it with a watercress salad. If you are doing it for a main course, I suggest accompanying it with wild rice.

Ingredients

8	Quail
1	Cup Soy sauce
1	Cup Water
4	Shallots, minced
¼	Cup Rice vinegar
2	Tbs Five-spice powder
2	Tbs Light brown sugar
1	Tbs Garlic, pressed or minced
1	Tbs Ginger, minced
1	Tbs Coarsely ground black pepper
2	Tbs Canola or peanut oil
2	Tbs Chopped parsley for garnish

(Recipe continues on next page)

Procedure

In a medium saucepan, combine the soy sauce with the water, shallots, rice vinegar, five-spice powder, brown sugar, ginger, garlic and pepper. Simmer over moderately high heat for 3 minutes, stirring occasionally. Cool to room temperature, then strain the sauce into a large bowl. Add the quail and turn to coat. Cover with plastic wrap and refrigerate for at least 3 hours or overnight. Bring to room temperature before proceeding.

Remove the quail from the marinade and pat dry. Heat the oil in a large skillet. Add the quail and cook over high heat until the skin is browned and the meat is rare, turning the birds to sear them evenly on all sides. This process should take no more than 10 minutes. Serve whole or cut in half lengthwise sprinkled with chopped parsley.

MY NOTES:

Braised Guinea Hen

About This Recipe

Unless you live in a rural area where a local farm is producing these birds, this dish ain't frugal. A whole dressed bird, weighing 2½ - 3½ pounds will set you back $25 - $35. In the event it may be worth it to you for a special occasion, here is some info you may be interested in:

Guinea hens, native to Africa, also known as Guinea fowl or Pintade, are very popular in Europe where they are universally known as the "Sunday Bird." They are a little smaller than a chicken and taste somewhere between a chicken and a pheasant. They are almost always braised or roasted.

You can buy Guinea hens online, or, if you have an upscale market in your neighborhood, they will order one for you. The main supplier to U.S. markets appears to be Grimaud Farms. Look them up online and they will give you a list of markets that will order one for you, or you can buy from them directly through their online store.

In any event, if you have never tried a Guinea hen, I think you will be impressed. This particular recipe comes from the English chef Jamie Oliver. His original recipe calls for using blood oranges, but since these are hard to find in America, you can substitute small navels or valencias.

You carve the Guinea hen as you would a whole roast chicken. Jamie recommends serving it with roast potatoes and a simple green vegetable like spinach or broccoli.

Ingredients

1	Guinea hen
8	Oranges
1	Stalk Celery
	Small handful of fresh thyme
2	Tbs EVOO
6	Cloves Garlic, unpeeled
6	Tbs Butter
6	Sage leaves
½	Cup White wine
	Salt and pepper to taste

Procedure

Pre-heat the oven to 425°.

Remove any excess fat from the cavity of each guinea fowl. Wash thoroughly inside and out and pat dry with paper towels. Rub the cavity with a little salt. Cut off the two ends of the oranges, stand them on end and carefully slice off the skin. Slice the oranges into five or six rounds each. Remove the tougher outside ribs of the celery until you reach the white, dense bulb and slice across thinly.

(Recipe continues on next page)

Put the orange slices and celery in a bowl, mix in the thyme and a small pinch of salt and pepper, then stuff the cavity of each guinea fowl with this filling. Pull the skin at the front of each guinea fowl's cavity forward, to cover the filling, and tightly tie/truss up.

Heat a large Dutch oven and add the olive oil and the guinea fowl, the skin of which has been rubbed in salt and pepper. Cook until lightly golden on all sides, then add the garlic, butter and sage and cook for 3-4 minutes until golden brown. Add the wine at intervals, enough to keep the pan slightly moist at all times. Place in the oven for 45 minutes, checking every 10-15 minutes and just topping up the wine as necessary. The guinea fowl will be roasted and partially steamed.

When cooked, carefully remove from the oven and place upside down on a dish, allowing all the juices and moisture to relax back into the breast meat for at least 5 minutes. While your meat is resting, make the gravy.

Remove all the fat from the roasting pan and place the pan on gentle heat. In the bottom of the pan will be your cooked, soft, sweet, whole garlic cloves and some gorgeous sticky stuff. When this gets hot, scoop out the stuffing from the guinea fowl cavity and add to the pan with about ⅔ cup of wine. As the wine boils and steams, scrape all the goodness with a spoon from the bottom of the pan into the liquor. When it has all dissolved, leave to simmer gently. Squash the cooked garlic out of their skins with a spoon (discard the skins); this will also thicken the gravy slightly, as well as give it flavor. Pour any of the juices that have drained out of the rested birds into the pan with the gravy, simmer and season to taste.

Carve the bird and serve with the pan gravy poured over it.

MY NOTES:

Brined and Steamed Duck

About This Recipe

This recipe is a bit of a misnomer as you will see. Its genesis is Alton Brown, the mad Food Channel chef who is wont to give a chemistry lesson on every show. I've modified it to make it a little less mad, but it is still, not only edible, but delicious. By the way, Alton calls this recipe "Mighty Duck." I told you he is a little off.

Alton used chard in this recipe. I hate chard, which, as you may know, is the green top of a beet plant that has been hybridized to grow the tops and not the root. Strangely enough, I like beets, but, because I hate chard, it is nowhere to be found in this recipe. Mikey does not like it.

I like to serve this with some steamed asparagus and sweet potatoes, cooked however you like them. I suggest you try frozen sweet potato fries and bake them for 20 minutes along with the final cooking of the duck.

Ingredients

1   Duckling
½   Cup Salt
1   Pint Orange juice, pineapple juice or a combination
1   Tbs Black peppercorns
1   Bunch Fresh Thyme
1   Head Garlic, cloves peeled and smashed

Procedure

Split the duckling (after removing the giblets and wing tips) and remove the backbone. Separate the hind and front quarters so that you are left with 4 pieces.

Combine the salt, juice, peppercorns, thyme and garlic and dump into a sealable plastic baggie. Put the duck pieces in the bag and seal it. Squish it around so that the duck is evenly coated with the brine. Allow to sit for 2-3 hours.

Remove the duck pieces from the brine and place in a steamer large enough to accommodate them. Steam for 45 minutes.

Pre-heat oven to 475°. While the oven is heating, place a large iron or copper skillet in it. You want it to get very hot. Add the duck leg quarters to the skillet, skin side down, and cook for 10 minutes. Add the breasts and cook an additional 7 minutes. The skin should be crisp. Remove the pan from the oven and tent with foil. Allow to rest for at least 10 minutes before serving.

MY NOTES:

Brined and Roasted Pheasant

4-6 Servings

About this Recipe

Discounting the $200 hunting license, the $1500 shotgun and the $1000 it cost to train your dog to retrieve, pheasant is free, and thus extremely frugal. You just have to be careful to pick out the buckshot. If getting the free kind is not appealing, you can buy farm-raised pheasant online or upscale markets will order one for you. One 2.5 - 3 pound pheasant will set you back $25 - $35 - definitely not frugal. However, if you have never tried pheasant, considered a great delicacy in many parts of the world, you owe it to yourself to try it at least once.

The biggest challenge to making pheasant taste good is the lack of fat in the bird. If overcooked for even a few minutes, the breasts will have the texture of cardboard. To compensate for that, I recommend brining pheasant before its cooked and then covering it with fat while it is cooking. This recipe uses both those techniques and produces a very tasty bird that you will remember for a long time.

This basis of this recipe comes from a local PBS TV show called "Outdoor Wisconsin." I couldn't find any Wisconsin recommendations for accompaniments, but I think some simple roasted potatoes and a green salad will do nicely.

Ingredients

BRINE

½	Gallon Water
½	Cup Kosher salt
1	Cup Brown sugar
¼	Cup Maple syrup
1	Onion, chopped
4	Cloves Garlic, smashed
¼	Tsp Ground cloves
	Juice of 1/2 lemon
1	Whole Pheasant

ROAST

2	Tbs Softened butter
6	Strips Blanched bacon
1	Cup Chicken stock, more if needed
6	Cloves Garlic, peeled
2	Tbs Brandy

(Recipe continues on next page)

Procedure

Heat the water and salt until all the salt is dissolved. Allow to cool. Add the rest of the brining ingredients and stir to combine. Add the pheasant, making sure that is it completely covered in the brine. If needed, place a weight on top of the bird. Refrigerate overnight.

Next day, pre-heat the oven to 350°. Remove the bird from the brine and dry it with paper towels. Discard the brining solution, but save the solids and use them to stuff the bird. Take some softened butter and rub it under the breast skin, then rub the rest of the butter over the entire bird. Put the bird on a rack in a roasting pan. Drape slices of blanched (to get rid of the smoky taste) bacon over the bird. Pour the chicken stock into the pan and toss in the garlic cloves. Roast about 1 – 1½ hours tented with foil until an instant-read thermometer registers 150° in the thickest part of the leg. During the roasting process, baste frequently with the pan juices. Remove the foil and bacon strips. Turn the oven up to 400° and roast another 10 minutes to brown the skin. Remove the bird to your cutting board, tent with foil and allow to rest at least 10 minutes. You'll want the internal temperature to be at least 160° before serving.

While the bird is resting, you can make a gravy out of the pan drippings. Put the roasting pan on top of the stove over medium-high heat. Mash the garlic cloves and deglaze the pan with a wooden spatula. Add a little more chicken stock if there is not enough liquid. Add brandy and flame off the alcohol. Season to taste. Reduce the liquid to the consistency you want. If you are in a rush, you can use a cornstarch slurry as a thickener. You can also enrich the gravy by swirling in a pat of butter,

MY NOTES:

Chinese Glazed Squab

4 Servings

About This Recipe

A squab is a variety of pigeon that has been raised for the table. Dressed, they weigh about 1 pound, enough for one person. The meat is all dark meat and has an extremely high protein content. I checked around for squab prices. Online they are $20 - $25 each. In upscale markets, they are about $15 each, but in an Asian market, you'll find them for $4 - $7 each.

This recipe comes from author Grace Young. She says that squab was a rare delicacy in her family, so it was always served in small pieces as part of a multi-dish meal. You can serve it that way too - or, eat a whole bird yourself maybe accompanied by steamed rice and a stir-fried veggie dish. This recipe contains a trick I'd never seen before. After you take the squab out of the cooking pan, you drizzle it with just a touch of vinegar. While it rests, the skin will crisp. Sounds weird, but it works!

The recipe calls for chopping the birds into bite-size pieces. If you are good with a cleaver, by all means use it. If not, kitchen shears will do.

Ingredients

2	Squab
1	Tsp Salt
½	Cup Cilantro sprigs
2	Scallions, finely shredded
2	Tbs Grated fresh ginger
2	Tbs Regular soy sauce
1	Tbs Black soy sauce
2	Tbs Chinese rice wine or dry sherry
½	Tsp Sugar
½	Tsp Distilled white vinegar

Procedure

Pre-heat the oven to 350°. Remove any fat pockets from the squabs and discard them., Rub the birds with salt and then rinse them in cold water. Pat them dry with paper towels inside and out.

In a medium bowl, combine cilantro, scallions, ginger, thin soy sauce, black soy sauce, rice wine and sugar, and stir to combine. Place half the cilantro, scallions, and ginger in each of the cavities and smear the soy sauce mixture in the cavities and on the outside of the squab. Marinate 30 minutes.

Pour ¼ cup boiling water into an 8-inch glass baking dish and place the squab breast-side down in the dish, reserving the marinade. Roast 30 minutes and turn the squab breast side up, basting with reserved marinade. Roast 30 more minutes. Baste with marinade in pan and cook 15 minutes more, or until squab are golden brown and just cooked.

Drizzle 1/4 teaspoon of vinegar on each squab. Allow squab to rest 10 minutes before chopping into bite-sized pieces. Serve immediately.

Citrus Braised Duck

4 Servings

About This Recipe

I never had braised duck until I had it at the Bull Valley Roadhouse in Port Costa, California. The chef-owner, Dave Williams says that he got the idea from a Mexican chef, but this recipe is more reminiscent of France that it is anything south of the border. Like most braising recipes, this one is easy to make, but takes 2-3 hours to cook and you need to start it the day before. Like duck a l'orange, this duck is flavored with citrus. The recipe specifies oranges, but you could use any combination of citrus that appeals to you. Meyer lemons or tangerines come to mind.

Ingredients

1	Pekin Duck, about 4 pounds
	Salt and pepper
2	Tbs Marmalade or apricot jam
2	Stalks Celery, cut into 2" lengths
2	Carrots, peeled and cut into 2" lengths
1	Large Onion, peeled and quartered
1	Bunch Fresh thyme
½	Bunch Italian parsley
½	Bunch Cilantro
1	Orange, halved
1	Bay leaf
1	Cup White wine
	Orange juice

Procedure

With kitchen shears or a sharp knife, cut along both sides of the duck's backbone. Remove the backbone and discard it. Then cut through the breast, separating the duck in half down the center. Generously salt and pepper the duck, cover with plastic wrap and refrigerate overnight.

Pre-heat the oven to 350°. Remove the duck from the refrigerator and slather the skin with marmalade or apricot jam. In a deep roasting pan or Dutch oven, place the vegetables and lay the thyme, parsley and cilantro on top of them. Squeeze the juice from the orange over, then toss in the fruit, peel and all. Add the bay leaf. Set the duck halves on top, then pour over the wine. Cover the pan tightly (with foil if using a roasting pan) and place it in the oven. Cook 2.5 - 3 hours or until the meat pulls from the bone easily. Remove the duck to a cutting board and carve it into pieces. Put the pieces on a warm serving platter and tent with foil.

Pour the braising liquid through a strainer into a saucepan, pressing to extract the most liquid that you can. Discard the solids. Remove the fat from the pan (save it) and reduce by about ⅓. Adjust the seasoning and add a bit of orange juice to taste. Serve at once with the sauce on the side.

Roast Glazed Duck, Low Temperature Method

2-4 Servings

About This Recipe

In Volume I, I included a roast duck recipe that called for cooking the duck at 225° for 6 hours. I received a few emails from readers who tried it and weren't happy with the result. I concluded that the difference is the oven. A restaurant-quality convection oven is needed to make it work. As a result, I came up with the alternative presented here in which you roast the bird for 4 hours at 300° followed by 20 minutes at 400°.

You can "stuff" the duck with one or more aromatics. You have a lot of choices. A peeled onion, a head of garlic cut in half, a quartered lemon or orange, sliced fresh ginger are all good choices. You can add herbs like thyme, rosemary or parsley.

The French and the Chinese make the skin extra crispy by covering the duck with boiling water and letting it sit for 5 minutes. You then dry off the bird with paper towels and place it in the refrigerator, uncovered, to dry further overnight.

You have a lot of options for the glaze. This recipe includes one made from orange juice and honey, but you can use any glaze that you like. Try one with reduced pomegranate juice or the juice from canned peaches or pears. Fruit preserves such as marmalade or currant jam also work very well. You have a zillion options. If you want to make the duck taste Chinese, put soy sauce, ginger, Hoisin sauce and five-spice powder in the glaze mix.

My favorite accompaniment to roast duck is wild rice cooked in chicken stock and mixed with caramelized chopped onions. Although almost any salad will do, I especially like a wilted spinach salad. I find it cleans the palate for the duck.

Ingredients

1   Pekin Duckling, about 4-5 pounds
    Aromatic stuffing (See description)
    Salt

GLAZE

¼   Cup Honey
¼   Cup Molasses or Brown Sugar
3   Tbs Orange juice
2   Tbs Soy sauce

Procedure

To make the glaze, put all the ingredients in a small pot and cook until the mixture coats the back of a spoon. If it cools off and thickens too much, just reheat it.

Remove the giblets from the duck and cut off the excess skin, fat and the wing tips. Save it all for other uses such as making a duck stock.

(Recipe continues on next page)

Pre-heat the oven to 300°. Liberally salt the duck inside and outside and insert your chosen aromatics into the body cavity. Cross the legs and truss them. Fold the wings under the bird and truss or pin them in place. Poke the bird all over in many places with the tip of a knife or the tines of a serving fork. Just pierce the skin, not the meat. The idea is to have the fat drain out. Place the bird on a non-stick or oiled rack in a roasting pan. You are going to turn the duck several times during the cooking process. If it sticks to the rack, the skin might pull off the bird.

Roast the bird for 3 hours, beginning back side up. Every half- hour, poke the bird all over and flip it. Remove it from the oven and turn up the oven temperature to 400°. While the oven is heating, remove the duck to a platter, remove and discard the aromatics and tent with foil. Pour off the fat to be saved for later use. You may have as much as a cup to a cup and a half of fat. Yum! Scrape up the bits on the bottom of your roasting pan and add them to your duck stock if you made some. Then wipe out the pan with paper towel. You want the pan to be fairly clean to minimize smoking.

Return the duck to the roasting pan and rack. Roast at 400° for 10 minutes. Brush with the glaze and roast 10 minutes longer. Keep an eye on the bird to make sure that the sugar in the glaze doesn't burn. Remove the duck from the oven and let stand 10-15 minutes tented before carving. Leftover glaze can be used as a dipping sauce or mixed with your duck stock and used as a gravy.

You can carve the duck any way you like, but I like to cut it into four pieces. Poultry shears are the best tool for this. Make a single cut through the longitudinal center of the breast. Then cut along each side of the backbone and discard it, leaving two halves of the bird. Next, separate the breast section from the leg section and you are done.

MY NOTES:

Turducken

20-30 Servings

Turducken is a turkey stuffed with a duck stuffed with a chicken. I could have put this recipe in the chicken chapter, but I like duck better than chicken so there you have it.

Turducken's invention is credited either to Paul Prudhomme, the well-known New Orleans chef, or to Herbert's Specialty Meats, a Houston meat market that sells it mail order. Herbert's charges around $75 for a frozen turducken and offers several different versions including "turduck" (no chicken) and "turken" (no duck). Check out the company's website. Regardless of who invented the dish, John Madden, the famous football coach and TV announcer, is responsible for popularizing turducken outside of Cajun country.

Preparing turducken from scratch is a chore because you have to bone out all three birds. I recommend that you buy it already boned, stuffed and assembled. A bit expensive perhaps, but something you aren't going to do very often. Because the title of this book stresses "Easy", I'm not going into what it takes to prep the three birds, so I'm assuming you are going to buy the finished, uncooked product. If you are up for preparing it from scratch, you will find several videos online that walk you through the process. If you would like to try Paul Prudhomme's original turducken recipe, buy a copy of his cookbook "Always Cooking", or check out the recipe online. Paul's recipe takes all day to make. Personally, I'd go out for dinner before attempting his version.

You can either roast your turducken, or, as Madden likes it, you can deep fry it. If you choose the latter method, use a deep fryer designed to do a whole turkey, and do it outdoors. You are dealing with a lot of very hot fat, and, if there is a problem, you do not want to have to deal with it in your kitchen. The turducken must be completely defrosted or it will explode when it hits the hot oil.

Your turducken may be stuffed or unstuffed, brined or not, seasoned or not. Regardless, you need to cook it until a thermometer that reaches the center reads at least 155°. Let it rest for half an hour before carving, and the temperature will rise another 10°. An issue that you have to live with is that the turkey and duck will, of necessity, be cooked at a higher temperature than the chicken. C'est la vie. If you roast it, you can use whatever method you would use for a turkey.

Prepared turduckens run 10 - 15 pounds and will feed 20 - 30 people, which works out to roughly $3/person. Not bad for a party dinner.

MY NOTES:

Chapter 9: Main Dishes: Lamb and Goat

This chapter in Volume I contained only lamb recipes. For this book, I decided to include a few that use goat. It is claimed that more goat meat is consumed in the world than that of any other animal. You can substitute lamb for goat in any of the goat recipes.

Berbere Lamb

6-8 Servings

About This Recipe

There is a terrific San Francisco restaurant called "Radio Africa and Kitchen". The chef/owner, Eskender Aseged, hails from Ethiopia, but has worked at several of San Francisco's upscale eateries. His menu combines cuisines from his native Ethiopia with those associated with the Mediterranean. I had this lamb dish there, and he was only too happy to share it with me. I asked him if he ever made this recipe with goat, and he said that goat would be more common in Ethiopia, but that it was a hard sell in the restaurant, and getting a reliable supply of quality goat meat isn't easy.

Berbere is an Ethiopian spice blend that is similar to garam masala. You can get it at markets catering to Africans, from online spice stores, or directly from the restaurant. It can be very hot since it contains ground chilis or cayenne, so if you are heat-averse, be careful.

Ingredients

2-3   Lbs Lamb shoulder or leg, boneless

1   Tsp Berbere powder or more to taste

1   Tsp Garlic, pressed

1   Tbs Lemon juice

1   Tbs EVOO

1   Tbs Chopped parsley

       Salt and freshly ground black pepper to taste

Procedure

Trim the fat and sinew from the lamb and cut it into 1.5" - 2" thick slices cross-grain. Put the lamb into a large sealable baggie. Mix the remaining ingredients together and pour into the baggie. Seal the bag and scrunch it around so that the meat is fully coated. Allow the lamb to marinate from 30 minutes to 2 hours. Remove the lamb and pat it dry with paper towels.

Cook the lamb on a grill and cook to desired doneness, about 7 minutes for medium rare. Alternatively, sear the meat in a skillet in a bit of EVOO and then put it in a 375° oven for 6 -7 minutes to finish cooking. In either case, allow the meat to rest for at least 10 minutes. Cut the meat into bite-size chunks and serve immediately.

Grilled Goat Chops

4 Servings

About This Recipe

This is a super easy recipe that is very similar to many that you will see for lamb chops. It comes from the Puglia region of Italy which is the heel of the Italian boot. You make a marinade paste, coat the chops, let them sit for a while and then grill them on an outdoor BBQ or on the stovetop. They are best when slightly pink in the center of the meat.

Although you can buy goat meat by mail order, it tends to be expensive. If you have a Latino, Caribbean or Filipino market in your area, you may find goat meat at a very reasonable price. For a Latino market, look for one that has a carniceria (butcher). Goat meat is known in such places as "cabrito." I have read that Pakistani halal (raised according to Islamic guidelines) markets usually carry it, but I haven't been able to verify that. Some farms that raise goats sell the meat directly. Since no middlemen are involved, farm prices can be very reasonable. Look around online for local sources.

Goat chops are small, so you will want at least 2 per person.

Ingredients

6	Cloves Garlic, peeled
1	Medium Onion, coarsely chopped
½	Cup EVOO
2	Lemons, grated zest and juice
½	Cup White wine
1	Tbs Oregano
½	Tsp Salt
½	Tsp Freshly ground black pepper
8	Rib or loin goat chops

Procedure

Combine all the ingredients except chops to make a marinade. Put the chops in plastic baggies and pour in the marinade. Squish it around to coat all of the chops. Marinate overnight in the refrigerator. Remove the chops and allow them to come to room temperature. Then grill to your desired degree of doneness.

MY NOTES:

Grilled Lamb Shoulder

8-12 Servings

About This Recipe

Lamb shoulder is a lot cheaper than leg of lamb, and, to my way of thinking, is just as good if it is cut right. In this recipe, a 4-5 Lb lamb shoulder is butterflied, marinated, grilled and sliced thinly cross-grain. Depending on what you put in the marinade, you can give the lamb different flavor profiles. The meat has a large surface area so that the flavor of the marinade is going to be prominent.

You could serve this with any sauce that goes well with red meat. If you want to give it a South American flair, try using a chimichurri sauce. If you want to Frenchify it, use a red wine sauce. Let your imagination be your guide!

I'd suggest serving this with garlic roast potatoes and a wilted spinach salad.

Ingredients

4   Tbs EVOO
2   Tbs Lemon juice
2   Tbs Red wine vinegar
4   Cloves Garlic, pressed or minced
2   Tbs Fresh oregano, chopped, or
2   Tbs Fresh rosemary, chopped
     Salt and pepper to taste
4-5 Lb Lamb shoulder, butterflied and any big chunks of fat removed

Procedure

Put all the ingredients except lamb in a small jar and shake vigorously to combine.

Roll out the butterflied lamb shoulder and coat both sides with the marinade. Roll it back up, put into a large Ziploc bag, pour in any remaining marinade and refrigerate overnight. Turn the bag a few times to distribute the marinade.

Grill until an instant-read thermometer is 120° (rare) or 130° (medium-rare). Let stand 10-15 minutes. Cut ¼" slices cross grain.

MY NOTES:

Jamaican Goat Curry

6-8 Servings

About This Recipe

If you can't find or don't want to eat goat, you can substitute lamb. Pound for pound, goat has half the calories but the same amount of protein as lamb or beef.

In any event, this is a classic Jamaican recipe. The key ingredient (besides the goat) is the Jamaican curry powder. If you can't find it, add allspice to your favorite brand of Indian curry powder. The recipe calls for a hot pepper, which is cooked along with curry, but removed before serving. The intent is to add a flavor component, not to make the dish hot. That said, some Jamaicans like it hot (shades of Marilyn Monroe), so you can feel free to heat up this dish.

This dish is better 1-3 days after you make it, so it is a good party dish that can be made ahead and simply reheated before serving. The traditional accompaniment is Jamaican "Rice and Peas. The recipe is in the Starch Side Dishes chapter.

Ingredients

3	Lbs Goat meat, cut into 2" - 3" cubes
	Salt
6-8	Tbs Jamaican curry powder (or more to taste)
2	Tbs Canola or peanut oil
2	Medium Onions, chopped
1-2	Hot peppers
1	2" Piece of ginger, peeled and minced
1	Head Garlic, peeled and chopped
4	Cups Coconut milk
3	Cups Water
1	14-oz Can of tomatoes, crushed
1	Tbs Dried thyme
	Water to cover the goat, 2-3 cups
2	Lbs Boiling potatoes, peeled and cut into 1" chunks

Procedure

Salt the meat and let it sit for half an hour. Heat the oil in a Dutch oven and add 2 Tbs of the curry powder. Cook until fragrant. Pat the meat dry with paper towels and brown well in the oil. You will probably have to do this in batches. Reserve the meat. Add onions and chili peppers to the pot and sauté until the onions start to turn brown. As they cook, sprinkle some salt over them. Add ginger and garlic and sauté another couple of minutes.

Put the meat back into the pot along with any juices that may have been exuded. Add coconut milk, water, tomatoes, thyme and 4 Tbs of curry powder. Stir to combine. Bring to a simmer and cook at least 2 hours. Add the potatoes and cook about 15 minutes longer or until potatoes are ready to eat.

Lamb Ragù

6 Servings

About This Recipe

When you think of the word ragù, you probably think of the stuff sold in jars by that name in every supermarket. You would be wrong. I looked it up and learned: "Ragù is a sauce of braised or stewed meat that may be flavored with tomatoes as opposed to a tomato sauce flavored with meat." To be honest, I don't understand that definition, but perhaps you can decipher it.

Making the subject even more complicated, l'Accademia Italiana Della Cucina has defined 14 types of ragù. It's enough to make your head spin. After reading all that stuff, I haven't a clue as to whether this recipe qualifies for the title, but since it doesn't involve braising meat for several hours, it is probably a misnomer. That said, this tastes good, is easy to make and will keep for months in the freezer.

You will need some basic marinara sauce for this recipe. You can buy it in a jar (OK) or make it yourself (better). The recipe is in Volume I.

I'd serve this sauce with a thick pasta such as ziti or rigatoni. Accompany with a green salad and some good bread and you have a complete meal.

Ingredients

1	Tbs EVOO
1	Clove Garlic, minced
2	Medium Shallots, minced
1½	Lbs Ground Lamb
1	Cup Red wine
1	Quart Marinara Sauce
2	Tbs Chopped Mint (optional)
½	Cup Ricotta cheese
1	Lb Pasta

Procedure

Heat the olive oil in a large sauté pan and cook the shallots and garlic in it for about 2 minutes. Add the lamb, break it up with a wooden spatula and cook until it is completely browned. Add the wine, deglaze the pan and cook until the wine is almost completely evaporated.

While the meat is cooking cook the pasta in lots of boiling salted water, about 12 minutes.

Add the marinara sauce to the meat and heat through. Stir in the mint and the ricotta. Add the pasta and toss. Serve at once.

MY NOTES:

Madras Lamb Curry

6-12 Servings

About This Recipe

Many years ago, I took a course in Indian cooking. The teacher was a lady from Sri Lanka who was a terrific instructor. She pointed out that the name of this dish is a misnomer because there is no such thing as Madras Curry in India! She claimed that it was an invention of an Indian restaurant that caught on in America, like Chinese chicken salad which does not exist in China.

However, she said it was representative of many Indian cuisines and worth learning. She also wanted to teach us how to make our own masala and that is included with this recipe. You can, of course, buy masala in a hundred varieties already prepared, but I encourage you to try making your own just for the experience.

That said, this is a great tasting dish that you can make as hot as you want by adding more or less chili powder. I would serve it with plain basmati rice, an Indian vegetable dish (see Volume I) and maybe some naan bread. In Southern India, it would probably be served with parathas, a flatbread similar to chipattis. You could pick some of them up at a local Indian restaurant, or make them yourself. You will find the recipe online.

Ingredients

MASALA

1	Tsp Cumin seeds
1	Tsp Poppy seeds
6	Peppercorns
6	Cloves
1	3" Cinnamon stick
1	Bay leaf
1	Tsp Fennel seeds
2	Tbs Coriander seeds
1	Tsp Red chili powder (or to taste)

COCONUT PASTE

½	Lb Fresh coconut meat, cut into thin strips
2	Tsp Garlic, pressed
1	Tsp Ginger, mashed into a paste

(Recipe continues on next page)

LAMB STEW

3	Tbs Canola or peanut oil
2	Onions, chopped fine
2	Lbs Lamb, cut into 1" - 2" chunks
1	14-oz Can Crushed tomatoes with their juice
1	Cup Thick coconut milk
1	Cup Hot water, more if needed
	Salt to taste

Procedure

To make the masala, put the first 9 ingredients into a skillet and toast them until fragrant. Allow to cool and grind them to a powder in a spice grinder.

To make the coconut paste, put the coconut slivers and the garlic and ginger into a food process and process to a paste consistency. If you cannot find fresh coconut, you can reconstitute dried, flaked or shredded coconut which you can usually find in the baking aisle or the bulk section of your local supermarket.

Heat the oil in a heavy pot. Sauté the onion in it until it starts to brown. Add the masala and the coconut paste and cook for a few minutes. Add a little water if needed to prevent the spices from burning. Now add the meat and brown it. Add the tomatoes, coconut milk and hot water. Season with salt, cover the pot and cook at a simmer until the meat is tender, 1- 2 hours depending on the cut. Keep an eye on it and add water if it appears to be drying out or if there is not enough gravy. Serve at once or reheat for later.

MY NOTES:

Roast Leg of Lamb

8-12 Servings

About This Recipe

Leg of lamb comes boneless and bone-in. The boneless variety is easier to carve and takes less time to cook, but the bone adds to the flavor. In either case, the cooking method is the same. First, marinate the roast using garlic, lemon and rosemary. Then roast it at high temperature for a little while, followed by a longer period at low temperature.

The meat will cook more evenly if you set it on a rack that is high above a drip pan, thus allowing the hot air to circulate around the meat. An even better choice is to use a rotisserie. In my case, my wife doesn't like me to cook lamb in the kitchen - she doesn't like the smell - so I do it on my gas grill. I prop the roast up onto a grate that has 3" feet set into a throwaway foil roasting pan, thereby eliminating cleanup. How clever is that?

You can make a gravy out of the pan drippings and marinade, use my cherry pepper sauce described in Volume I, or serve it with traditional mint preserves. I prefer potatoes with roast lamb, and I recommend you try my easy seasoned potatoes recipe from Volume I.

Ingredients

4½   Lbs Leg of lamb, boneless, tied, or
1   6 Lb Leg of Lamb, bone-in
8   Cloves Garlic, peeled and slivered
4   Rosemary sprigs, chopped or
1   Tbs Dried rosemary, crushed
½   Cup EVOO
½   Cup Lemon juice
1   Tbs Salt
½   Tbs Black pepper

Procedure

Stab the roast all over with the tip of a knife and fill the slits with garlic slivers. Mix together the EVOO, lemon juice, rosemary, salt and pepper and pour into a 1 or 2 gallon freezer bag. Add the roast to the bag, squeeze out the air and seal it. Squish it around until the meat is coated with the marinade. Refrigerate overnight. Every few hours, move it to be sure everything is well-coated with the marinade. A couple of hours before cooking, take it out of the refrigerator and let it come to room temperature. Reserve the marinade if you want to make a sauce out of it.

Pre-heat oven to 425°. Place the roast on a grate in the middle of the oven, fattiest side up, and put a drip pan on the bottom of the oven with a little water in it to prevent the drippings from smoking. Roast for 20 minutes and then turn the temperature down to 325°. Cook an additional 40 - 60 minutes until a meat thermometer registers the temperature that you want. Remove the roast from the oven, set it on a platter, tent with foil and let it rest for 15-20 minutes before carving.

Stuffed Seared Lamb Tenderloin

4 Servings

About this Recipe

I first ran into this dish at a restaurant in San Francisco called La Ciccia where it was called Pezza de Angioni. Pezza literally means bolt of cloth or patch, and Angioni is a name of a person or a place. The dish supposedly hails from Sardinia, but I could not find a place named Angioni on a map.

In any event, you take a lamb tenderloin, stuff it with something, sear it and then finish it off in a hot oven. The dish is finished with a sauce made from a reduced wine. La Ciccia uses "Saba" which is a grape must from Sardinia, but you can use Marsala or a medium sweet sherry.

The stuffing can be anything you like. One chef uses pecorino cheese, prosciutto and basil leaves. Pecorino, by the way, means 'sheep' in Sardinia, so it is nice to use a cheese from the region. I've included that stuffing in this recipe. La Ciccia use a stuffing based on bread crumbs. To each his own.

Ingredients

2	8-12 oz Lamb tenderloins
	Salt and pepper to taste
4	Slices Prosciutto or ham
4	1/4" slices Pecorino
4	Large Basil leaves
	EVOO for sautéing
½	Cup Saba, Marsala or Sherry
½	Cup Chicken stock
2	Tbs Butter
	Chopped basil for garnish

Procedure

Cut a pocket in each tenderloin large enough to insert the stuffing. Lay 2 cheese slices and 2 basil leaves on top of two slices of prosciutto and roll it up into a wrapped packet. Place each packet into one of the pockets you cut into the tenderloin. Tie up the tenderloins with butchers twine so that the stuffing won't fall out. Salt and pepper the tenderloins.

Pre-heat an oven to 400°. Sear the tenderloins in a little EVOO in a hot skillet, browning on all sides. Put the tenderloins in an oiled baking pan and roast them in the oven to about 130° on an instant-read thermometer. This will take only about 10-15 minutes. Remove the tenderloins from the oven and allow to rest while you make the sauce.

Pour any pan juices from the oven into the skillet and add the wine and stock, salt and pepper. Deglaze the pan. Bring to a boil and reduce by half. Your sauce is done.

Slice the meat crosswise into 1/2" thick slices. Reassemble the loins and pour over the sauce.

Chapter 10: Main Dishes: Pork

No meat offers more bang for the buck than pork. Roasted, BBQ'd, sautéed, grilled, in a sandwich – they all work. And what food do you know that is more American than BBQ'd ribs? Here are 12 pork recipes that run the gamut.

Baby Back Ribs a al Greque

4-8 Servings

About This Recipe

This recipe comes from Iron Chef Michael Symon who claims that his Greek grandmother made this twice a month.

You need to make this outdoors unless you have a fantastic exhaust system in your kitchen to handle the smoke. If you have a charcoal grill, put the coals on one side only and place soaked and drained wood chips on top of the coals. If you have a gas grill put the wood chips in a foil pan, cover with foil and poke holes in the foil. Place the foil pan on top of the cool side of the grill, close the grill lid and when the chips start to smoke, you are ready to cook. Symon says the right temperature for cooking the ribs is about 275°.

You start with a rub that features coriander seeds, a popular Greek seasoning. Although you can cook right away, it is best to let the ribs sit overnight in the rub refrigerated before you start cooking. To prep the ribs for cooking, place the slab in a package made out of heavy-duty aluminum foil. Poke holes in the sides of the package so that the smoke will penetrate the meat and steam escape.

After the ribs have cooked for a couple of hours, open the package and pour over a glaze. Cook another 45 minutes. Remove the slab from the package and place it on the hot side of the grill, meat side down to char slightly. To finish the dish, drizzle the ribs with lemon juice, honey and EVOO and dust with kosher salt.

Accompany the ribs with Greek olives, tzatziki, Greek salad, pita bread, taramasalata, hummus and/or other Greek specialties.

Ingredients

2-4 Racks of baby back ribs

RUB

1 Tbs Coriander seeds, dry toasted in a skillet
1 Tbs Dried oregano
1 Tbs Smoked Spanish paprika
1 Tbs Garlic salt
2 Tbs Fresh lemon juice
2 Tbs Kosher salt

(Recipe continues on next page)

GLAZE

1	Clove Garlic, smashed
1	Medium Onion, coarsely chopped
2	Tbs Coarsely chopped fresh oregano
1/4	Cup Red Wine vinegar
1/4	Cup Honey

FINISH

2	Lemons, halved
	Honey for drizzling
	EVOO for drizzling
	Kosher salt

Procedure

In a spice grinder or mortar, put all the dry ingredients. Grind until the coriander seeds are coarsely chopped. Coat the ribs on both sides with lemon juice and salt. Put the rub on the ribs and massage it into the meat on both sides of the slab. Make a package out of a piece of heavy-duty foil with the ribs inside. Make sure that the air space is left on top of the ribs. Poke several holes in the sides of the package. You can start cooking right away, but the ribs will be more flavorful the longer they sit in the rub.

Set up the grill with a hot side and a cool side. Add soaked wood chips as described in the introduction. When the wood starts smoking, place the package on the cool side of the grill. Put a lid on the grill and cook for 1½ to 2 hours.

Make a glaze by combining the garlic, onion, oregano, wine vinegar and honey. Remove the ribs from the grill and open the package. Pour the glaze over the ribs and reclose the package. Place the ribs back on the cool side of the grill and cook an additional 40 minutes.

Remove the package from the grill and take the ribs out of the foil, being careful not to let the juices out. Scrape off the onions and reserve them. Place the ribs on the hot side of the grill, meat side down and cook until they are lightly charred, about 5 minutes. Put the lemon halves cut side down on the hot side of the grill at the same time.

Remove the ribs and lemon halves from the grill. Place the ribs on a serving platter and pour over the juices from the foil package. Drizzle the ribs with a little honey and EVOO. Squeeze the juice from the grilled lemons over the ribs and sprinkle them with kosher salt. Garnish with chopped parsley or oregano if desired. Serve at once with the grilled lemon halves on the side for those that want more lemon.

MY NOTES:

Braised Pulled Pork

6-12 Servings

About This Recipe

The genesis of this recipe came from Jenny Rosenstrach's "Dinner, A Love Story." She calls it Ragu (sans accent), but I think the word is misleading because it evokes, at least in my mind, the stuff that comes in a jar with the u accent turned the wrong way.

Ingredients

3	Lbs Pork shoulder roast, boneless
1	Onion, chopped
3	Cloves Garlic, chopped
	Salt and Pepper to taste
2	Tbs EVOO
1	Tbs Butter
1	28-oz Can of Tomatoes
1	Cup Red or white wine
½	Tbs Dried thyme
½	Tbs Dried oregano
2	Tbs Fennel seeds
	Hot sauce to taste (optional)
	Grated Parmagiano Reggiano or Pecorino Romano

Procedure

Heat EVOO and butter in a Dutch oven. Salt and pepper the meat and brown it on all sides. Reserve the meat.

Add onion and garlic and sauté 1 minute. Add the remaining ingredients except cheese and bring to a boil. Put the meat back in the pan. The liquid should come up to at least ⅓ of the way up the meat. If not, add a little water, wine or chicken stock until it does. Cover the pot and braise about 3 hours or until meat is practically falling apart. Keep your eye on the liquid level and top off with water, wine or stock as needed. Also turn the meat every half-hour or so. The braising can be done in a pre-heated 325° oven, but I prefer doing it on top of the stove because I don't have to keep taking it in and out of the oven to turn the meat.

Put the meat on a cutting board and pull it apart using two forks, then put the shredded pork back in the pot. Heat and serve over pasta in large bowls, garnished with the grated cheese.

MY NOTES:

Chinese Pork and Noodle Stir-fry

4 Servings

About This Recipe

This dish can be one dish in a multi-course Chinese meal or it can be a complete meal in that it contains meat, starch and vegetables. Like most stir-fried dishes, it cooks very quickly.

There are many choices that you can make. Since the pork is going to be sliced thin, you can use almost any cut, but I recommend using the tenderloin for best results. The veggies can be anything you like. Carrots, mushrooms, celery, broccoli florets, Chinese cabbage, bean sprouts, onions, red or green bell peppers, water chestnuts, bamboo shoots, snap peas are all suitable choices.. The noodles can be rice noodles, bean threads, udon, or linguine. You can add heat by putting in hot chilis or red pepper flakes. Lastly, you can use many types of sauce. Brown sauce, black bean sauce, garlic sauce hoisin sauce, oyster sauce or sweet-and-sour sauce are all worthy choices.

Ingredients

1	Lb Pork tenderloin
2	Tbs Soy Sauce
1	Tbs Cornstarch
	Salt and pepper to taste
1	Tbs Canola or peanut oil
½	Tbs Sesame oil
1	Clove Garlic, pressed or minced
1	2" piece of fresh ginger, peeled and minced
3	Cups Mixed veggies, cut into bite-sized pieces
6	Tbs Prepared sauce of choice
½	Cup Chicken stock
2	Tbs Cornstarch slurry
12	Oz Noodles, cooked according to package instructions
	Chopped coriander for garnish

Procedure

Remove visible fat and silverskin from the tenderloin. Cut it in half lengthwise and then cut thin slices across the grain from each half. Put the meat into a bowl. Mix the soy sauce with the cornstarch, salt and pepper and pour over the meat and toss. Heat the canola and sesame oil on high heat in a large skillet. Add the garlic and ginger and stir fry 30 seconds. Add the meat and stir-fry until it is browned on all sides, working in batches if necessary. Reserve the meat. If needed, add a bit more oil to the pan and stir-fry the vegetables, just until wilted, about 2 - 3 minutes. Add the chicken broth and the sauce. Bring to a boil. Add the cornstarch slurry, a little at a time until the sauce reaches the consistency you want. Add the pork and the noodles, stir to combine and heat through. Serve immediately, garnished with fresh chopped coriander.

Creole Paella

12 Servings

About This Recipe

This dish is better known by its Louisiana sobriquet, "Jambalaya". According to my research, when the Spanish came to the Louisiana area, they lusted for home-cooked paella. Given the availability of American veggies like tomatoes and peppers, the influence of the French who loved parsley and thyme, great preserved pork products like ham and sausages and a cornucopia of seafood from the Gulf, Jambalaya was born.

The list of ingredients may be intimidating at first glance. However, it is truly an easy recipe, so don't be put off.

I've been told that there are as many recipes for jambalaya as there are residents of Louisiana, but there are two main styles, the Creole and the Cajun. This recipe falls into the creole camp. That said, the variations you can perform are nearly infinite. Virtually any kind of meat or poultry that won't fall apart can be used in place of or in addition to the proteins mentioned in this recipe. Feel free to experiment with different herbs and/or seasonings. I'll bet that, with a little experimentation, you can come up with something that beats my recipe hands down.

Although there is a fair amount of chopping associated with this recipe, the whole thing gets made in one pot which can serve as the serving vessel. In addition, there is a lot of stirring, so you need to keep an eye on the pot and make sure that everything is mixed well. It is a great party dish that can be easily scaled to serve many. You don't need to serve anything with it except maybe some bread and a green salad.

Ingredients

1	Lb Kielbasa, Spanish chorizo or andouille sausage
1	Tbs EVOO
1	Lb Ham, sliced ⅜" thick
1	Red bell pepper, medium dice
1	Green bell pepper, medium dice
1	Large Onion, medium dice
4	Stalks Celery, medium dice
1	Tbs Butter
1	14-oz Can Tomatoes
6	Cloves Garlic, chopped
1	Jalapeno, seeded and chopped fine, or
½	Tsp Cayenne or Tabasco sauce (optional)
2	Tbs Tomato paste
1	Tbs Fresh oregano leaves or ½Tbs dried

(Recipe continues on next page)

1	Tbs Fresh thyme or ½ Tbs dried
½	Tbs Salt
1	Tsp Black pepper freshly ground
3	Bay leaves
6	Cups Chicken or vegetable stock
3	Cups Basmati rice, well-rinsed
¼	Cups Chopped parsley
¼	Cup Chopped scallions
¼	Cup Lemon juice
1	Lb Medium shrimp, peeled and deveined
24	Clams or mussels in shell, cleaned
2	Tbs Chopped parsley for garnish
2	Tbs Chopped scallions for garnish
	Tabasco sauce (optional)

Procedure

Slice the sausage into pieces about ¼" thick. Brown them in a large Dutch oven in EVOO until browned, about 8 minutes. Reserve the sausage.

Dice the ham into ⅜" cubes and brown them in the Dutch oven, about 8 minutes. Reserve the ham with the sausage.

Melt the butter in the Dutch oven, and add the vegetables. Cook until the onions are transparent, about 5-7 minutes.

Add the tomatoes with their juice, crushing them with your hands, the garlic, jalapeno or cayenne (if using), the tomato paste, salt, pepper, oregano, thyme, and bay leaves and cook 5 minutes to combine. Add the reserved sausage and ham. Add the chicken stock and bring to a boil. Add the rinsed rice, return to the boil, lower the heat to a bare simmer, cover and cook for 15 -20 minutes until all of the liquid has been absorbed by the rice.

Stir in the parsley, scallions and lemon juice. Then add the shrimp and clams or mussels, making sure that they are buried. Take the pot off the heat, cover and let sit for 10 minutes. The shrimp and shellfish will steam to perfection during that time.

Serve at once, garnished with a little more parsley and scallions. Pass around a bottle of Tabasco sauce for heat lovers.

MY NOTES:

Orzo with Sausage, Peppers and Tomatoes

4 Servings

About This Recipe

This is my own variation on the common pasta with sausage and peppers dish. I got the idea on a trip to Athens when I had a dish a bit like this made with lamb and tomatoes.

Most of the orzo sold in US markets is very small - about the size of long-grain rice. In Greece, they have larger varieties. If you can find the larger ones, use them.

Although the dish calls for fresh tomatoes and peppers, you can substitute canned tomatoes and roasted peppers that come in a jar. The dish will taste different, but still good and you won't have to mess around with roasting peppers and peeling tomatoes. Use any kind of sausage that you like. Sweet, hot, Italian, German, Louisiana are all good

This dish is great for an outdoor meal. You can serve it in the pan it was cooked in

Ingredients

1	Lb Sausage, any kind you like
1	Tbs EVOO
3	Cloves Garlic, chopped
2	Sweet Bell Peppers, roasted, peeled, seeded and cut into 1/4" strips
2	Sweet tomatoes, peeled, seeded and coarsely chopped
1	Cup Chicken stock
12	Oz Orzo
1	Tsp Red pepper flakes (optional)
	Salt and Pepper to taste
3	Tbs Chopped fresh herbs such as oregano, basil and parsley alone or in combination
	Parmagiano Reggiano

Procedure

Use a deep skillet or sauté pan. Cut the sausage into bite-size pieces and sauté them in EVOO until cooked through. If there is an excessive amount of fat, pour it off, leaving a couple of tablespoons. Add the garlic and sauté a minute. Add the tomatoes, peppers and red pepper flakes and sauté 2 minutes. Pour in the chicken stock and bring to a boil. Add the orzo, stir and cook about 8 minutes or until the orzo is al dente. The orzo should be a bit creamy - like risotto. If it is too dry, add more chicken stock.

Add the chopped herbs, salt and pepper to taste and pass around a block of parmagiano and a grater.

MY NOTES:

Pasta alla Carbonara

4 Servings

About This Recipe

This classic Italian pasta dish has a sauce made from bacon, eggs and grated cheese, but within that basic framework you have a lot of latitude in the selection of ingredients and their relative amounts. Traditionally, the dish was made with "guanciale" (cured pork jowl), but you can use regular bacon, slab bacon or pancetta. This entire dish can be made in less than 15 minutes. The only way to screw it up is to allow the eggs to scramble instead of smoothly incorporating them into the sauce.

Purists don't use onions, wine, cream or peas in this dish, but I think they are all OK and give you the option to make the dish differently each time so you don't get bored with it. One cook I know likes to add a bit of cinnamon. I haven't tried it, but he swears by it.

Ingredients

1   Lb Pasta such as spaghetti, linguine, tagliatelle or bucatini.

1   Tbs EVOO

¼   Lb Guanciale, pancetta or bacon, chopped

1   Onion, chopped fine (optional)

4   Cloves Garlic, pressed or minced

¼   Cup White wine (optional)

2-4   Eggs at room temperature

½   Cup Grated parmagiano or pecorino cheese

2   Tbs Heavy cream (optional)

     Salt and pepper to taste

½   Cup peas, kept warm (optional)

2   Tbs Chopped parsley, chives or scallions for garnish

Procedure

Cook the pasta al dente in boiling water. Drain and toss with a little EVOO to prevent sticking. Reserve the pasta and a bit of the pasta water.

While the pasta is cooking, fry the bacon or pancetta in EVOO in a large skillet or sauté pan until crisp. Drain the bacon on paper towels and pour off all but a couple of tablespoons of fat. Add the onion (optional) and garlic to the fat and sauté a few minutes. Deglaze the pan with white wine (optional). Add the pasta, the meat and a little of the reserved pasta water. Over high heat, stir until most of the water has evaporated.

Combine the eggs, cheese and cream (if using) together in a bowl. Off-heat, add the egg mixture to the pan, whisking briskly to prevent the eggs from scrambling. Add a little more pasta water if the sauce needs thinning. Season with salt and pepper. Careful on the salt since the bacon and cheese are already salty. Add the optional peas and stir to combine.

Garnish with parsley, scallions or chives and serve immediately. Serve with help-yourself grated cheese.

Pork Adobo

6-8 Servings

About This Recipe

Adobo is a Spanish or Portuguese word that was co-opted by Filipinos to characterize what has become that country's unofficial national dish. Adobo originally referred to meat or seafood that was cooked in a mixture of salt and vinegar that prevented spoiling. Today, adobo recipes still contain salt (or soy sauce) and vinegar as basic ingredients, and there are now as many adobo recipes as there are Filipinos.

You can use any type of vinegar that suits your fancy. Cider vinegar is quite popular, although they certainly do not grow apples in the Philippines. There, cane sugar vinegar is a staple. Personally, I like sherry vinegar.

It is traditional to serve the adobo over steamed rice. I like it with long grain basmati rice, but, in the Philippines, sticky short grain rice is popular.

Ingredients

2	Lbs Pork shoulder, fat removed and cut into 1" cubes
½	Cup Soy sauce
	Light cooking oil
1	Small Head of garlic, cloves peeled and smashed
1	Tsp Peppercorns
4	Bay leaves
½	Cup Vinegar of choice
1	Pint Coconut milk or chicken stock
	Red pepper flakes or hot chilis (optional)
3	Tbs Chopped scallions for garnish

Procedure

Put the pork cubes in a plastic bag and add the soy sauce. Squish it around to coat the meat evenly and allow to marinate for an hour or so. Remove the meat and dry it off with paper towels, reserving the soy sauce. Brown the meat in a large skillet or sauté pan in a little oil. Remove the meat and pour off the fat.

Add the remaining ingredients except scallions to the pan and Bring to the boil. Add the meat, reduce to a simmer and cook 45 - 90 minutes depending on the quality of the meat. Remove the meat to a warm platter or bowl and reduce the pan liquid until it thickens slightly, about 5 minutes. Remove the bay leaves, garlic cloves and peppercorns. Pour the sauce over the meat, sprinkle with chopped scallions and serve at once. The dish will keep several days refrigerated or up to several months in the freezer.

MY NOTES:

Roast Pork Loin

6-10 Servings

About this Recipe

Pork loin is one of the most economical cuts of meat that, properly prepared, can be designated "gourmet." There are three secrets to making it delicious. First, brine the meat. Second, flavor it. Third, don't overcook it.

Volume I contains the instructions for brining, so I won't bother to repeat that here. Brine your loin for at least 12 hours but no more than 24 hours. You can add flavoring ingredients to the brine if you wish, but I don't think it is necessary since the loin will b e flavored before it is roasted. You can choose different herbs to flavor the roast. This recipe suggests garlic and rosemary, but sage, thyme, marjoram and others are good too.

I recommend serving your roasted pork loin with a sauce such as the Port and Dried Fruit Sauce that you will find in the Sauce chapter. Just about any side dishes or salads go well with pork roast. I am partial to serving it with lightly candied yams or carrots and a green vegetable such as spinach sautéed with sliced garlic.

Ingredients

3   Lbs Pork loin, boneless
4   Cloves Garlic, pressed
1   Tbs Rosemary, fresh or dried, chopped
2   Tsp Salt
1   Tsp Freshly ground black pepper
3   Tbs EVOO

Procedure

Brine the meat as described above.

Pre-heat oven to 400°. Combine the herbs, salt, pepper, garlic and EVOO and mash it into a paste. Cut small slits in the meat with the tip of a sharp knife and stuff them with the paste. Rub the meat all over with the remaining paste.

Place the roast in a roasting pan on a rack. Roast for approximately 1 hour, turning every 15 minutes so that the roast will brown evenly on all sides. Take the roast out when a thermometer registers140°. Let the roast rest at least 15 minutes before carving.

MY NOTES:

Sausage, Artichoke and Sun-dried Tomato Pasta

4-6 Servings

About this Recipe

This 15-minute recipe is what I think of as a "personality" dish. That is, the dish will take on the personality of the ingredients. For example, if you want it to taste Italian, use Italian sausage and Italian herbs like basil and oregano. Want Polish? Use kielbasa and some celery seed in addition to parsley. German? Use bratwurst and herbs such as caraway seeds, thyme and chives. French? Try merguez (lamb) sausages with a bit of rosemary or maybe some Moroccan spices. American? Try some of the interesting varieties of chicken sausages, especially ones containing artichoke and an interesting cheese such as Gruyere.

At the end, you can add some grated or crumbled cheese. For Italian, use Parmagiano or Asiago; for Greek, use feta; American, try blue cheese.

Ingredients

1	Lb thick pasta like bucatini or fusilli
	Salt
1	Lb Sausage, cut into bite-size pieces
1	Lb Artichoke hearts, packed in water and drained or frozen (defrost before using)
3	Cloves Garlic, pressed or minced
1	Cup Sun-dried tomatoes, packed in oil, roughly chopped
1½	Cups Chicken stock
½	Cup White wine
	Fresh or dried herbs and spices
	Salt and freshly ground black pepper to taste
	An appropriate cheese, grated or crumbled (optional)

Procedure

Cook the pasta as usual. If the sausage you will be using is raw, sauté it in a little oil from the sun-dried tomato jar until it is cooked through.

In a large skillet or sauté pan, heat a couple of tablespoons of oil from the sun-dried tomatoes. Add the garlic and cook 1 minute. Add the artichoke hearts, the sausage and the sun-dried tomatoes and heat through, about 3-4 minutes. Deglaze the pan with the wine and cook off the alcohol. Add the chicken stock and cook about 5 minutes to concentrate the sauce. Add whatever herbs and spices you are using and stir to combine. Drain the pasta and add it to the skillet. Mix thoroughly. Taste and adjust seasoning. Serve at once.

If you are using cheese, you can add it now or just pass it around for people to help themselves

MY NOTES:

Spareribs with an Asian Flair

4-8 Servings

About this Recipe

I derived this recipe from one that Chef Bobby Flay did years ago on his *Throwdown* TV show. Bobby's recipe lost the competition, but, trust me, it is delicious. I've simplified the recipe a bit, but I don't think the final product suffers.

This recipe takes time to make, but nowhere near as long as smoked ribs. I recommend that you make lots of them and freeze them prior to the last cooking stage. You can then defrost and finish them off on the grill.

You need to make three items for this dish: a spice rub, a cooking liquid and a glaze. You can make all of them well ahead of time and store them in the fridge or the freezer.

Ingredients

THE RIBS

2	Racks Spareribs or St. Louis ribs

THE RUB

½	Cup Smoked Spanish paprika
2	Tbs Dry mustard
2	Tbs Chinese five spice powder
2	Tbs Dried ground ginger
1½	Tbs Ground black pepper
1	Tbs Ground allspice
1	Tbs Salt
1	Tbs Cayenne or red pepper flakes (optional)
	Canola oil

THE ROASTING LIQUID

1	Quart Water
2	Cups Soy sauce
	Salt and pepper
1/4	Cup Coarsely chopped fresh ginger
1	Tbs Whole black peppercorns
1	Tbs Whole coriander seeds
1	Tbs Whole black mustard seeds

(Recipe continues on next page)

THE GLAZE

3	Tbs Canola oil or other vegetable oil
3	Shallots, peeled and minced
6	3-inch-long strips lemon zest
3	Cloves Garlic, pressed
2	Chilis, finely chopped, preferably Thai chilis
3	Tbs Fresh ginger, finely chopped
2	Tbs Curry powder
1	Tsp Ground cinnamon
2	Whole Star anise
1	Large Can of plums with juice
¼	Cup Hoisin sauce
2	Tbs Soy sauce
¼	Cup Honey
¼	Cup Brown sugar
3	Tbs Powdered ginger
1	Cup Water

Procedure

Mix together all the dry ingredients for the Rub. Stir in just enough oil so that the rub coats the ribs without dripping off. Coat the ribs on both sides with the rub and allow to sit for half an hour. Grill the ribs about 5 minutes on each side to set the rub.

Fit a rack into a roasting pan large enough to hold both racks. Pre-heat the oven to 500°. Mix all the ingredients for the roasting liquid together and pour into the bottom of the pan. Roast the ribs for an hour. There is a good chance that your kitchen will get smoky, roasting at that temperature. You can avoid that by cooking outdoors on an enclosed grill.

Mix all the ingredients for the glaze together. Paint the racks with the glaze and return to the grill. Grill about 45 minutes, basting every 10 minutes with the glaze.

Slice the ribs and serve.

MY NOTES:

Stinco

6 Servings

About this Recipe

Stinco in Italian translates to the English word "shank", and this recipe is a braised and roasted pork shank. It is similar to osso buco and braised lamb shank, but is uniquely flavorful. To be honest, I never heard of it until I encountered it at *Maestro's*, an Italian restaurant in Saratoga Springs, New York. Even though the waiter told me it was the best thing on the menu, I ordered it only because I couldn't resist anything that rhymed with "stinko."

I don't know why I was so surprised that this dish is so good. Pork shanks have all the fat, gelatin and marrow that a great braising sauce requires. I think it is every bit the equal of osso buco, and, given the price of decent veal these days, it is a great bargain.

Basically, pork shanks are braised in a sauce containing wine, porcinis and prosciutto (or bacon) and then browned in a hot oven. If the shanks are small enough, you could serve one to a person. If they are large cut the meat off the bone and serve it in chunks on top of pasta or mashed potatoes.

Ingredients

1	Oz Dried porcinis
1½	Cups Boiling water
5	Lbs Pork shanks
	Salt and pepper to taste
3	Tbs EVOO
2	Oz Prosciutto or blanched bacon
2	Cups Onions, chopped
1	Cup Finely chopped carrots
½	Cup Finely chopped celery
1	Cup Chopped leeks (white part)
2	Tbs Garlic, pressed
1	Cup White wine
1	Cup Chicken stock
2	Tbs Mixed fresh herbs such as sage and rosemary

Procedure

Soak the mushrooms in the boiling water for at least 45 minutes. Strain the soaking liquid to remove any grit and reserve it. Chop up the mushrooms and reserve them.

Pre-heat oven to 325°. Tie each shank with butcher's twine,. Usually, 3 loops will do the job. Heat 2 Tbs EVOO in a braising pot or large Dutch oven over medium-high heat. Sprinkle the meat with salt and pepper and brown the shanks, working in batches, about 10 minutes per batch. Reserve the shanks and pour off all but about 2 Tbs of fat.

(Recipe continues on next page)

Add the prosciutto and chopped vegetables to the pot and cook until they are soft, about 10 minutes, scraping any browned bits into the mix. Add the garlic, porcinis and wine and bring to a boil. Add the reserved mushroom liquid, chicken stock and half the fresh herbs. Bring to a boil and add the shanks.

Cover the pot and bake it in the oven for 30 minutes. Then turn the shanks, re-cover and bake another 30 minutes. Repeat this process over about 3 hours or until the meat is almost falling off the bone. During this cooking, add more chicken stock whenever necessary if too much liquid evaporates.

Transfer the shanks to a roasting pan. Increase the oven temperature to 425°. Brush the shanks with the remaining EVOO, sprinkle with the remaining fresh herbs and more salt and pepper. Roast for 15-20 minutes until nicely browned.

While the meat is roasting, return the pot to the stovetop. Degrease the liquid and reduce it to the sauce consistency you want if it is too thin. Adjust seasoning to taste.

If you are going to serve the meat off the bone, discard the twine and cut the meat in large chunks off the shanks. If the shanks are small enough to feed one person, just get rid of the twine and serve whole. Ladle on a bit of sauce and serve the rest on the side.

MY NOTES:

Tuscan Sausages and Grapes

4-6 Servings

About this Recipe

There is an upscale Italian restaurant in Providence, Rhode Island called *al Forno* that has been there for decades. A friend took me there, and I ordered this dish which I was told is a house specialty. It is very simple to make, inexpensive and amazingly good. It is basically Italian sausage, either hot or mild, cooked with seedless grapes. The waiter told me that it was a specialty of Tuscany, but I've been in Tuscany several times and never saw anything like it. You can do the whole dish in about 40 minutes.

If you are not a fan of pork, you can use chicken or turkey sausages. I haven't tried it, but I think this dish would go very well with merguez, the lamb sausages that originated in North Africa. You can buy them in Mediterranean markets or make them yourself.

The restaurant served the dish with mashed potatoes, but I prefer oven-roasted new potatoes or French fries. Add a green salad for a complete meal.

Ingredients

2	Lbs Italian sausage, sweet or hot or both
2	Lbs Seedless grapes, red, white or both
3	Tbs Butter
2	Tbs Red wine

Procedure

Pre-heat the oven to 500°. Boil the sausage for 8 minutes to eliminate some of the fat. While the sausage is boiling, remove the grape stems. In a large baking pan, melt the butter and then add the grapes. Stir well to coat all the grapes. Add the wine and cook most of it off, stirring constantly. Add the sausages, making sure that they touch the bottom of the pan. Put the pan in the oven. After 15 minutes turn the sausages so that they cook evenly, and return the pan to the oven for another 15 minutes. Serve immediately.

MY NOTES:

Chapter 11: Main Dishes: Seafood

Here are 13 varied recipes for seafood main dishes. I am not a good fish cooker. Therefore, none of the recipes in this chapter are challenging. If I can make them, anyone can.

Baked or Grilled Lemon Halibut, With or Without Crust

2 Servings

About This Recipe

You may well ask why halibut, at around $20/lb, is in this cookbook. Maybe you fish for it yourself, so outside of the airfare to Alaska, the fishing license and the tackle, it is free. That said, halibut is an excellent fish that is sturdy enough to stand up to grilling and tender enough to be treated like sole.

This recipe is the simplest, and to my mind, the best way to cook halibut. You marinate the fish in lemon juice, EVOO and herbs, then grill or bake it. If you like, you can cover one side of the halibut with a crust made from dried mashed potato flakes mixed with chopped fresh herbs. My mother used to make this dish with a crust made from crushed cornflakes. I haven't had it for 50+ years, but I remember that I liked it.

Ingredients

1	Lb Halibut
1	Lemon, juiced
2	Tbs EVOO
	Salt and Pepper to taste
	Herbs such as rosemary, paprika, thyme, marjoram, etc., chopped
	Mashed potato flakes
1	Egg

Procedure

Put the fish in a shallow baking dish. Mix the rest of the ingredients together and pour over the fish. Allow to marinate 30-60 minutes. Bake in a pre-heated 450° oven for 10-15 minutes, depending on thickness, or grill 3-4 minutes per side. Serve at once.

If you want to make a crust, combine enough potato flakes with herbs to form a crust about ¼" – ½" thick. Make an egg wash by mixing 1 egg with 1 Tbs water. Dip one side of the fish in the egg wash and then into the crust mixture. Repeat. Sauté the fish, crust side down in a skillet in a little hot EVOO until the crust has browned, about 5 minutes. Remove the fish and place on a rack positioned over a drip pan and bake 5 or 6 minutes in a 350° oven or until fish is cooked through.

Grilled Fish Filets with Citrus Sauce

4 Servings

About This Recipe

This recipe involves grilling fish filets about 2 minutes per side and topping the filets with a quickly made sauce flavored with citrus. If you have ever been afraid of cooking fish, this is the recipe that will cure you of that fear. I got this recipe from a restaurant on the Isle of Capri where I had it for lunch. I haven't a clue what the fish was. The chef told me, but I'd never heard of it.

Be sure to pick fish filets that will stand up to grilling and won't fall apart when you flip them. Tilapia, snapper and similar fish work well. Most soles are too tender.

Ingredients

3	Tbs Butter
2	Tbs EVOO
2	Cloves Garlic, pressed or minced
1	Tbs Orange juice
1	Tbs Lemon juice
	Grated zest from half an orange
	Grated zest from half a lemon
½	Tsp Salt
	Chopped herbs such as basil or rosemary
4	Fish filets
	EVOO to coat filets
	Salt and pepper to taste

Procedure

Toss all the ingredients except the last three into a pan and cook for about 5 minutes. Your sauce is finished. Keep warm while the fish is cooking.

Coat the filets with EVOO and sprinkle with salt and pepper on both sides. On a well-greased grill, cook over high heat about 2 minutes per side. Remove the filets to a serving platter and drizzle the sauce over them.

MY NOTES:

Mediterranean Shellfish with Fennel and Tomato

4 Servings

About This Recipe

This dish is fabulous and easy to make. This recipe is for four, but can easily be doubled to serve eight. I like to serve it in the pan it is cooked in. If you have a paella pan, that would be perfect. If not, a large skillet will do nicely for four people, 2 skillets for eight.

The idea here is to build a base with fennel and tomatoes flavored with a fennel or anise-based liquor. The base is then topped with your choice of shellfish topped with seasoned breadcrumbs topped with grated or crumbled cheese. The pan is then cooked in a hot oven until the shellfish is cooked. Although this recipe calls for canned tomatoes plus tomato paste, you can substitute any marinara sauce that you might have on hand.

You have lots of choices to make. Appropriate seafoods are shrimp, scallops, calamari, mussels, clams and firm fish. Use a combination of two or more if you wish. There is also a wide choice of fennel-flavored liquors to choose from: Finocchietto from Italy, Ouzo from Greece, Pernod and Ricard from France, Ojen from Spain, Kasra from Libya and Arak from several middle-eastern countries.

Pick the cheese you want depending on what part of the Mediterranean you want to emphasize. e.g., feta for Greece, Manchego for Spain or Parmagiano for Italy. Serve this dish with a green salad and plenty of great bread for sopping.

Ingredients

1	Large Fennel bulb, coarsely chopped
¼	Cup EVOO
3	Cloves Garlic, minced
½	Cup White wine
1	14-oz Can Tomatoes with juice
2	Tsp Tomato paste
1	Tsp Dried oregano or 2 Tsp fresh
2	Tbs Fennel/anise flavored liquor
1	Tsp Salt
½	Tsp Pepper
1	Cup Fresh--made or Panko breadcrumbs
3	Tbs Chopped parsley
	Grated zest of 1 lemon
1+	Lbs Shellfish (shrimp, calamari, scallops, clams, etc.)
1	Cup Grated or crumbled cheese

(Recipe continues on next page)

Procedure

Sauté the fennel in 2 Tbs EVOO 8-10 minutes. Add the minced garlic and cook an additional 30 seconds, stirring. Add the white wine and deglaze the pan. Cook until the wine is reduced by half. Add the tomatoes and the tomato paste, breaking up the tomatoes by hand or with a wooden utensil. Add the oregano and liquor, salt and pepper and cook 15 minutes, stirring often.

While the tomatoes are cooking, mix together the breadcrumbs, lemons zest, the chopped parsley and 2 Tbs EVOO.

Layer the seafood on top of the base, sprinkle with the breadcrumb mixture and then with the grated or crumbled cheese. Up to this point, you can refrigerate the pan to be cooked at a later time.

Pre-heat the oven to 450°. Place the pan in the upper third of the oven and bake for 10-15 minutes until the seafood is cooked and everything is heated through.

Drizzle EVOO and lemon juice over the dish and serve immediately.

MY NOTES:

Pan-seared Filet of Sole Meunière

2 Servings

About This Recipe

Pan-seared filet of sole, known as "meunière" in France, is a dish favored by restaurants because it is easy to make and you can charge a lot for it. You can make it just as good as any restaurant can and save a ton of money. Total make time for 4 filets (2 per person) is less than 15 minutes. You can use any kind of sole for this recipe. Trout filets also work well.

If you add sliced, toasted almonds, you can call the dish "Sole Amandine" which enables a restaurant to add $5 to the price.

Sole meunière is often served alone as a separate course. If you want to make a meal course out of it, I'd suggest rice or a vegetable couscous and maybe some sautéed French stringbeans. I had it served once with pommes frites and it was a terrific combination.

Ingredients

4	3-4 Oz Sole filets
	Salt and pepper
½	Cup Flour for dredging
2	Tbs Canola oil
2	Tbs Butter

SAUCE

4	Tbs Butter
2	Tbs Chopped parsley
1	Tbs Fresh lemon juice
	Splash of White wine (optional)
2-4	Tbs Sliced, toasted almonds

Procedure

Pre-heat oven to 200°. Pat the filets dry with paper towels and sprinkle with salt and pepper. Heat oil and butter in a 12" skillet until just before it reaches the smoke point. Dredge two filets in the flour, shake off the excess and place in the pan. Cook 2-3 minutes. Carefully turn the filets and cook on the other side 1-2 minutes. Transfer the filets to a warm platter, place in the oven, and repeat the process for the other two filets.

To make the sauce, wipe out the skillet and cook the butter until it turns light brown. Add the lemon juice, a splash of white wine and the parsley. Add almonds if using. Heat the sauce through, plate the fish and pour the sauce over the fish.

MY NOTES:

Red Curry Steamed Mussels

4 Servings

About This Recipe

Despite my vast experience, I had never heard of red curry mussels until I had a fabulous dish by that name at the Fog Harbor restaurant in San Francisco. Although the menu lists it as a starter, they give you enough for a main course, assuming you have their excellent sourdough bread to accompany it.

The next day, I looked online and found more than a dozen recipes called red curry mussels, including a few from famous chefs. Those recipes are all much the same and are quite different than Fog Harbor's creation despite having the same name. In any event, I unsuccessfully tried to bribe the manager for the recipe, so I emailed them, promising to include their recipe in my next book if they would share it. Obviously, that strategy worked.

Please use PEI (Prince Edward Island) or equivalent mussels. Green-lips and other beasties just don't have the right texture and sweetness. This recipe assumes that 3 pounds of mussels will do for 4 people. That could be a gross understatement!

The recipe calls for Kaffir lime leaves and Thai basil, both of which are readily available in Asian markets. You can substitute lime zest for the Kaffir leaves and regular basil or mint for the Thai variety.

Ingredients

SAUCE

1	Pint Chicken stock
1	Pint Clam juice
2	Cans Light coconut milk
1½	Tbs Red curry paste, mild or hot as you wish
1½	Tbs Chicken base
½	Cup Powdered ginger
1	Bunch Cilantro, chopped
¾	Cup Garlic, minced
2	Kaffir lime leaves or zest of a lime
2	Tbs Sesame oil
1	Pinch Salt

THE MUSSELS

2	Tbs Canola or peanut oil
2	Cloves Garlic, pressed or minced
1	Onion, halved and thinly sliced
1	Red bell pepper, julienned
1	Green bell pepper, julienned

(Recipe continues on next page)

2   Tbs Cilantro, chopped

3   Lbs PEI mussels, cleaned

2   Tbs Thai basil, chopped

Procedure

Put all of the sauce ingredients in a pot. Bring to a boil, then allow to cool. Strain the sauce through a sieve.

In a large pot, heat the oil and add the garlic, onions and peppers. Sauté until the vegetables begin to soften, about 4 minutes. Add the mussels and as much sauce as you want. Bring to a boil, cover and steam until mussels have opened, about 5 minutes. Stir in some freshly chopped cilantro and Thai basil.

Serve at once in large bowls with plenty of the broth..

MY NOTES:

Salmon en Croute

4 Servings

About This Recipe

You' have probably enjoyed an entrée labeled "en croute" at a restaurant and were totally impressed. I'm here to tell you that it is no big deal. You can do it yourself at home and it will be every bit as good as the $25 (a la carte) restaurant version. All you gotta do is wrap up the food in puff pastry which you can buy at any supermarket and bake it. This recipe calls for salmon, but you can use any fish that is not likely to fall apart under prolonged heat.

Since this dish looks sexy as all getout, you might serve it with sexy sides like roasted asparagus drizzled with bernaise or hollandaise sauce and buttered new potatoes sprinkled with chopped parsley.

The en croute technique can be used with any filling you like. For example, Beef Wellington (described in the Beef chapter) is just a chunk of meat en croute.

Ingredients

4	Tbs Softened butter
	Handful of Watercress or arugula, chopped
	Juice and zest of ½ a lemon
1	Tbs Chopped fresh tarragon
½	Tsp Salt
4	Salmon filets, about 6 Oz each
1	Sheet Puff pastry
1	Egg, beaten, for glaze and seal
½	Tbs Chopped fresh chives

Procedure

Mix the first 6 ingredients together to make a paste. Pat the filets dry with paper towels and spread the paste on one surface of the filets.

Defrost a frozen puff pastry sheet and roll it out on a floured surface. Cut into four squares. Wrap each piece of salmon in one of the squares and seal the edges with beaten egg applied with a pastry brush. Brush all over the top with the egg and cut a couple of slits in the tops. Bake for 20 minutes or until golden. Serve immediately.

MY NOTES:

Scallops Gratinée

6 Servings

About This Recipe

This dish is elegant, but is super-easy to make. It can be served as a starter course or a main dish. For a main dish, use 5-6 oz of scallops per person. For a starter, use half that amount. To make serving easy, prepare it in individual gratin dishes of appropriate size. You can use deep sea scallops or bay scallops. If the scallops are large, cut them in half or quarters.

Ingredients

2	Lbs Scallops
6	Tbs White wine
6	Tbs Butter, softened
6	Cloves Garlic, finely chopped
2	Shallots, minced
2	Oz Prosciutto or cooked bacon, finely chopped
4	Cup Parsley, minced
2	Tbs Lemon juice
2	Tbs Pernod or Ouzo (optional)
2	Tsp Salt
1	Tsp Black pepper
¾	Cup EVOO
½	Cup Panko bread crumbs
	Lemon wedges
	Chopped parsley for garnish

Procedure

Pre-heat oven to 425°. Cut scallops into bite size pieces. Put 1 Tbs of wine into each gratin dish. Dry the scallops with paper towels and distribute them evenly in the gratin dishes.

In a large bowl, (a stand mixer is most convenient) put the butter, garlic, shallots, prosciutto or bacon, parsley, lemon juice, Pernod or Ouzo, salt and pepper. Mix well. While the beater is running add the EVOO in a stream. By hand, stir in the Panko. The topping is finished. Dollop it over the scallops in each dish.

Put the dishes on trays and into the oven for 10 - 12 minutes until bubbling. Serve at once.

Instead of cooking right away, the dish can be assembled hours ahead of time and placed in the refrigerator until it is time to cook.

MY NOTES:

Shellfish Ravioli with Olive Oil Poached Tomato Cream Sauce

2-4 Servings

About This Recipe

There is a small company in Benicia, California called Pasta Prima. It makes the best fresh raviolis I have ever eaten outside of Italy. Indeed, their stuff is better than much of what is served over there. The pasta has that silky texture which is difficult to achieve. The fillings are amazing, and the best of them is Dungeness crab. I ran across this dish at a local Costco tasting. I asked one of the attendants what she recommended as a sauce and she gave me this recipe that takes less than 15 minutes to make.

Ingredients

1	Lb Seafood stuffed ravioli
½	Cups EVOO
1½	Pints Cherry tomatoes cut in half
8	Cloves Garlic, smashed
5	Sprigs Thyme
3	Tbs Chopped Italian parsley
¾	Cup Heavy cream
	Salt and pepper to taste

Procedure

Boil a pot of water, Salt it well and cook the ravioli for about 8 minutes. Drain them, coat with EVOO to prevent sticking, cover and keep warm.

Combine the rest of the ingredients in a large pot and cook over medium heat until the tomatoes start to pop. Do not let the tomatoes fry, so keep an eye on the heat. Drain most of the oil from the pot. Discard the thyme. Add the cream and the parsley and cook 2 minutes until everything is well incorporated. Toss with the ravioli and serve immediately.

MY NOTES:

Shellfish with Ptitim

4 Servings

About This Recipe

I put a recipe for Israeli "pearl" couscous in Volume I. Subsequently, I got curious about the origins of the dish and learned that it was invented just after the Israeli War of Independence because the country was in economic doo-doo and couldn't afford rice. Since then, it has been made into many shapes, but the little round pearl shape is best-known outside of Israel. The Israelis call it "ptitim".

I've developed a fondness for it and serve it often. Most recipes you'll find for it advise toasting the kernels, but you may be able to find it already toasted in the bulk foods section of your local market. Here is a simple all-in-one main dish based on ptitim that takes very little time to prepare.

Ingredients

	EVOO for sautéing
1	Lb Shellfish (shrimp, calamari, scallops, clams, etc.)
1	Lb Zucchinis, sliced ¼" thick
½	Medium Onion, coarsely chopped
1	Lb Tiny tomatoes
	Salt and pepper to taste
	EVOO for sautéing
1	Clove Garlic, minced
1	Shallot, thinly sliced
2	Cups Toasted Ptitim (or Pearl Couscous)
2½	Cups Water or stock
½	Cup Toasted pine nuts
½	Cup Scallions, chopped
	Lime wedges

Procedure

In a large pot, sauté the garlic and shallot in a little EVOO for 2 minutes. Add the ptitim and stir to coat the kernels. Cook for a couple of minutes to infuse the flavored EVOO. Add salt and pepper to taste and stir in. Add the water or stock, bring to a boil, cover and simmer for 10 minutes.

While the ptitim is cooking, in a skillet, add a little EVOO and sauté, separately, the seafood, zucchinis, tomatoes and onions. As you finish an item, put it in a large serving bowl, adding the other items as you go. When the ptitim is finished cooking, add it to the bowl. Add the scallions and pine nuts and stir to combine everything. Serve with lime wedges for spritzing lime juice on the dish.

Singapore Noodles

6 Servings

About This Recipe

When I was researching this recipe, I learned that there is no agreement on its origins, except that everyone says that it did not originate in Singapore. Most say it originated in Hong Kong. Some say Europe, and a few say America where it has become a staple in thousands of Chinese restaurants. There are only two ingredients in common to all: curry powder and rice noodles.

A neat thing about this dish is that, because it can contain veggies, proteins and starch, it can be a complete meal. You can make it for one person or a big party. It can also be a side dish in a varied Chinese meal. Versatile, delicious and economical

You have lots of choices for veggies and proteins. The most popular proteins are shrimp and pork. Chinese barbecued pork (if you can get it) is more or less traditional, but you can just slice up a pork chop and be happy with the result. Chicken strips are also popular. For veggies, mushrooms (dried or fresh), bell peppers, onions, shallots, Chinese cabbage, scallions and bean sprouts are good choices, but almost anything you choose that can be stir-fried will do nicely.

Preparation of the rice noodles is controversial. Some chefs insist that they be soaked in cold water for at least 2 hours. Some say you need to soak them in water for 30 minutes, then spread them out on paper towels and let them dry for an hour. A YouTube chef puts them in boiling water for 30 seconds and they are ready to go.

This recipe is an amalgam of several recipes. I've chosen to use a method wherein the noodles, proteins and veggies are prepared separately and tossed together to make the final product. I think this method takes the guesswork out of the cooking process, but does add extra cooking time.

Ingredients

1	Lb Rice stick noodles
¾	Cup Canola or peanut oil
2	Tsp Sesame oil (optional)
½	Tsp Cayenne (optional)
½	Lb Shrimp
1	Chicken breast, skinned and boned
1	Small Pork chop, boneless
3	Tbs Soy sauce
¼	Cup Chinese wine or dry sherry
1	Tbs Cornstarch
3	Eggs, beaten
1	Tbs Minced ginger
1	Tbs Pressed garlic

(Recipe continues on next page)

1	Red bell pepper, julienned
½	Onion or 3 shallots, julienned
½	Lb Mushrooms, any kind, cut into bite-sized pieces
½	Lb Chinese cabbage, shredded
1	Cup Chicken stock
½	Lb Bean sprouts
4	Scallions, 1/2" dice
	Juice of 2 limes

Procedure

NOODLES

Put the noodles in a large colander or strainer and set it into a pot of boiling water. Heat a 12" skillet and add 3 Tbs of oil. Add the curry powder and optional sesame oil and cayenne and cook 2-3 minutes stirring constantly. Empty the drained noodles into a large bowl. Add soy sauce, sugar and the curry oil. Toss to coat all of the noodles and set the noodle bowl aside.

PROTEINS

Shell, devein and cut the shrimp into two or three pieces. Cut the chicken breast and pork chop into strips cross-grain. Place all the meat in a bowl. Combine the soy sauce, wine and cornstarch and pour over the meat. Toss to coat the meat evenly. Allow to marinate for 15 - 30 minutes. Put 1½ Tbs of oil in the skillet on high heat. Add the meat and stir-fry for 2 - 3 minutes. Reserve the meat in a large bowl.

Add the beaten eggs to the skillet and cook until the eggs are dry. Remove the eggs to a cutting surface and chop them. Add the eggs to the reserved meat.

VEGGIES

Wipe out the skillet and add 1½ Tbs of oil over medium heat. Add the ginger and garlic and fry 30 seconds. Add the veggies and stir-fry 2 - 3 minutes until crisp tender. Add the veggies to the meat bowl.

FINAL STEPS

Pour the stock into the skillet and bring to a simmer. Add the noodles, toss well and cook until the noodles have absorbed all the liquid.

Add the contents of the meat bowl to the noodles and toss to heat everything through. Add the bean sprouts, lime juice and scallions and toss again. Transfer to a platter and serve at once while piping hot.

MY NOTES:

Sole Rolls with Asparagus

4 Servings

About This Recipe

This is a simple, but very good way to fix filets of sole. You coat the inside surface of the roll with a flavored breadcrumb mix, then roll the filets around a filling and bake them drizzled with EVOO and lemon juice. The filling in this recipe is a stalk of asparagus, but you can use anything that strikes your fancy.

The dish is fine as proscribed, but I like to enhance it with a sauce. My personal preference is hollandaise sauce (See Volume I), but you could make a beurre blanc (See Sauce Chapter) or any other sauce that goes well with fish.

Ingredients

¼	Cup Breadcrumbs
¼	Cup Grated Parmagiano Reggiano
2	Tbs Chopped parsley
1	Tsp Chopped oregano
½	Tsp Grated lemon zest
	Salt and Pepper to taste
4	Sole filets
4	Stalks Asparagus (optional)
	Lemon juice
	EVOO

Procedure

Pre-heat oven to 400°. Mix the first six ingredients together and coat the inside surface of the filets with the mixture. Place stalks of asparagus on the surface and roll the filets. Place the filets in a glass baking dish, sprinkle with salt and pepper and drizzle with lemon juice and EVOO. Bake 10 minutes and serve immediately.

MY NOTES:

Spaghetti con Vongole

2-4 Servings

About This Recipe

Spaghetti con Vongole (spaghetti with clams) is popular all over Italy and much of America. Outside of the fact that it tastes good, it is fast and easy to make.

You can use whole fresh clams such as cockles, Manilas, cherrystones or littlenecks. Or, to save time and mess, use canned or chopped clams and forget the shells. If you want to serve them in the shells, steam them in a covered pot until they open. You then have the choice of serving them in the shells (bad idea in my opinion) or shucking out the meat.

Ingredients

1	Lb Linguine, spaghetti or fettuccine
2	Tbs EVOO
4	Cloves Garlic, sliced thin
1	Pinch Red pepper flakes (optional)
2-3	Lbs Clams in the shell, or
1	Can Clams, or
1	Pint Chopped fresh clams
½	Cup White wine
2	Tbs Fresh lemon juice (optional)
1	Small bottle Clam juice or more white wine
3	Tbs Butter (optional)
	Salt and pepper to taste
2	Tbs Chopped Italian parsley for garnish

Procedure

Make the pasta as usual.

If using fresh clams in the shell, steam them open. Shuck the meat if you don't want any shells in your final product.

While the pasta is cooking, sauté the garlic and red pepper flakes in EVOO in a large skillet. Add the clam juice, lemon juice and wine. Bring to a boil and reduce until you have the sauce texture you desire. 5 minutes or so will generally suffice. Season the sauce with salt and pepper to taste, and add the clams. Enrich the sauce with the butter if desired.

Add the cooked pasta to the pot, stir to combine, sprinkle with chopped parsley and serve at once.

MY NOTES:

Stir-fried Shrimp

2 Servings

About This Recipe

Although this recipe serves two people, it easily scales to serve 4-6. If you are in a hurry and want to prepare a lo-cal meal, this dish fits the bill. Depending on your chopping technique, it should take half an hour at most to make this dish. You can do this dish with a different kind of seafood. Calamari, bay scallops, "rock lobster" tails, or clams are good choices.

Ingredients

1-2	Tbs	Canola or peanut oil
1	Tsp	Pressed garlic
1	Tsp	Crushed fresh ginger
½	Lb	Shrimp, peeled
		Salt and pepper to taste
¾	Cup	Chicken stock
1	Tbs	Soy sauce
1	Tsp	Sesame oil
1	Tbs	Cornstarch
1		Medium Carrot, peeled and thinly sliced
1		Red bell pepper, cut into strips
1		Medium Celery stalk, thinly sliced
½		Medium Onion, cut into wedges and layers separated
¼	Lb	Mushrooms, cut into bite-sized pieces (optional)
1	Tbs	Toasted sesame seeds (optional)
		Chopped scallions or chives for garnish (optional)
		Chinese crispy needles (optional)

Procedure

Cover the bottom of a 12" skillet (or a wok if you have one) with oil. When the oil is hot, add the garlic and ginger. Stir-fry about 30 seconds or until fragrant. Dry the shrimp in paper towels and sprinkle them with salt and pepper, add them to the hot pan and cook 15 seconds per side until just opaque. Reserve shrimp.

Add the prepared veggies to the pan and stir-fry for a few minutes until tender but still crisp. Add a bit more oil if necessary.

While veggies are cooking, mix together the chicken stock, soy sauce, sesame oil and cornstarch in a small bowl. When veggies are cooked, add the mixture to the pan along with the reserved shrimp and stir-fry until the sauce has thickened and is hot. Adjust seasoning, sprinkle with garnishes and serve immediately.

Chapter 12: Main Dishes: Veal

Like chicken, veal can take on a wide variety of personalities. Unfortunately, good veal may be difficult to obtain. Nevertheless, if you can find it, try one of the 6 recipes in this Chapter.

Moroccan Veal Stew

8 Servings

About this recipe

Trust me, this recipe is dynamite. Although it calls for veal shanks, you could make this with other cuts. First the meat sits in a garlic-ginger marinade for 6 - 24 hours. Then it is braised for 2-3 hours with vegetables, all flavored by ras el hanout (See recipe in the Miscellaneous Chapter)

I would serve this with couscous or rice pilaf and a tabbouleh salad, accompanied by a flatbread such as pita.

Ingredients

MARINADE

8	Lbs Veal shanks, cut in 2" pieces
2	Tbs Garlic, pressed or minced
1	Tbs Fresh ginger, minced
¼	Cup EVOO
½	Cup Soy sauce
2	Jalapeños, seeded and chopped

BRAISE

2	Tsp Salt
1	Tbs Ras el hanout
¼	Cup Canola oil
1	Cup Red wine
¼	Cup Dry sherry
5	Cloves Garlic, chopped
1½	Quarts Chicken or veal stock
1	Tbs Harissa (optional)
1	Large Onion, 1" dice
4	Stalks Celery, 1" pieces
2	Red bell peppers, 1" dice
3	Large Carrots, cut into 3" batons, 1/2" thick
½	Cup Dried apricots, halved if large

(Recipe continues on next page)

Procedure

Remove any membranes from the meat. Tie string around each piece of shank to keep it together during the cooking process. Mix the marinade ingredients together and rub onto the meat. Place the meat in plastic bags and put them into the refrigerator for 6 - 24 hours. Every once in a while squish the bags around to distribute the marinade.

Pre-heat oven to 325°. Remove the meat from the marinade and dry it with paper towels. Sprinkle with salt and ras el hanout. Heat 2 large Dutch ovens or 1 large roasting pan on top of the stove. Add oil and brown the pieces of meat on both sides. Deglaze the pan(s) with wine and sherry.

Add the remaining ingredients, bring to a simmer, then cover the pans (use foil for the roasting pan). Put the pans in the oven and braise for 2 hours.

Remove the meat and half the vegetables to a serving dish, cover and place in a warm oven. Put the pan back on the stove and boil until juices have reduced to a sauce-like consistency, about 15 - 20 minutes. Spoon off excess fat if any. Pour the sauce over the meat and vegetables and sprinkle with chopped parsley. Serve at once or reheat for later.

MY NOTES:

Swedish Meatballs (Fricadella)

Yields 50 Meatballs

About This Recipe

If you have been to an IKEA store and had lunch there, you have probably tried their Swedish meatballs, known in Scandinavia as Fricadella. They are inexpensive and quite good, but this recipe is better and takes less than half an hour to make, replete with a tasty sauce.

Fricadella can be served as an appetizer, finger-food (on toothpicks) or as a main course. Lingonberry jam is a traditional accompaniment. Normally I don't like mixing sweet and savory, but, in this case, it works pretty well. If you are serving them as a main course, I'd suggest sides of potatoes and a green vegetable like stringbeans.

Ingredients

2	Tbs EVOO
1	Medium Onion, chopped fine
1	Lb Ground beef
1	Lb Ground veal
½	Cup Panko bread crumbs
2	Egg yolks, beaten
¼	Tsp Allspice
¼	Tsp Nutmeg
	Salt and pepper to taste
2	Tbs Butter
⅓	Cup Flour
1	Quart Chicken or veal stock
¾	Cup Sour cream
	Salt and pepper to taste
2	Tbs Chopped parsley for garnish (optional)

Procedure

In a large skillet, sauté the onions in 1 Tbs EVOO for 3 minutes. Combine meat, onions Panko, egg yolks, allspice, nutmeg and seasoning in a bowl. Roll the mixture into 1¼" diameter balls using your hands. In the same skillet, brown the balls in 1 Tbs EVOO in all sides, working in batches. Reserve the meatballs.

In the same skillet, melt the butter, stir in the flour and cook 1 minute. Whisk in the stock and cook 2 minutes. Whisk in the sour cream and season with salt and pepper. Add the meatballs, cover the skillet and cook 10 minutes., turning the meatballs occasionally.

MY NOTES:

Veal Marengo with Truffles

4-8 Servings

About This Recipe

Don't get upset. I entitled this dish "with truffles" just to get your attention. At as much as $1000/pound, white truffles from Italy are definitely unfrugal. Now, if you are in a position to get your hands on some truffles that fell off the back of a truck, by all means use them. If not, drizzle some truffle oil over the dish or use US-grown black truffles. You can also use reconstituted dried porcini mushrooms or sliced morels.

I recommend serving this dish over linguine, pappardella or fettuccini.

Ingredients

2	Tbs EVOO
2	Lbs Veal, preferably from the shoulder, cut into 1½" cubes
½	Cup Flour for dredging
½	Red bell pepper, chopped
½	Green bell pepper, chopped
1	Medium Onion, chopped
2	Cloves Garlic, pressed or minced
1	Cup White wine
½	Cup Chicken stock
1	14-oz Can of tomatoes with juice
½	Tsp Dried tarragon
½	Tsp Dried thyme
½	Lb Crimini or button mushrooms, sliced
1	Bay leaf
	Salt and pepper to taste
2	Tbs Italian parsley, chopped
	Truffle oil

Procedure

Heat half the EVOO in a Dutch oven. Dredge the veal in flour and sauté until browned, in batches if needed. Reserve the veal.

Sauté the peppers, onion and garlic in the remaining EVOO until tender. Add the wine and stock and cook 10 minutes until the liquid is reduced by half. Add the veal and the tomatoes with their juice. Add the herbs and seasonings and stir in. Cover and cook for 45 minutes. Add the mushrooms and cook another 15 minutes.

Plate the veal and sprinkle with chopped parsley, drizzle with truffle oil or scatter chopped reconstituted porcini over all.

Veal Marsala

4 Servings

About This Recipe

Most Marsala sold in the US is sweet, but I think this recipe works better if you use ½ sweet and ½ dry. If you can't find dry Marsala, use dry Vermouth instead.

Finding high quality veal that is cut right, namely across the grain may be problematic. If you live in places with a large Italian contingent like New York, Boston or Chicago, you can get very good veal at just about any Italian market. Like most veal dishes that call for thin pieces of meat, you can substitute pounded chicken breasts or pork loin filets. Like the veal they should be no more than ⅛" – ¼ " thick.

Ingredients

8	3-oz Veal scallops, cut or pounded to ⅛" – ¼" thick
3	Tbs Butter
2	Tbs EVOO
	Salt and pepper
1	Large Shallot, finely chopped
4	Cloves Garlic, pressed or minced
4	Oz Mushrooms, sliced
¼	Cup Sweet Marsala
¼	Cup Dry Marsala or dry Vermouth
¾	Cup Veal, chicken or beef stock
1	Tbs Fresh thyme, chopped, or 1 Tsp dried thyme
	Chopped parsley for garnish

Procedure

Heat 1 TBS each of butter and EVOO in a large skillet. Dry the veal scallops with paper towels and sprinkle with salt and pepper on both sides. Sauté the scallops in batches about 1-2 minute on each side until golden brown. Reserve the scallops.

Add the shallot and garlic to the pan with a little more EVOO and butter if the pan is dry. Sauté 1 minute until fragrant. Add sliced mushrooms and cook until they give up their water, 3-5 minutes. Add the wines, deglaze the pan and cook about 3 minutes to get rid of most of the alcohol. Add the stock and thyme and reduce by half over high heat, about 4 minutes. Stir in 1 Tbs of butter to enrich sauce. Correct seasoning. Return scallops to pan and cook just long enough to heat them through. Serve at once sprinkled with chopped parsley.

MY NOTES:

Veal Martini

4 Servings

About This Recipe

This recipe is from Chef Tony Tommero of the Palm Restaurant in New York City. If you don't know it, the Palm is one of New York's best steakhouses and has been around since 1926. I like this recipe because you can make up component parts ahead of time and then assemble the dish at the last minute just as a restaurant would do.

Ingredients

3	Cups Veal or chicken stock
1	Cup White wine
4	Tbs Butter
8	Oz Shiitake mushrooms, thinly sliced
¾	Cup Sun-dried tomatoes in oil; drained and coarsely chopped
¼	Cup Shallots, minced
¼	Cup Flour
½	Tsp Salt
¼	Tsp Pepper
1½	Lb Veal scallops, pounded to ⅛ " thick
1½	Cups Canned diced tomatoes, drained (optional)
¼	Cup Shredded basil leaves

Procedure

Combine the stock and wine in a small pot and reduce by half. This is the sauce base. If you make a lot of it, it will keep nicely in the freezer.

In a large skillet, heat 2 Tbs butter and sauté mushrooms, shallots and sun-dried tomatoes for about 5 minutes. Reserve. This too can be saved and kept in the freezer for later use.

Combine the flour, salt and pepper in a shallow dish. Dredge the scallops in the seasoned flour and sauté in the skillet for a minute on each side, cooking in batches if necessary. Keep the scallops warm.

Deglaze the pan with the sauce base. Return the veal and the mushroom mix to the pan. Stir in the optional tomatoes and basil. Serve immediately.

MY NOTES:

Veal Medallions with Mushrooms

6 Servings

About This Recipe

This is a takeoff on a classic French dish. You can substitute pork tenderloin or pounded chicken breasts.

To make this dish successful, you need a strong contribution from the mushrooms. I use dried mushrooms because they offer more concentrated flavor than fresh ones. My first choices are morels or porcinis (morels are classic in France, porcinis in Italy). In any event, this dish takes only half an hour to make and will work for an everyday meal or an elegant dinner party. You can do the meat and the sauce ahead of time, and, at the last minute, add the meat to the sauce and heat for a couple of minutes.

The recipe calls for white wine, but you could use a robust fortified wine such as sherry, Marsala or Madeira. To add a touch of class, add a pinch of saffron threads to the sauce.

Ingredients

12	3-oz Veal, pork or chicken medallions, pounded ¼" thick
2	Cups Boiling water
2	Oz Dried mushrooms, preferably morels or porcinis
	Salt and Pepper to taste
2	Tbs Butter
1	Tbs EVOO
2	Cloves Garlic, minced or pressed
3	Shallots, finely chopped
1	Tsp Dried thyme
½	Cup White wine or alternative fortified wine like Marsala or Madeira
½	Cup Chicken stock
½	Cup Heavy cream
1	Pinch Saffron threads (optional)
1	Tbs Lemon juice
	Chopped parsley or chives for garnish
	Lemon wedges

Procedure

Prepare the meat by slicing and/or pounding to the desired thickness.

Soak the dried mushrooms in the boiling water for at least 30 minutes. Chop the mushrooms and reserve them and the soaking liquid, but strain the liquid if it is sandy.

(Recipe continues on next page)

Season the meat with salt and pepper. Sauté the medallions over high heat in a Tbs of butter and a Tbs of EVOO for about 2 minutes on each side. Reserve the medallions to a platter, cover with foil and keep them warm.

Add the remaining butter to the skillet and sauté the garlic, shallots and thyme over low heat about 3 minutes. Add the wine and deglaze the pan over high heat. Cook until the wine has mostly evaporated, about 4 minutes. Add the mushrooms and their liquid. Simmer about 5 minutes. Add the chicken stock and any meat juices that may have collected in your warming platter, and cook over medium-high heat until reduced by half, about 5 minutes. Add the cream and simmer until thickened, about 4 minutes. Stir in the lemon juice and correct seasoning. Add the meat to the pan and cook until heated through.

Serve at once garnished with parsley or chopped chives and lemon wedges to squeeze over the veal.

MY NOTES:

Chapter 13: Main Dishes: Vegetarian

I'm not a vegetarian and rarely make vegetarian main course dishes. Nevertheless, here are 5 recipes for vegetarian entrées that I like.

Cheese Fondue

4-6 Servings

About This Recipe

Fondue was all the rage in America in the 1970s. For reasons I don't understand, it went out of fashion 30+ years ago. Although many types of cheese will work, if you want it to be authentically Swiss, gruyère is essential. The most common addition is Emmenthaler, but other cheeses that aren't stringy when melted will work as well. This recipe calls for the addition of a wedge of *Laughing Cow* cheese which imparts a creamy texture.

The Swiss use a wine called Fendant, very dry and crisp. However, the Swiss drink most of it themselves, so it is difficult to find in North America. Some alternates that will work well include a dry white Burgundy such as Macon Village, a dry Riesling from Germany or Washington State, a Gruner Veltliner from Austria or a Muscadet from France. Wines like California Chardonnays tend to overpower the cheese.

You can add many different flavoring ingredients if you wish. The Swiss generally use a bit of garlic and a dash or two of kirsch (cherry brandy). Paprika and thyme are also popular. If you want it very garlicky, toss in a teaspoon or so of pressed garlic.

Usually, a starch is added that helps to stabilize the fondue. Most recipes call for flour, but I prefer cornstarch.

Traditionally, cubes of crusty French bread are dipped into the melted cheese, but you can use vegetables, either raw or cooked and meats such as chunks of precooked ham or sausage.

Any pot that you can keep warm enough to melt the cheese will do. You will need a way to keep the fondue hot while it is on the table. Fondue specialty pots generally come with Sterno burners, but an electric hot plate is even better. I use an enameled cast iron pot and a gel-filled tile that is heated in the microwave for 5 minutes. It stays hot for a couple of hours and I don't have to worry about adjusting the flame.

When the fondue is almost all used up, it may form a crust on the bottom of the pot. This crust is incredibly delicious. If you are nice, you will cut it up and share it, but, if no one is looking, I recommend that you scarf it up all by yourself.

(Recipe continues on next page)

Ingredients

1	Clove Garlic, peeled and cut in half
1	Cup Dry white wine
1	Lb Gruyère cheese, shredded
½	Lb Emmenthaler or other cheese, shredded
2	Tbs Cornstarch
1	Wedge *Laughing Cow* cheese
2	Tbs Kirsch or other white brandy
2	Cloves Garlic, pressed or minced (optional)
1	Tbs Lemon juice (optional)
	Salt and white pepper to taste
	Pinch Ground nutmeg (optional)
	Pinch Dry mustard (optional)
	Pinch Paprika (optional)
½	Tsp Chopped fresh thyme (optional)

Procedure

Rub the garlic all over the inside of the pot in which you will be making the fondue. Pour in the wine and bring to the simmer. Toss the cheese with the cornstarch and add it, a little at a time, stirring to melt it evenly.

Add the kirsch and the seasonings. Stir the pot until everything is melted together and is lightly bubbling.

You can also make fondue in the microwave if you use a ceramic pot. Throw everything into the pot and nuke it for a couple of minutes. Stir well and nuke it a minute more. Keep stirring and nuking until the consistency is right.

MY NOTES:

Linguine with Onion Sauce

4 Servings

About This Recipe

You can make the sauce while the pasta is cooking, so dinner can be on the table about 10-15 minutes after the pasta water boils. The dish lends itself to long thin pasta. You can use spaghetti, linguine or fettuccini. For reasons I can't explain, I prefer linguine.

Use sweet onions such as red onions, Walla Wallas or Vidalias. The red ones add some nice color, but not all red onions are sweet, so be careful if you use them.

Lemon is an important flavoring ingredient to this dish. You can buy lemon-infused EVOO, but you can make your own by steeping lemon zest strips in EVOO for a few days, or you can simply add a bit of lemon juice to the onions while they are cooking. Either regular or Meyer lemons will work.

Ingredients

1	Lb Linguine or other thin pasta
2	Tbs Lemon infused EVOO
2	Sweet onions, thinly sliced
	Salt and freshly ground black pepper to taste
2	Tbs Fresh oregano or marjoram, chopped
¼	Lb Crumbled goat cheese

Procedure

Put the pasta into a large pot of salted boiling water and cook 8-12 minutes depending on how al dente you like it.

Put 2 Tbs of lemon-infused EVOO or 2 Tbs regular EVOO and the juice of a lemon in a skillet and sauté the sliced onions until they begin to caramelize, 15 - 20 minutes. Add the oregano or marjoram and cook 1 minute. Drain the pasta and dump it into the skillet. Toss well, season with salt and pepper, top with the crumbled cheese and toss again. If the pasta seems too dry, add a bit of pasta water, a little at a time until you get what you want. Serve immediately.

MY NOTES:

Pasta with Mushroom Sauce

4 Servings

About This Recipe

This isn't quite vegetarian, because it contains a small amount of pancetta. If you are a strict vegetarian, you can use veggie bacon, but you may want to add additional EVOO if it is too lean. In any event, if you are hankering for pasta with meat sauce, but don't have the time, this dish is a great solution since it takes 45 minutes start to finish and has the heartiness associated with a meat sauce.

Ingredients

1	Oz Dried porcini mushroom
1	Cup Chicken stock
4	Oz Pancetta, cut into 1/2" dice
2	Portabella mushrooms
3	Tbs EVOO
1	Tbs Chopped fresh rosemary, thyme, basil or oregano
1	Tbs Tomato paste
4	Cloves Garlic, thinly sliced
	Salt and pepper to taste
1	14-oz Can of tomatoes
½	Cup Grated Pecorino Romano or Parmagiano Reggiano cheese
1	Lb Pasta such as spaghetti, linguine, tagliatelle or bucatini.

Procedure

Put the porcinis and a cup of chicken stock in a microwave-proof container and partially cover to prevent spatter. Nuke for 2 minutes and let stand for 10 minutes. Remove the porcinis, chop them finely and strain the soaking liquid through a coffee filter or fine-mesh sieve to get rid of any dirt. Reserve the porcinis and the liquid.

In a large skillet, sauté the pancetta until its fat has rendered and the bits are browned, about 5 minutes.

Remove the stems and the gills (scrape them off with a spoon) from the portabellas and chop the caps into ½" dice. Add the portabellas, the porcini, tomato paste, EVOO, garlic and herbs to the skillet and cook until the mushrooms have given off their liquid and everything in the pan is brown. This should take about 7 minutes.

Add the canned tomatoes, crushing them with your hands and the porcini liquid. Cook over low heat until the sauce has thickened, about 15 minutes. Season to taste.

While the sauce is thickening, cook the pasta as usual. When it is done, drain the pasta, but retain a cup of the pasta water.

Pour the sauce over the cooked pasta and add the grated cheese. Mix well and serve. If the sauce is too thick, add a bit of pasta water to thin it out to the consistency you want.

Stuffed Peppers

2 Servings

About This Recipe

My wife makes the best stuffed peppers ever from a recipe handed down from her Eastern European ancestors. They do, however, contain meat. An admitted meat lover, I was skeptical when I first saw this recipe. Although it doesn't hold a candle to my wife's stuffed peppers, it is pretty good, frugal, simple to make and a good choice for a dinner for two. The only downside is that there will be three pots and pans to clean. Serve it with a salad and a crusty baguette.

Ingredients

2	Green Bell Peppers, halved and seeded
1	Tbs EVOO
2	Shallots, thinly sliced
1	Tsp Dried oregano
1	Tsp Dried basil
1	14-oz Can of diced tomatoes, drained
4	Oz Goat cheese or feta
	EVOO for drizzling (optional)
½	Cup Tomato sauce (optional)
	Chopped parsley for garnish (optional)

Procedure

Pre-heat oven to 400°. Roast the peppers on an oiled baking sheet for 20 minutes until softened and beginning to brown.

In a large skillet, heat the EVOO and cook the onions, herbs and seasonings for 3 minutes. Add the tomatoes and rice, stir to combine and heat through. Off heat, stir in the cheese and adjust seasoning. Stuff the peppers with the onion/tomato/rice mixture. Heat in the oven for 5 minutes before serving.

You could drizzle some EVOO or tomato sauce over the peppers if you wish.

MY NOTES:

Tomatoes Stuffed with Mushrooms and Onions

6 Servings

About This Recipe

This dish could be a side dish or the main course of a lunch or a light dinner. The secret is to get very sweet, delicious tomatoes. Chances are that you will find them only in your own garden or a farmer's market. You can use any kind of mushrooms you like. Chanterelles, porcinis, morels, shiitakes are all good choices, but be sure and remove and discard any tough stems.

Ingredients

3	Large Tomatoes
3	Cups Dried wild mushrooms
2	Cups White wine
1	Cup Boiling water
2	Tbs EVOO
3	Cloves Garlic, pressed or minced
2	Medium Shallots, chopped
1	Medium Onion, finely diced
1	Cup Panko bread crumbs
1	Tomato, seeded and chopped
¼	Lb Goat cheese
2	Tbs Chopped Parsley

Procedure

Cut the tomatoes in half perpendicular to the stem and scoop out and discard the insides. Sprinkle the insides with salt and place them on a grate, cut side down, for 15-30 minutes to get rid of excess moisture.

Put the mushrooms in the wine and boiling water and allow to sit for 30 minutes. Drain, reserving 1 cup of the liquid (strain if it is sandy). Coarsely chop the mushrooms.

In a large skillet, sauté the garlic, shallots and onions in EVOO until the onions are soft. Add the mushrooms and the reserved liquid and cook over high heat until most of the liquid has been cooked off. Then stir in the panko and the chopped tomato. Continue to cook about 5 minutes longer. If the mixture seems too wet, add some more panko. If too dry, add a bit of white wine.

Fill the tomatoes with the mushroom mixture. Top each one with a teaspoon of goat cheese that has chopped parsley mixed into it. Bake the tomatoes for about 7 minutes under the broiler in the middle of the oven. The cheese should be bubbly and the tomatoes heated through.

MY NOTES:

Chapter 14: Salads and Salad Dressings

This Chapter contains 15 recipes for salads and salad dressings. Some of them could serve as main courses. All are easy.

Arugula Salad with Figs, Bacon and Cheese

4 Servings

About This Recipe

Figs have snuck into the high-end food scene over the past decade, but you might not eat them if you knew that figs contain digested wasps! Fig flowers blossom inside the actual fruit itself. It is these tiny flowers that produce the seeds that give figs their crunchy texture. Cross-pollination happens thanks to an extremely small wasp. But not to worry. The fig you eat does not contain wasps. The males chew holes through the fig's skin for the hatched females' escape. Then they mate. Parenting duties fulfilled, the males die (so what else is new) and are absorbed by special enzymes.

Now that you know the whole story, here's a recipe for a fig-containing salad that I think you will enjoy. The recipe calls for fresh figs, which are seasonal.

Ingredients

2	Tbs EVOO
2	Oz Bacon or pancetta, diced
1	Clove Garlic, minced
6	Fresh black or green figs, chopped
1	Tbs Balsamic vinegar
	Salt and pepper to taste
4	Handfuls Arugula
4	Oz Goat, blue or feta cheese
	Toasted walnuts, chopped (optional)

Procedure

In a skillet, heat the EVOO and add the chopped bacon or pancetta. If you are using bacon and don't want the smoky taste, blanch the bacon first. Cook until the bacon bits are crispy. Add the garlic and cook 30 seconds. Add the figs and cook 2 minutes more. Add the vinegar and deglaze the pan off-heat, scraping up all the bacon leavings. Season the dressing with salt and pepper to taste.

Arrange the arugula on salad plates and top with the fig dressing. Add a few small knobs of cheese and sprinkle on a few toasted walnuts if desired. Be aware that the hotter the dressing, the more the arugula will wilt.

Blue Cheese Dressing

About This Recipe

Blue cheese dressing is an American staple. Most people buy it made, but it is extremely simple to make at home if you have a food processor, and you get to choose from gorgonzola, Roquefort, stilton or many artisanal American blue cheeses.

This recipe calls for a bit of vinegar, and you can change the flavor profile by using different vinegars. You can also add some chopped fresh herbs although that is not usually a feature of blue cheese dressings. My favorite is chives, but you might like cilantro, chervil, or parsley. Other additions could be horseradish, Tabasco sauce or garlic.

Most bottled blue cheese dressings contain preservatives that I think make the product taste "off". If you make your own, it will be preservative-free.

Ingredients

4	Oz Blue cheese
1	Cup Mayonnaise
1	Cup Cream
2	Tsp Vinegar, plain white wine or flavored
1	Tsp Salt
½	Tsp Freshly ground black pepper
	Chopped herbs (optional)
	Other flavorings (optional)

Procedure

Put everything in a food processor. Some like it chunky, some like it smooth. Pulse until you get the consistency you want. Serve immediately or refrigerate until ready to use. It will keep refrigerated for several days.

MY NOTES:

Caprese Salad

4 Servings

About This Recipe

Caprese salad supposedly originated on the Isle of Capri. In its basic form, it is a combination of tomatoes, fresh mozzarella and basil leaves, sprinkled with salt, pepper and EVOO. When well-made, it is absolutely delicious. Served with a great bread and a crisp white wine, it can be a meal in itself.

That said, there are a lot of myths about this salad. Perhaps the most prevalent is that the mozzarella has to be made from buffalo milk. Since, in recorded history, there has never been a buffalo on the Isle of Capri, this is clearly baloney. The fresh mozzarella available on Capri, called "fior de latte", is made from cow's milk and you can get very good cow's milk fresh mozzarella in the US at virtually every market in the country. Another myth is that Caprese must be dressed only with EVOO, salt and pepper.

In fact, Caprese salad lends itself to all sorts of flavoring agents. A few you might want to consider are chopped garlic, chopped parsley, capers, and almost any kind of vinegar or lemon juice. You can also try different kinds of salt such as the French "fleur de sel" for a different flavor profile. I particularly like to use the juice from Meyer lemons. Unfortunately, Meyers are at their best in the winter, while tomatoes and basil are at their best in the summer and early fall months. You can, however, freeze the juice of Meyers in winter and use it in the summer.

Regardless of which flavoring agents you want to use, the key to a successful Caprese is the quality of the ingredients. Only the best tomatoes, mozzarella and basil will do, and, while you will no doubt be happy with any EVOO, this is one of those dishes where the really special stuff will shine.

Ingredients

2	Lbs Vine-ripened tomatoes, sliced
1	Lb Fresh Mozzarella, sliced
1	Handful Fresh basil leaves
	Salt and Pepper to taste
2	Tbs EVOO
2	Tbs Vinegar, any kind or lemon juice
	Chopped oregano, parsley, capers, garlic, shallots, etc. (optional)

Procedure

Alternately stack tomato slices, mozzarella slices and basil leaves in a serving dish. Sprinkle with salt and pepper, drizzle with EVOO, lemon juice or vinegar, and top with chopped herbs if you are using them.

MY NOTES:

Chicken Salad with Roasted Bell Peppers

6 Servings

About This Recipe

If you like chicken salad - and most people do - try this easy variant. Makes a great lunch served with artisan sourdough bread. You can use any dressing that you like. Best of all, you can make this dish in less than 15 minutes if you buy a freshly roasted chicken from your market and the roasted peppers in a jar. If you don't have any slivered almonds handy, you can add a similar crunch from the crispy Chinese noodles that come in bags or cans at the market.

Ingredients

1	Roasted chicken, skinned and the meat shredded
2	Roasted red or yellow bell peppers, cut into thin strips
½	Red onion, thinly sliced
1	Stalk Celery, sliced
¼	Cup Slivered almonds, toasted
	Salad dressing of choice
6	Large Bibb lettuce leaves, or
	Shredded Romaine or head lettuce
	Shaved Parmagiano Reggiano for garnish

Procedure

Mix the salad ingredients together in a large bowl. Spoon the salad into the lettuce leaves or on top of a bed of shredded lettuce and top with the shaved cheese.

MY NOTES:

E.A.T. Tomato Salad

4-6 Servings

About This Recipe

On Madison Avenue in the 80s in New York City, there is a sandwich cum deli cum bakery called E.A.T. that has been there for nearly 50 years. The reason for its continued popularity is simple. The food is terrific and reasonably priced. That the place does a huge takeout business attests to the quality of the food. Try this extremely simple salad recipe, and you will understand.

The main ingredients are tomatoes and pancetta. I recommend using halved cherry tomatoes or quartered Campari tomatoes. Whichever you choose, they should be excellent. You can substitute blanched thick-sliced bacon for the pancetta, or, if you want to keep the bacon smoky taste, don't blanch it. Not counting the cooking time for the pancetta, this salad takes less than 3 minutes to prepare.

After I made this at home, my wife suggested adding cucumber. Turns out that is a good suggestion.

Ingredients

8	Oz Pancetta, 1/4" dice, or blanched bacon
1	Tbs EVOO
1	Tbs Sherry vinegar
1	Tbs Dijon mustard
2	Lbs Tomatoes, cut into bite-size pieces
1	Cucumber, peeled, seeded and diced
	Chopped parsley for garnish

Procedure

Sauté the pancetta or bacon until crisp. Discard the fat left in the pan. Allow to cool. This can be done well ahead of time.

Put the EVOO, vinegar, and mustard in a small jar, put on the lid and shake vigorously to combine. Put the tomatoes, cucumber and pancetta in a bowl, pour over the dressing, toss to coat and sprinkle with the chopped parsley.

MY NOTES:

Greek Salad

4 Servings

About This Recipe

What makes a salad Greek? Good question, since there are a thousand recipes with that title. Most people agree, however, that a Greek salad has olives in it and a dressing made with lemon juice. This recipe comes from a salad I had a plaza-side restaurant in central Athens. It was an extremely hot, humid day, and the salad hit the spot.

You can use any kind of cucumber. I like the so-called English variety, but, if you use the more common kind, scoop out the seeds. It goes without saying that the tomatoes have to be garden fresh and sweet. This recipe uses a green bell pepper, but you could also use red or yellow bell peppers by themselves or in addition to the green.

My Athens salad was served on a bed of Bibb lettuce leaves, primarily for decoration, but they didn't add anything to the taste of the salad, and you can include greens or not as you wish.

Ingredients

1	Cucumber, peeled and diced
3	Roma tomatoes, seeded and diced
1	Medium Red onion, sliced into thin rings
1	Green bell pepper, cut into rings
¾	Cup Kalamata olives, pitted
¾	Cup Crumbled feta cheese
6	Tbs EVOO
1½	Tbs Lemon juice
1	Tbs Wine vinegar
1	Clove Garlic, pressed or minced
	Salt and pepper to taste

Procedure

Unless the onion is sweet, soak the onion rings in ice water for 10 minutes. That will get rid of the acrid taste.

Put all the vegetables and the cheese in a bowl. Put the EVOO, lemon juice, vinegar, garlic, salt and pepper in a small jar with a tight-fitting lid. Shake it vigorously and pour it over the vegetables. Toss well. Spoon the salad onto serving plates on a bed of greens if you wish.

MY NOTES:

Grilled Lettuce Salad

About This Recipe

4-6 Servings

It turns out that bitter lettuces are transformed into something delicious when lightly cooked over high heat. In order to make this recipe work, you need lettuces that will hold together on the grill. My choices are romaine, radicchio and Belgian endive.

A dressing with a quality balsamic vinegar in it works well. The result is a bittersweet salad that will go great with steaks or chops.

Ingredients

1   Head Romaine lettuce

1   Head Radicchio

2   Heads Belgian endive

    EVOO

    Salt and pepper to taste

    Aged Balsamic Vinegar

    Grated Parmagiano Reggiano (optional)

Procedure

Cut the lettuces in half or quarters depending on size. Leave enough of the stem end intact so that the lettuce won't fall apart. Sprinkle the lettuces with EVOO and salt.

Grill the lettuces on all sides until char marks show. Coarsely chop the lettuces and toss in a dressing consisting of EVOO, aged balsamic vinegar, salt and pepper.

Serve with optional grated Parmagiano Reggiano.

MY NOTES:

Kicked Up Cole Slaw

6 Servings

About This Recipe

Cole slaw is one of the most popular salads served in America. In its simplest form, it consists of shredded cabbage and carrots dressed with mayonnaise. Also popular are vinegar based dressings. Nothing wrong with these variations. They are good, but boring. I decided to try a few things, and came up with the recipe presented here.

Ingredients

VEGETABLES

4	Cups Shredded cabbage
2	Large carrots, peeled and shredded
1	Red or yellow bell pepper, cut into thin strips about 1.5" long
2	Stalks celery, thinly sliced

DRESSING

1	Cup Kraft Miracle Whip®
½	Cup Sour Cream
½	Tbs Sugar
	Juice of a lemon
¼	Cup White wine vinegar
½	Tsp Salt
¼	Tsp Ground white pepper
½	Tsp Dijon mustard
¼	Tsp Celery seeds

Procedure

Toss all the vegetables together in a large bowl. Put all the dressing ingredients in a jar, tighten the lid and shake like crazy to combine everything. Pour enough of the dressing over the vegetables to coat them well. Toss and serve. Leftover dressing will keep for several days in the refrigerator.

MY NOTES:

Kohlrabi and Carrot Salad

4-6 Servings

About This Recipe

This recipe comes from Israel via the Joy of Kosher Cooking website. It is very, very good. If you have never had kohlrabi, seek it out. A member of the cabbage family, it is popular in central Europe (where it is known as German turnip) and in southern India. It tastes like the heart of a cabbage, but is milder and sweeter. Some kohlrabi bulbs are as crisp and juicy as apples.

In any event, this is a terrific salad. Great to serve when you want a departure from the ordinary. No more than 10 minutes prep time.

Ingredients

2	Kohlrabi bulbs, peeled
4	Medium Carrots, peeled
3	Scallions, thinly sliced
3	Tbs EVOO or walnut oil
	Juice from one lemon
	Juice from one orange
1	Tbs Honey
1	Tbs Dijon mustard
3	Tbs Fresh dill, chopped
½	Cup Toasted walnuts, chopped
½	Cup Dried cranberries
	Salt and pepper to taste

Procedure

Cut the carrots and kohlrabi into thin sticks like you would cut potatoes for French fries. Put everything else in a small jar. Cover and shake well to combine.

Toss all the ingredients together in a large bowl. Let stand for 15 minutes to allow flavors to blend.

MY NOTES:

Moroccan Beet Salad

4 Servings

About This Recipe

I don't know why this salad is Moroccan, except that it is popular there and is often served as one of many vegetable salads in a Moroccan mezze spread. In any event, it's pretty simple, and, if you like beets, you will be happy.

You can prepare the beets by roasting them wrapped in foil (takes 50 - 90 minutes), boiling them an hour plus), cooking them in a pressure cooker (about 30-40 minutes) or nuking them (about 15 minutes for 4 beets). The skins slip off easily if you boil or pressure cooker them. If you roast them, you have to peel them. Some people swear that roasting concentrates the flavor the best, but I can't tell the difference. If you nuke them, make sure you pierce the skins to allow steam to escape. You may have to experiment, because microwave ovens are not the same.

Many markets carry pre-cooked shrink-wrapped sliced beets in the refrigerated section of the produce department. Although they are more expensive than raw beets, they get rid of the hassle of preparing them. Depending on what you want your salad to look like you can either dice the beets or slice them.

Ingredients

4   Medium beets, prepared as above and chilled
2   Handfuls of lettuce greens, roughly chopped if necessary
1   Red onion, thinly sliced
¼   Lb Goat cheese or feta
½   Cup Slivered almonds or pine nuts, toasted
2   Tbs EVOO
1   Tbs Lemon juice
        Salt and freshly ground black pepper to taste

Procedure

Put some greens on a plate and spoon the beets on top. Top with a few rings of red onion and a few knobs of goat cheese and sprinkle with toasted almond slivers.

In a small jar with a tight-fitting lid, add the EVOO, lemon juice and salt and pepper. Shake very well and drizzle the dressing over the salad. Serve at once.

MY NOTES:

Panzanella

8 Servings

About This Recipe

Panzanella is Italian bread salad that was conceived to make use of stale bread. The bread is cubed, mixed with tomatoes and dressed with vinaigrette.

This version calls for using oven-toasted fresh bread and adds onion or shallots and cucumber. The secret to making this dish fabulous is to use first quality tomatoes and a great artisan rustic bread. My preference for the latter is sourdough, but any of the Italian breads like ciabatta will do nicely. In any case, you will find this salad is delicious, and best of all is sooooo easy to make.

While this recipe calls for the addition of cucumber and shallots or onions, you could add other veggies. Bell peppers are a good choice. Some cooks like to add a few capers. Feel free to experiment. You really cannot go wrong. Instead of toasting the bread, you could also sauté the pieces in garlic flavored EVOO.

Ingredients

1	Loaf Artisan rustic bread
2	Tbs EVOO
1	Tsp Salt
2	Lbs Tomatoes
1	Cucumber, peeled, halved, seeded and thinly sliced
1	Large Shallot or small red onion, thinly sliced
3	Tbs Chopped fresh basil
6	Tbs EVOO
3	Tbs Red wine vinegar
	Salt and freshly ground black pepper to taste

Procedure

Pre-heat oven to 400°. Cut the bread into bite-size pieces and toss the pieces in a bowl with EVOO and salt. Spread the bread pieces on a rimmed cookie sheet and toast them in the oven for about 15 minutes or until golden. Put the pieces in a large bowl and let them cool.

Halve the tomatoes and scoop out the insides. Chop them into bite-size pieces.

Make a dressing with the EVOO, vinegar, salt and pepper. Combine the bread, tomatoes, cucumber, shallot and basil and pour over the dressing. Toss the salad (hands are best) and allow the salad to stand for at least 15 minutes for the bread to absorb some of the dressing.

MY NOTES:

Pickled Cucumber and Onion Salad

4 Servings

About This Recipe

This is an inexpensive, easy-to-fix salad that is a great accompaniment to hearty meats. You can use either regular or English cucumbers, and you don't have to peel them unless they are coated with wax.

Wine vinegar works well, but you can use any sort of vinegar that strikes your fancy and goes with whatever else you are serving. Raspberry, cider, sherry and champagne vinegars are all good choices.

Ingredients

1	Large Cucumber, thinly sliced
1	Small Red onion, halved and thinly sliced
½	Cup Vinegar
1	Tsp Pressed garlic
1	Tsp Salt
¼	Tsp White pepper
1	Tsp Sugar
¼	Tsp Red pepper flakes (optional for heat)

Procedure

Put everything except the cucumbers in a medium size pot. Stir and bring to a boil. Turn off the heat and add the cucumber slices. Let stand for at least one hour, stirring occasionally. Refrigerate for an hour or so if you want to serve it chilled.

MY NOTES:

Potato Salad with Roasted Red Peppers

2-4 Servings

About This Recipe

Americans love potato salad. The deli department of my local supermarket caries five different kinds.

This dish, a bit out of the ordinary, but super-easy to fix, can be served hot as a side dish or cold as a salad. In either case, don't add the chopped parsley until the last minute.

Ingredients

1	Lb Red potatoes
1	Roasted red bell pepper, peeled and julienned
2	Stalks Celery, diced
1	Tbs Dijon mustard
1	Tbs Sherry vinegar
2	Tbs EVOO
	Salt and pepper to taste
1	Handful Parsley, chopped

Procedure

Boil the potatoes until tender, about 10 - 15 minutes depending on their size. When cool enough to handle, cut them into bite-size chunks.

Combine all the ingredients and serve.

MY NOTES:

Roasted Fennel and Onion Salad

2 Servings

About This Recipe

Roasting caramelizes fruit and vegetable sugars, intensifying their flavor. In this salad, I roast fennel and onion together in the oven, and eat them by themselves or in combination with other veggies. You may find that you don't need a dressing with these ingredients, but, if you do, I suggest a simple lemon juice or balsamic vinaigrette.

Ingredients

1	Fennel Bulb
1	Medium Red onion
	Salt
	EVOO
	Other veggies such as lettuces, cucumbers, carrots, etc. (optional)
	Vinaigrette (optional)

Procedure

Pre-heat oven to 400°. Cut the top off the fennel bulb and slice of the root end. Cut the bulb in half with the grain and then make three or four cuts on each half with the grain. Peel the onion, cut in half cross-grain and then cut thick slices. Arrange the fennel and onions on a parchment lined baking sheet in a single layer. Sprinkle with salt and drizzle with EVOO. Roast for 20 minutes or until the fennel and onions begin to brown. Serve as is or with other veggies. Dress with a simple vinaigrette if desired.

MY NOTES:

Wilted Spinach Salad

About This Recipe

Wilted spinach salad was once a staple of many West Coast restaurants. For reasons that make no sense to me, it has gone out of favor. Nonetheless it is very good to eat and very easy to make. You can add anything you like to enhance the basic salad. Some of the additives I like are bacon bits, chopped hard-boiled eggs, sliced radishes, croutons (see Volume I for a recipe), toasted sesame seeds, toasted pine nuts, etc. Use your imagination.

The ratio of EVOO to vinegar is important. I like it 1:1, but you may like it more or less vinegary. Besides red wine, other good vinegar choices are raspberry, fig and sherry. Try them all. This is a super healthy inexpensive dish, so have it often.

Ingredients

Spinach Leaves

EVOO

Red wine vinegar

Salt and pepper to taste

Additives (see above)

Procedure

Place the spinach in your salad bowl. Put the EVOO, vinegar, salt and pepper in a small pot. Bring to a boil. Whisk briskly and pour it over the spinach while still very hot. Toss. Add your additives and toss again. Serve immediately.

MY NOTES:

Chapter 15: Sauces, Dips, Spreads, Marinades and Rubs

A great sauce can transform an otherwise plebian dish into a triumph. Here are 17 ideas to take you on that transformative path. The stated yield amounts are approximate.

Asian Marinade

Yields 1½ Cups

About This Recipe

I adapted this recipe from one I saw Bobby Flay make. He used it to marinate grilled veal chops, but it can be used on any type of meat and even a sturdy fish like swordfish. He described this dish as "Mongolian", but I'm skeptical that the Mongolians invented it. He used peanut butter in it, but I think it works better without. I also think it is better with pork than with veal.

I did a bit of research on Mongolian fare and learned, among other things, that the most popular meat dish there is called "Boodog", which is marmot or goat cooked with hot stones in the stomach. There are elaborate instructions on how to remove the fur with a blowtorch. Think I'll pass on that one.

Ingredients

2	Tbs Sesame oil
2	Tbs Honey
2	Tbs Sriracha or equivalent (optional)
4	Cloves Garlic, pressed or minced
1	Tbs Ginger, minced
1	Shallot, minced
¼	Cup Cilantro, chopped
½	Cup Rice wine vinegar
3	Tbs Hoisin sauce
2	Tbs Soy Sauce

Procedure

Mix all the ingredients together. Spread on meat or fish and allow to marinate for several hours.

MY NOTES:

Beurre Blanc

About This Recipe

Beurre blanc (literally "white butter") is a classic French sauce that marries beautifully with fish, light meats such as chicken breasts, and vegetables such as asparagus. It is a great sauce to know about, because it can be whipped up at the last minute. In its most basic form it contains only two ingredients, wine and butter, but you can add chopped fresh herbs, shallots, garlic or whatever strikes your fancy.

The Culinary Institute of America posted a very good 3-minute YouTube video that shows how to make beurre blanc, and I encourage you to look for it. The chef in the video adds peppercorns to the wine/vinegar/shallot reduction. If you do that, you will need to strain the sauce.

Ingredients

½   Cup White wine

2   Tbs White wine vinegar

1   Bay leaf (optional)

3   Tbs Heavy cream

     Salt and white pepper to taste

1   Tbs Chopped shallot

1   Lb Cold unsalted butter, cut into 1/2" cubes

1   Tbs Chopped fresh herbs such as tarragon, parsley, chives or basil (optional)

Procedure

In a large skillet, bring the wine, vinegar, bay leaf and shallots to the boil and cook until it reduces to about 2 tablespoons of liquid, about 5 minutes. Remove and discard the bay leaf and add the cream, salt and white pepper and bring to the boil. Boil 1 - 2 minutes, stirring, then immediately reduce the heat. The recipe can be done ahead of time up to this point.

Over very low heat, add the cold butter cubes, one or two at a time, whisking constantly. Incorporate the last couple of cubes off heat. Stir in the chopped herbs if using. The finished sauce should be thick and smooth. You can strain out the shallots if you wish, but I don't think that is worth the effort.

To keep the sauce warm, put it in a bowl sitting in a hot water bath. If you try to warm it on the stove, the butter is likely to separate and the sauce will become watery.

MY NOTES:

Black Currant Mustard Sauce

About This Recipe

Black currant mustard is a French product from Dijon. As far as I know, there is only one company that makes it, *Edmond Fallot*. You can find it online for as little as $4 a jar.

The sauce in this recipe is perfect with game dishes, duck, venison, etc. Very easy to make. You can make a lot of it and freeze it. It will keep for months in the freezer.

Ingredients

2	Tbs EVOO
1	Onion, finely chopped
2	Tbs Sherry wine vinegar
1½	Cups Stock (Beef, veal or chicken)
1½	Tbs Black currant mustard

Procedure

Sauté onions in EVOO until caramelized, about 25 - 30 minutes. Deglaze the pan with the sherry vinegar. Add stock and simmer for 20 minutes. Whisk in mustard.

You can add a bit of EVOO at the end if you wish. You can also strain the sauce before whisking in the mustard if you want a very smooth final product.

MY NOTES:

Brown Butter

About This Recipe

Brown butter is simply butter that has been cooked long enough for the solids to turn brown. It is an amazing flavoring ingredient, and is a favorite pasta sauce in Italy. Mix it into your mashed potatoes, spoon it over boiled new potatoes or gnocchi, add it to your potatoes au gratin, etc.

The Italians often add chopped sage leaves to brown butter, especially when it is used as a pasta sauce.

Procedure

Place half a stick of butter in a skillet and melt it over a high heat. Turn the heat down to medium and cook until the butter is a medium brown color. This takes only a few minutes, but it needs to be watched because, if the butter burns, it will be ruined.

MY NOTES:

Chocolate Sauce

Yields 2 Cups

About This Recipe

Making a great-tasting chocolate sauce at home is easy. You can make a lot of it if you wish and freeze it in serving size packets, then defrost and reheat as needed. This one is orange-flavored, but you can use any kind of flavoring you wish.

An important consideration is the quality of the chocolate. Use good stuff and you will be happy. There are two ingredients that you may think are strange. The first is corn syrup. It gives the final product a glossy finish. The second is instant coffee. (You could use finely ground coffee like the stuff you find in the eastern Mediterranean.) You won't taste the coffee, but it enhances the taste of chocolate like no other ingredient..

Chocolate melts at 94°. If the temperature gets much higher, the chocolate will "burn" and ruin the dish, so be careful not to allow the chocolate to get too hot. If you want to be safe, make this recipe in a bowl that is sitting over a pot of steaming water without the bottom of the bowl touching the water surface. If you think you can keep the temperature under control, take a chance and just cook it in a pot.

This sauce is great over ice cream and is terrific for dipping strawberries or biscotti.

Ingredients

1   Cup Heavy cream

        Grated zest of an orange

½   Lb Chocolate, coarsely chopped or chocolate bits

2   Tbs Orange liqueur

2   Tbs Corn syrup

1   Tbs Instant coffee

Procedure

Warm the cream in a pot, double boiler or a bowl set over hot water and add the zest. Add the chocolate and stir until all the chocolate is melted and the mixture is smooth. Stir in the remaining ingredients and you are done! Serve in a pitcher for pouring over ice cream or in a bowl for dipping.

MY NOTES:

Crème Anglaise

Yields 3 Cups

About This Recipe

In the UK, nine out of ten desserts are accompanied by a pitcher of Crème Anglaise (translation "English Cream"), a simple thin custard.

The classic recipe is flavored with vanilla, but you can choose other flavors such as almond, orange, lemon, even spices like cinnamon. You can use flavoring extracts, liqueurs, or zests. Purists will use vanilla beans, but I find that vanilla extract works just as well and you may not have to strain the sauce which should be quite smooth. You can make this recipe using heavy cream, half-and-half, whole milk or a mixture of them. The higher the fat content, the richer the sauce. This recipe is about as simple as it gets. You just have to be careful to mix the hot milk or cream and the egg yolks carefully so that the eggs don't curdle. Other than that, the recipe is a cinch. It can be served cold, at room temperature or warmed.

Crème Anglaise is also the basis for pastry cream. Simply add cornstarch.

Ingredients

2	Cups Heavy cream, half-and-half, whole milk or a mixture
1	Tsp Vanilla extract or other flavoring
5	Egg yolks
½	Cup Sugar

Procedure

Heat the cream and vanilla in a sauce pan, but do not let it boil. In a bowl, whisk the egg yolks and sugar together until the mix is pale yellow and forms smooth ribbons.

Take the sauce pan off the heat and stir in the egg mixture a little at a time until fully incorporated. Put the sauce pan back on the heat and heat it to a temperature of 155° to 180° as measured on a candy thermometer, stirring constantly to prevent the eggs from curdling or sticking to the bottom of the pan. The higher the temperature, the thicker the sauce, so stop heating when you have reached the consistency that you desire. At this point is best to stop the cooking process by pouring the sauce into a bowl that is sitting in an ice bath. This may not be necessary, but it does add a bit of insurance in case you have allowed the sauce to overheat.

To be absolutely sure that the sauce is as smooth as possible, you can strain the sauce as you pour it into the bowl. This will remove any bits of egg that may have curdled.

You can serve the crème hot, at room temperature or cold. The cold sauce is the base for the famous "Floating Island" recipe given in the Dessert Chapter.

MY NOTES:

Cuban Citrus Salsa

Yields 1½ Cups

About This Recipe

The Cubans are justly famous for their salsas. This one is orange-based, but you could use mangos instead and it will be just as good. There is no cooking involved. Just mix up all the ingredients, let it sit for a while to meld the flavors and serve alongside roast pork, grilled fish, chicken or veal.

I prefer to use Valencia oranges, but, if they are not available, navels will do. Just keep in mind that navel oranges turn bitter after a day's exposure to air, so this recipe won't keep long if using navels. If the orange segments are large, cut them in half. Be careful not to allow any of the orange segment membranes into the dish.

Ingredients

5	Medium Oranges, segmented
	Grated zest of 1 orange
1	Jalapeno pepper, seeded and chopped fine
½	Medium Onion, chopped fine
2	Cloves Garlic, pressed or minced
	Grated zest of 1 lime
	Juice from 1 lime
2	Tbs Chopped fresh cilantro
1	Tbs EVOO
2	Tsp Brown sugar
2	Tsp White wine vinegar
½	Tsp Ground cumin
½	Tsp Salt
½	Tsp Freshly ground black pepper

Procedure

Combine all the ingredients in a bowl. Mix thoroughly. Allow to stand for at least 15 minutes before serving.

MY NOTES:

Green Peppercorn Sauce

Yields 1 Cup

About This Recipe

Green peppercorn sauce was once de rigueur at fine steakhouses and was also the traditional sauce accompaniment to Beef Wellington. It has since gone out of fashion. I don't know why. Perhaps because it is rich, and many people these days prefer rabbit food, but, if you are willing to splurge on the calories, you can easily make it at home. It will keep in the fridge for a few days and can be gently reheated without losing anything.

Green peppercorns are immature black peppercorns. Although you can buy them dried like black peppercorns, for this recipe you need to buy them in a jar, packed in brine. A 4-oz jar costs around $4. You can make this sauce separately, but, if you make it in the same pan that you cooked the steaks in, you can use the fond from the meat to enhance the flavor.

You'll find dozens of recipes for this dish. They are all similar but there are variations. The demi-glace and thyme are my additions.

Ingredients

1	Tbs EVOO
1	Large Shallot, thinly sliced
2	Cloves Garlic, pressed or minced
1	Tsp Chopped fresh thyme leaves or more to taste
½	Cup Brandy or Bourbon
1	Pint Beef, chicken or veal stock
1	Tbs Concentrated demi-glace
1	Cup Heavy cream
1	Tbs Dijon mustard
2	Tbs Green peppercorns in brine, drained
1	Tbs Vinegar

Procedure

Sauté the shallots, garlic and thyme in the EVOO for 1-2 minutes. Deglaze the pan with the brandy or bourbon (flambé it if people are watching.) Add the stock and the demi-glace, stir well to dissolve the demi-glace, then bring to a boil and reduce to 1 cup of liquid. Add the cream and mustard and reduce by half. Add peppercorns and vinegar. Adjust seasoning.

MY NOTES:

Honey Balsamic Sauce

Yields 2 Cups

About This Recipe

This is a quick sweet-sour sauce that goes very well with pork, lamb or even duck. Besides the fact that it tastes good, I like it because it doesn't have to be cooked and can be made at the last minute. It will also keep for a long time if you leave out the fresh garlic and add it at the last minute before serving.

Ingredients

½	Cup Balsamic vinegar
1	Cup Canola or peanut oil
2	Cloves Garlic, pressed or minced
1	Tbs Grated lemon zest
3	Tbs Honey
	Chopped herbs for garnish

Procedure

Whisk together all the ingredients and you are done. Allow to sit for a while to meld flavors.

MY NOTES:

Lime Sour Cream

Yields 1½ Cups

About This Recipe

Here is a way to jazz up sour cream. It can be used as a dip, as a topping for Mexican food or almost any time you would use plain sour cream.

Ingredients

1	Cup Sour cream
1	Tbs Grated lime zest
2	Tbs Fresh lime juice
2	Tbs Chopped fresh cilantro
1	Tbs Unflavored rice vinegar
	Salt to taste

Procedure

Mix everything together and let sit at least an hour in the refrigerator to meld flavors.

MY NOTES:

Lobel's Coffee Steak Rub

About This Recipe

This rub comes from one of New York City's most famous butcher shops, Lobel's. If you aren't familiar with it, I encourage you to go to their web site, lobels.com. There you will find dozens of great recipes for cooking meat of all kinds. You can also order their meat direct, but make sure that your wallet is full.

This rub features ground coffee. Sounds weird, but it is delicious in the final product, grilled steak. I won't kid you that applying this recipe to one of Lobel's dry-aged prime rib steaks at $60/pound is frugal, but this rub will taste just as good on a $6/pound tri-tip.

Ingredients

1	Tbs	Brown sugar
1	Tbs	Salt
1	Tsp	Pepper
½	Tsp	Cayenne
1	Tbs	Ground coffee
1	Tbs	Garlic powder
1	Tbs	Smoked Spanish paprika

Procedure

Prepare a grill with one side very hot and the other side turned off.

Mix all the rub ingredients together, varying proportions to your taste as desired. Coat the meat with EVOO and then the rub. Allow the meat to sit for an hour or so at room temperature.

Grill the meat on both sides over high direct heat, about two minutes per side. The meat should be well-seared. Place the meat on the cold side of the grill, close the cover and cook 20 minutes or until the internal temperature reaches 120°. Remove meat to a platter, tent with foil and allow to rest 15 minutes before serving.

MY NOTES:

Mango or Peach Chutney

Yields 2 Quarts

About This Recipe

A little 6-oz bottle of mango chutney in your local market costs around $6. This is a ridiculous price. You'll be lucky if it lasts for more than one meal. If you can find a local Indian market, you can do much better, but why not consider making your own? It's easy, and you can tweak the recipe to suit your own taste.

Mangos and peaches are virtually interchangeable in this recipe, but mangos are available year round while peaches are only available for a few months, so if you want it in the winter, mangos it is. You can make this chutney as hot or as mild as you wish. Just add more cayenne or use hot curry powder. In any case, it will last a long time in the freezer.

Ingredients

4	Lbs Ripe peaches or mangos
1	Tbs Canola or peanut oil
1	Medium Red onion, finely chopped
1	Red bell pepper, finely chopped
½	Cup Brown sugar
½	Cup Mango, pineapple or peach juice
½	Cup Apple juice or cider
2	Tbs Lemon juice
1	Tbs Curry powder
½	Tsp Cayenne (optional)
2	Tbs Fresh ginger, minced
2	Tsp Salt
1	Tsp Ground black pepper
½	Cup Raisins (optional)
½	Cup Chopped Macadamia nuts (optional)

Procedure

Peel and pit the mangos or peaches. Coarsely chop the flesh and reserve.

In a suitable pot, heat the oil and sauté the onions and pepper until soft, about 7 minutes. Add the rest of the ingredients, bring to the boil and simmer for 40 minutes. Adjust seasoning including the curry powder. Allow to cool.

Keep out what you need short term and freeze the rest.

MY NOTES:

Mediterranean Yogurt Sauce

Yields 1 Cup

About This Recipe

This recipe makes a sauce that goes great with grilled lamb or as a dip for chips, veggies or whatever you like to dip. There is no cooking involved. Everything is made in the food processor. You want to be sure and use a quality so-called Greek yogurt, or, if you can't find that, regular yogurt that has been strained overnight through paper towel or cheesecloth. You want the yogurt to be very thick with a low water content.

There is a huge variation in the quality and water content of commercial yogurt brands. Experts rate the Fage and Trader Joe's brands tops among brands that are readily available nearly everywhere.

Ingredients

½	Cup Chopped fresh mint leaves
2	Tbs Chopped fresh dill
6	Scallions, coarsely chopped
1	Pinch Red pepper flakes (optional)
1	Tbs EVOO
1	Tbs Fresh lemon juice
1	Tsp Salt
½	Tsp Freshly ground black pepper
7	Oz Yogurt

Procedure

Put everything except the yogurt in the food processor and process to a paste consistency. Add the yogurt and process until everything is well combined.

MY NOTES:

Pomegranate Molasses

Yields 2 Cups

About This Recipe

I got this recipe from Tori Avey whose online moniker is the "Shiksa." For those of you who need that translated, a shiksa is the Yiddish word for a gentile woman. (Tori says she converted!)

In any event, pomegranate molasses is a staple of Middle Eastern cuisine. You can buy it in bottles from food stores that cater to a Middle Eastern clientele or get it online for around $7 plus shipping. Or, you can make it yourself if you follow the Shiksa's directions.

It is amazing that this stuff is not more popular in American cooking. Anytime you can think of a dish that would benefit from an addition that is both tart and sweet at the same time, think of pomegranate molasses. It is a fabulous added to a BBQ rib glaze. Add a little to a salad dressing. Mix it with chicken stock and chopped fresh thyme for a sauce to accompany roast chicken. The uses are endless. If you Google "pomegranate molasses recipes", you will quickly find dozens of great ideas. Check out the recipe for Brussels sprouts in the vegetable side dish chapter. You'll be glad you did.

This dish will keep for a few weeks in the fridge or many months in the freezer.

Ingredients

1	Quart Pomegranate juice
⅓	Cup Fresh lemon juice
⅔	Cup Sugar

Procedure

Put all the ingredients into a saucepan and bring to a boil stirring to dissolve the sugar. Cook over moderate heat for 1 - 2 hours until the molasses is the consistency you want. Do not let it get too thick, or it will harden as it cools. The Shiksa says "coating the back of a spoon" is about right.

MY NOTES:

Port and Dried Fruit Sauce

Yields 1½ Cups

About This Recipe

This is a great sauce for roast meat, especially pork. You can use almost any dried fruit you like. My favorite is cherries, but other good choices are peaches, apricots, plums, currants, pears, cranberries or figs. This sauce can be made ahead of time. It will keep several days in the fridge or months in the freezer.

If the fruit pieces are large as they would be for pears or peaches, chop them up before using. You do not need to use 100-year old Port. Inexpensive, U.S. ports are fine. There is a wide range of sweetness in ports, so choose the level of sweetness that you think will go best with what you are serving. For example, pork can handle a sweet sauce, beef not so much.

Ingredients

2	Tbs Butter
1	Large Shallot, minced
3	Tbs Brandy
1	Tbs Chopped fresh thyme or rosemary
	Salt and pepper taste
2	Cups Port
2	Cups Beef, veal or chicken stock
1	Cup Dried fruit, finely chopped
2	Cinnamon sticks (optional)
2	Tbs Butter as enrichment

Procedure

In a sauce pot, sauté the shallot for about 2-3 minutes. Add the brandy, thyme or rosemary and salt and pepper. Cook until liquid evaporates, about 3 minutes. Add the port, fruit and stock. Bring to a boil and reduce to about 1½ cups. Just before serving, stir in 2 Tbs butter off-heat. If you are going to use it later, do the butter enrichment just before serving.

If you wish, you can strain the sauce, but I don't think it is necessary.

MY NOTES:

Red Wine Sauce Rapide

Yields 1 Cup

About This Recipe

In Volume I, I gave you a couple of sauce recipes that go well with red meat. Here is another one, and this one is the simplest of all. You can make it in the same amount of time that it takes to grill and rest a steak or a lamb chop.

Ingredients

2	Tbs Butter
1	Onion, thinly sliced
	Salt and freshly ground black pepper to taste
2	Cloves Garlic, pressed or minced
1	Tsp Dried oregano
½	Tsp Dried thyme
1	Tbs Tomato paste
2	Cups Red wine

Procedure

Sauté the onion in the butter for about 5 minutes. Add the garlic, oregano and thyme and cook two minutes. Stir in the tomato paste until it is dissolved and then pour in the wine. Reduce the sauce by half over high heat until it coats the back of a spoon. Strain out the solids, leaving a smooth delicious sauce. Correct seasoning.

MY NOTES:

White Clam Sauce

Yields 1 Cup

About This Recipe

This sauce goes great with pasta or gnocchi or used as a pizza topping. You can use fresh clams in the shell or canned clams. I prefer the canned clams - makes it easy - but the fresh clams will make a better product.

You can do your own pizza-like dish using a flatbread like lavosh, naan or the piadine described in the starch chapter. Coat the bread with the sauce and dot it with the clams. Broil until it is bubbling, then drizzle with EVOO and fresh lemon juice and sprinkle with chopped parsley.

If you are using fresh clams, you will need to buy clam juice which normally comes in an 8-oz bottle. I recommend that you buy clam juice that comes from New England or Italy.

You can make a large batch of this recipe and freeze it in serving size packages. It will keep frozen for many months. You can enrich the sauce with the addition of a little butter which I would add after the cream has reduced.

Ingredients

2	Tbs EVOO
1	Onion, coarsely chopped
4	Cloves Garlic, minced
½	Cup White wine
½	Cup Clam juice
1	Can Clams or 12 fresh clams
½	Cup Heavy cream
	Salt and pepper to taste
¼	Tsp Red pepper flakes (optional)
1	Tbs Butter

Procedure

In a large skillet, sauté the onion and garlic until the onion is soft, about 5 minutes. Add the wine and clam juice, bring to a boil and reduce the liquid by half.

If using fresh clams, add them to the skillet, cover and steam them until they open. Remove the clams and shuck them when cool enough to handle. Add the clams (fresh or canned) to the skillet and cook 2 minutes. Add the cream and reduce the liquid by half. Stir in the red pepper flakes if using and season to taste. Off heat, stir in the butter if desired.

MY NOTES:

Chapter 16: Soups

As I said in Volume I, I'm not a big soup fan, but there are a few that I like, and I've put 7 of them in this chapter. Some could serve as a main dish.

Avgolemono Soup

6-8 Servings

About This Recipe

If you have never had this soup, try it next time you are in a Greek restaurant. It is one of Greece's national dishes, and it is delicious. This is a quick version that takes 10 minutes of prep time and less than 30 minutes of cook time. There are versions that take all day, and I don't see much difference. In any event, the key to this soup is the egg/lemon sauce. It turns what is basically ordinary chicken soup into a silky, tangy concoction that has no equal in the soup world.

That sauce starts with raw eggs which must be tempered, otherwise you will end up with a scrambled mess. Further, NEVER LET IT BOIL once the sauce has been added. The soup will break and you will wind up with something that looks like Chinese egg drop soup. Use the same caution if you reheat it.

Ingredients

2	Tbs EVOO
1	Large Onion, finely chopped
6	Cups Chicken stock
1	Cup Diced cooked chicken breast meat (optional)
	Salt to taste
3	Tbs Fresh lemon juice
3	Eggs
	Chopped parsley or chives for garnish

Procedure

Heat the EVOO in a large pot and sauté the onions in it until they are translucent.

Add the chicken stock to the pot and bring to a bare simmer. Add the diced chicken meat if you are using it. Cook for 4-5 minutes and add salt to taste.

In a large bowl, beat the eggs. Whisking constantly to emulsify, add the lemon juice, then, still whisking constantly, slowly add a ladle of hot stock. Repeat the process with another ladle of stock, then pour the egg/lemon mix into the stock pot (off heat), whisking as you pour. Serve at once, garnished with chopped herbs.

MY NOTES:

Cold Berry Soup

6-8 Servings

About This Recipe

The only work to this recipe is cleaning the parts of your food processor. You just toss in some berries, thick dairy like sour cream, yogurt or mascarpone, flavor with honey and cinnamon, process and serve. You can use fresh or frozen berries as you wish. Makes a terrific first course for a summer meal.

You can use blueberries, raspberries, strawberries or blackberries depending on what is on sale or strikes your fancy. Blueberries are my personal favorite, but all of them are good.

If you want to thin the soup, add a little milk until you get the texture that you want.

Ingredients

2   Cups Berries, fresh or frozen
5½   Cups Sour cream, plain yogurt, clotted cream, crème fresh, etc.
1   Tbs Honey
½   Tsp Ground cinnamon
        Mint leaves for garnish

Procedure

Put everything in the food processor and process until smooth. Garnish with mint leaves. If not cold enough, chill in the refrigerator.

MY NOTES:

Exotic Mushroom Soup with Goat Cheese

6-8 Servings

About This Recipe

There is a recipe for mushroom soup in Volume 1. This variation is a bit more elegant. You can use any kind of mushrooms that you like or can easily find. Portobellos are a good choice as are porcinis, chanterelles, or morels. You can also use reconstituted mixed wild mushrooms. These are available inexpensively from Costco or Asian markets.

This recipe derives from one that appeared in the Wine Spectator magazine and calls for the addition of truffles, hardly a frugal ingredient. If you like the idea, but aren't interested in investing your life savings in truffles, you may be able to find truffle oil in your market at a reasonable price. A few drops of the oil added to the soup at the end, will give you the truffle flavor while ensuring that you remain solvent.

Ingredients

2	Slices Bacon, coarsely chopped
5	Shallots Peeled and finely chopped
2	Small Heads of garlic, cloves separated and peeled
1	Small Leek, white part, cleaned and sliced
5	Portobello (or other) Mushrooms, 1/2" cubes
2	Cups Red Wine
1½	Quarts Chicken stock
2	Cups Heavy cream
1½	Tbs Butter
4	Tbs Goat Cheese
1	Tbs Chopped chives for garnish

Procedure

In a large sauce pan or Dutch oven, sweat the bacon, shallots, garlic and leeks for about 20 minutes. Add a little EVOO if more fat is needed.

Add mushrooms and cook until the mushrooms have given up most of their moisture. Add wine and reduce by 3/4. Add chicken stock, bring to the simmer and cook about 45 minutes. Add cream and bring to a boil.

Purée the soup with an immersion blender or in a food processor in batches. Stir in the butter off-heat. If you want the soup to be very smooth, pass it through a sieve. Serve the soup, topped with goat cheese and chopped chives. Pass around a bottle of truffle oil.

MY NOTES:

Onion Soup

4 Servings

About This Recipe

Onion soup is a popular restaurant dish. Know why? Because it is easy to make, inexpensive and you can charge a lot for it. In other words, a high-margin item. You can make excellent onion soup at home which you can tailor to your taste buds.

Although gruyère is the traditional onion soup cheese, you have a lot of choices. It just has to be a cheese that melts well. Some good ones besides gruyère are Emmenthaler, asiago, fontina, cheddar, Cabot, Muenster, and Monterey jack. Every one of these cheeses has a different taste, so you never have to make the soup taste the same way twice.

Different onions have differing amounts of sugar in them. If you want your soup on the sweet side, use sweet onions. You can use different stocks or a combination of stocks depending on how strong you want the final product to taste. Beef is the strongest, chicken the lightest. Veal is in between. Whatever stock you use, make sure that it is not too salty.

Ingredients

4	Onions, halved and sliced
4	Tbs Butter
	Salt and pepper to taste
1	Quart Stock (Beef, veal or chicken)
4	Sprigs Thyme
2	Bay Leaves
1	Tbs Worcestershire Sauce (optional)
1	Tbs Balsamic vinegar (optional)
4	Slices Baguette, sour or sweet
4	Slices Cheese

Procedure

Sauté the onions in the butter with a bit of salt and pepper over medium-low heat in a large sauté pan or Dutch oven for about 30 minutes until the onions are well caramelized.

Add the stock, thyme, bay leaves and optional sauces. Bring to a boil, cover and simmer for 20 minutes.

Under a broiler, toast the bread slices. Ladle the soup into oven-proof serving bowls, top with a slice of bread and then with sliced cheese, enough to cover the dish opening. Place the bowls under the broiler and cook until cheese melts, is bubbling and forms a seal over the bowl, about 5 minutes. It is OK, in fact desirable, if the cheese laps over the sides of the bowl.

MY NOTES:

Pho

2 Servings

About This Recipe

If you live in the US and have visited Vietnamese restaurants, you are probably under the impression that Pho (pronounced "fa") is Vietnam's national dish. You may be right. I've never been to Vietnam, but Pho is ubiquitous in this country. It is a flavored soup, usually made with beef, but could be made with almost any protein you can think of.

If you want to make a truly authentic Pho, you need to make the stock from beef marrow bones, a process which takes all day. You are welcome to do that, but this recipe, which takes 30 minutes, is 85% as good as the made-from-scratch version.

You can make this Pho with rice or wheat noodles, but be sure to prepare them separately, otherwise they will make your Pho cloudy. Some rice noodles merely need soaking and rinsing, so read the package instructions if you use them. Cook wheat noodles as usual in plenty of salted boiling water.

The Vietnamese use any cut of meat that can be cut thin, but as a general rule, I use flank steak which can be sliced very thin while partially frozen.

One of the hallmarks of Pho is the garnishes. The most common are bean sprouts, fresh cilantro, Thai basil, lime wedges, hot peppers like serrano or jalapeno and Southeast Asian hot sauce (sriracha).

Ingredients

1	Quart Beef or chicken stock
1	Medium Onion, peeled and quartered
6	Cloves Garlic, coarsely chopped
2"	Piece Fresh ginger, peeled and sliced
6	Whole Cloves
1	Star Anise, bruised
	Salt and pepper to taste
2	Tbs Sugar
2	Tsp Fish sauce
8	Oz Rice or wheat noodles
8	Oz Steak, sliced thin

GARNISHES

Fresh coriander

Thai Basil

Serrano or jalapeno chilis, or sriracha

Bean sprouts

Lime wedges

(Recipe continues on next page)

Procedure

Combine the first 9 ingredients in a large pot. Bring to a boil and simmer for 20 minutes. Strain through a fine sieve and discard the solids. Return the liquid to the pot and return to the simmer.

While the stock is simmering, make the noodles according to package directions. Put half the noodles in each of 2 large serving bowls. Pour the hot stock into the bowls and add the sliced steak. The heat from the broth will cook the meat. Serve immediately with all the garnishes on the side.

MY NOTES:

Roasted Tomato Basil Soup

4-6 Servings

About This Recipe

This recipe comes from the Tra Vigne restaurant in Napa Valley, which was founded many years ago by the now-famous chef Michael Chiarello. I don't know if he personally invented this recipe, but I'm including it, because, by roasting the tomatoes, you get a wonderful flavor that is quite different from the usual. Although you have to dirty an extra pan, I think it is worth it.

I like to serve the soup either hot or cold garnished with a dollop of sour cream, a basil leaf and garlic croutons, but that is up to you.

Ingredients

1	14-oz Can Tomatoes
	Salt and pepper to taste
¼	Cup EVOO
1	Stalk Celery, diced
1	Carrot, diced
1	Onion, diced
2	Cloves Garlic, chopped
1	Cup Chicken stock
1	Bay leaf
2	Tbs Butter
¼	Cup Chopped basil
½	Cup Heavy cream (optional)
	Basil leaves for garnish (optional)
	Sour cream for garnish (optional)
	Garlic croutons for garnish (optional)

Procedure

Pre-heat the oven to 450°. Strain the tomatoes, reserving the juice and chop them. Spread them out on a baking sheet, sprinkle them with salt and pepper and drizzle EVOO over them. Roast them until caramelized, about 15 minutes.

While the tomatoes are roasting, sauté the celery, carrot, onion and garlic in 1/2 cup EVOO in a pot until soft, about 10 minutes. Add the roasted tomatoes, the reserved tomato juice, the chicken stock, bay leaf and butter. Simmer 15 minutes and add the chopped basil and the optional cream. Remove the bay leaf and purée the soup with an immersion or standard blender. Serve at once or reheat as needed, adding desired garnishes.

MY NOTES:

Thai Coconut Chicken Soup

4-6 Servings

About This Recipe

If you look online, you will quickly find about 100 variations of this soup. They are all tasty. I'm not going to tell you that my recipe is better or worse than any of the others, but I think it is very good, and I suggest substitutes for the more exotic ingredients called for in the "authentic" Thai recipes.

You can make this recipe with either raw or cooked chicken breast or thigh meat. If you use raw, you will have to cook it in the boiling liquid for a few minutes. Cooked chicken can be added at the last minute and just heated. Although chicken is my personal favorite, you can substitute shrimp or another protein, or you can leave out the protein altogether for a vegetarian soup.

Although the Thai's often make this soup spicy hot, you can control the amount of heat or leave the hot stuff out altogether. Heat can be provided with hot peppers and/or chili paste.

Lemongrass, galangal and kaffir lime leaves are traditional ingredients, but, if you don't have an Asian market where you live, you may not be able to find them. You can substitute lemon peel for the lemongrass, ginger for the galangal and lime zest for the lime leaves. The result won't be exactly the same, but it will still be quite good.

You can dress up the soup with strips of red bell pepper, sliced mushrooms or carrots, etc. If you want to make the soup heartier, you can add rice or noodles. One recipe I found uses the noodles out of a ramen package. I haven't tried it, but I think that is a good idea because they will cook right in the soup and don't have to be cooked separately. Just toss them in at the end and cook them for a couple of minutes until they have softened.

The soup base can be prepared ahead of time and kept in the freezer for months. Finishing the soup once the base is done takes less than 15 minutes.

Ingredients

2	Tsp Canola or peanut oil
1	2" piece Galangal or ginger, peeled and smashed
2	Stalks Lemongrass, chopped or zest of a lemon
10	Kaffir lime leaves or zest of 2 limes
2	Tsp Thai red curry paste (more or less as desired)
1	Seeded jalapeno or Thai chili pepper, chopped (optional)
4	Cloves Garlic, chopped
1	Quart Chicken stock
1	Pint Light coconut milk
4	Tsps Thai or Vietnamese fish sauce
1	Tbs sugar
	Salt and pepper to taste
2	Cups Chicken meat, cut into thin strips

(Recipe continues on next page)

    Carrots, sliced

    Red bell pepper (optional), cut into thin strips

    Mushrooms (optional), sliced

    Cooked rice or noodles (optional)

3   Tbs Chopped fresh cilantro

2   Tbs Lime juice

4   Tbs Chopped scallions for garnish (optional)

Procedure

In a stock pot of at least 2 quarts capacity, sauté the galangal, lemongrass, lime leaves, curry paste, chilis and garlic for 2 minutes in the oil. Add the chicken stock and bring to the boil. Simmer 15 minutes. Strain the soup into another stock pot and discard the solids.

Add the coconut milk, fish sauce, sugar, salt and pepper. Return to the simmer and cook 10 minutes. If you are using raw chicken or shrimp, add it now along with any veggies. Simmer an additional 5 - 10 minutes or as long as it takes to cook the meat and veggies. Add the rice or noodles if you are using them along with the cilantro and lime juice. Cook just long enough to heat the soup. Serve immediately with chopped scallions sprinkled on top.

Note: If the coconut milk you use is thick, mix it with a little water to thin it.

MY NOTES:

Chapter 17: Starch Side Dishes

If you are one of those people who thinks he or she ought not to eat anything "white", skip this chapter. Pasta, potato, bread and rice – Mikey likes them all.

Baked Orzo with Mushrooms and Peas

8 Servings

About This Recipe

I stole this recipe from Giada De Laurentiis. It is a terrific side dish to just about any kind of meat or poultry. I made a couple of minor changes. This is my book, not hers.

I think this dish benefits from some fancy mushrooms such as shiitakes or porcinis. In addition, the type of wine you use will have an impact on the final product. I haven't tried it, but I suspect that a bit of brandy instead of wine will work well, especially if you are serving this dish with lamb or beef. The peas just make the dish look pretty.

Ingredients

4	Cups	Chicken stock
1	Lb	Orzo
1	Medium	Onion, chopped
½	Lb	Fresh mushrooms, coarsely chopped
3	Tbs	Butter or EVOO or combination
1	Cup	Marsala, sweet Sherry or Madeira wine
½	Cup	Heavy cream
¼	Lb	Fontina or other cheese you like, grated or shredded
1	Cup	Fresh or thawed frozen peas
		Salt and pepper to taste
¼	Cup	Grated Parmagiano Reggiano
½	Cup	Breadcrumbs
1	Tsp	Dried thyme

Procedure

Pre-heat oven to 400°. Butter or non-stick spray a 9" x 13" baking dish. Bring chicken stock to a boil and add the orzo. Cook for 7 minutes only (it will finish cooking in the oven later). Remove from heat.

Sauté the mushrooms and onion in butter and/or EVOO for about 10 minutes. Add the wine, deglaze the pan and cook until the liquid is reduced by half. Add the mushroom/onion mix, cream, grated cheese, peas, salt and pepper to the orzo and stir to combine. Pour the orzo into the baking dish. In a small bowl combine the Parmagiano, breadcrumbs and thyme. Sprinkle this mix over the orzo and bake for 20-25 minutes until the top is golden brown.

DIY Foccacia

About This Recipe

Foccacia bread has become very popular in America in the last few years. You can make it yourself using pizza dough that you can buy at your local pizzeria. You just roll it out, top with whatever toppings you like and bake it for 20 minutes or so. It is terrific eaten hot out of the oven.

The difference between foccacia and pizza dough is the amount of leavening. Pizza dough uses less yeast than foccacia dough. You can approximate the real thing using pizza dough if you don't roll the dough out as thinly as you would for pizza.

Here are a few topping suggestions, but I'll bet that you can think of some more imaginative ones.

Topping Ideas

Potatoes and/or sweet potatoes

EVOO

Grated Parmagiano Reggiano

Paprika

Thyme

Garlic Powder

Salt and pepper, to taste

Procedure

Pre-heat the oven to 400°. Roll out the dough to the shape you want ¼" – ½" thick. Paint with EVOO, sprinkle on the toppings and bake 20-25 minutes. For a crispier crust, bake directly on the oven grate. For a softer crust, bake on a baking sheet or pizza pan.

MY NOTES:

French Potato Casserole

6-8 Servings

About This Recipe

I've had variations on this 2-3 times in France. Although I didn't get the recipes from the restaurants, I looked it up online and was amazed to find several well-known chefs offering exactly the same recipe, each claiming to have invented it!

Who am I to take issue with so many famous personalities? With no pride of authorship, I offer here the very same recipe touted by the rich and famous. If you have a mandoline or V-slicer, the recipe is trivial to prepare.

Ingredients

12	Oz Thick-sliced bacon, coarsely chopped
1	Large Onion, halved and thinly sliced
	Salt
2	Tsp Fresh thyme, chopped, or 1 Tsp dried thyme
	Freshly ground black pepper
1¼	Cups Chicken stock
1¼	Cups Beef stock
3	Lbs Yukon gold potatoes
2	Tbs Butter, cut into small pieces

Procedure

Pre-heat oven to 425°. In a saucepan, cook the bacon until all the fat is rendered. Reserve the bacon bits and pour off all but a tablespoon of the bacon fat. Add the onions to the pan with a couple pinches of salt and sauté them until they are caramelized to a rich brown color, about 30 minutes. Stir every few minutes so that the onion cooks evenly. Add water a tablespoon at a time if the onions are getting too dry. Be careful not to let them burn.

A few minutes before the onions are done, peel the potatoes and cut them into ⅛" thick slices. Put the potato slices in a large bowl. When the onions are done, add them to the potatoes along with the bacon bits, thyme and salt and pepper to taste. Mix everything together (hands are best). It is common practice to put cut potatoes in water to prevent them from turning brown. Resist this temptation because it washes away much of the starch that this dish needs.

Add the beef and chicken stocks to the saucepan and bring to the boil. Spread the potato mixture in a 9" x 13" baking dish and pour over the hot stocks. Dot the top of the casserole with butter. Put the dish, uncovered, into the oven and bake for 45 - 55 minutes or until all the liquid is absorbed and the top is crisply browned. Remove from the oven and let stand at least 20 minutes before serving.

MY NOTES:

Jamaican Rice and Peas

4 Servings

About This Recipe

I don't know how this dish got its name because there are no peas in it. It does, however, contain kidney beans, so the dish is similar to Cuban black beans and rice (See Volume I). In this recipe, the rice is cooked in a combination of stock and coconut milk. Like the Jamaican goat curry dish described elsewhere in this book, a hot pepper is cooked along with the rice. It is used as a flavor component, not to make the dish hot, and it is discarded before serving.

When you buy coconut milk for this recipe, don't use the Southeast Asian kind that is concentrated and thick. If you do, thin it with water.

Ingredients

2	Tbs Canola or peanut oil
½	Medium Onion, chopped
4	Cloves Garlic, chopped
2	Cups Long-grain rice
1	Tsp Salt
1	Tsp Grated ginger
2	Cups Coconut milk
2	Cups Chicken or vegetable stock
1	14-oz Can of kidney beans
2	Tsp Dried thyme
1	Hot chili pepper
	Fresh lime juice (optional)

Procedure

In a medium pot, sauté the onions for 5 minutes. Add the garlic and the rice. Stir, and cook for two minutes. Add the rest of the ingredients, stir well to combine, bring to a boil, cover and cook until rice is done, about 15 minutes. Turn the heat off and allow to sit for 10 minutes. Discard the hot pepper, fluff the rice with a fork, sprinkle on lime juice and serve.

MY NOTES:

Kasha Varnishkas

8-12 Servings

About This Recipe

This is a classic dish from Eastern Europe. I grew up with it, and it has always amazed me that it hasn't caught on as a common side dish in America. It is inexpensive, easy to make, and utterly delicious. Fantastic accompaniment to roast chicken or pot roast. It will keep in the fridge for several days, and it will keep in the freezer for 3 months.

The dish is nothing more than noodles (bowties are traditional) mixed with buckwheat groats that have been cooked in chicken stock (You could use vegetable stock if you want a vegetarian dish). Groats are the kernels of the buckwheat plant. They come in several grinds ranging from fine to whole. For varnishkas, my choice is the medium grind, most commonly available in markets under the Wolff brand name. In case you can't find this cookbook, you will find this recipe on the Wolff box!

Ingredients

1	Lb Bowtie noodles (farfalle)
2	Cups Chicken stock
2	Tbs Butter
1	Tsp Salt
¼	Tsp Pepper
1	Cup Wolff's medium, ground kasha
1	Egg

Procedure

Cook the noodles in plenty of salted water as usual for pasta.

Put the stock, butter, salt and pepper in a pot, bring to the boil and keep on the simmer.

In a small bowl, beat the egg and add the kasha. Stir to thoroughly coat the kernels.

Heat a 12" skillet and add the kasha. Stir constantly for about three minutes. You want the egg to have dried on the kasha and the kernels to be separated, not clumped. Reduce the heat to low and (carefully) add the boiling stock. Cover the pan and simmer 7-10 minutes until kernels are tender and liquid is absorbed.

Mix the kasha and the noodles together. If you like, you can add a little butter (chicken fat is traditional). Serve at once or reheat before serving. Feel free to add more salt and/or pepper if you wish.

MY NOTES:

Kicked Up Champagne Risotto

4 Servings

About This Recipe

Why a recipe for risotto in this cookbook? It is in practically every Italian-food cookbook that was ever printed. I just thought I would share with you a few tips I've garnered after making it dozens of times.

There are two keys - and only two - to making a successful risotto. The first is to use a short or medium grain rice that will properly absorb the liquid. The second is to add the liquid, a little at a time, so that the absorption is controlled. The Italians, who invented risotto, would have you believe that it can't be made with anything but Arborio rice from Italy, but that is B.S. Good ole short-grain rice from the US of A works just as well and is a helluva lot cheaper than the imported stuff. The process of adding the liquid should take no more than 15 minutes. If you go beyond that, you have messed up.

To be honest, you can use just about any kind of dry red or white wine in this recipe. My champagne suggestion has more to do with impressing your guests than with the bubbles that will inevitably disappear in the cooking process. The other thing is, that, while you are cooking your risotto, you can indulge in a glass or two or three of champagne. I guarantee that, after a few glasses, you will know you have made the world's best risotto.

Ingredients

2½	Cups Chicken stock
2	Tbs EVOO
1	Small Carrot, chopped or coarsely grated
1	Stalk Celery, finely chopped
1	Small Onion, finely chopped
2	Cloves Garlic, chopped fine
1	Sprig Fresh thyme (optional)
½	Tsp Red pepper flakes (optional)
1	Cup Short or medium grain rice
1½	Cups Champagne
	Salt and white pepper to taste

EXTRAS

Chopped sun-dried tomatoes

Cooked or reconstituted mushrooms

Grated Parmagiano Reggiano

Asparagus cut into 1" pieces

Chopped parsley

(Recipe continues on next page)

Procedure

Put the chicken stock in a pot, bring it to the simmer and keep it there.

In a Dutch oven or heavy sauté pan, sauté the carrot, celery, onion, garlic, thyme and red pepper flakes for about 10 minutes. Add the rice and cook 2-3 minutes, stirring to be sure all the grains are coated. Add 1 cup of champagne and cook until the wine is almost completely evaporated., about 5 minutes. Add 1 cup of the hot stock and cook, stirring, until the rice has absorbed the liquid. Continue adding the stock and champagne, ¼ cup each at a time until liquid has been absorbed, stirring constantly. When you are all done the rice should have a creamy texture, but still be a bit al dente.

Add any extras you like and serve.

MY NOTES:

Mashed Potatoes with Celeriac

6-10 Servings

About This Recipe

Here is a twist on mashed potatoes that I think you will enjoy. Adding celery root (celeriac) gives the potatoes an interesting flavor profile. As an option add chopped, toasted hazelnuts or walnuts and/or nut oil.

Ingredients

2	Lbs Yukon Gold or russet potatoes, peeled and cut into chunks
1	Celeriac, cleaned, peeled and cut into chunks
	Salt
½	Cup Heavy cream
3	Cloves Garlic, pressed or minced
2	Tbs Chopped parsley
	Fresh-ground black pepper
2	Tbs Chopped hazelnuts or walnuts, toasted (optional)
3	Tbs Hazelnut or walnut oil (optional)
3	Tbs Melted butter (optional)

Procedure

Boil the potatoes and celeriac chunks in salted cold water for about 15 minutes. Reserve vegetables and save some of the cooking liquid.

While vegetables are cooking, simmer the garlic in the cream in a covered pot for about 10 minutes.

Mash potatoes and celeriac with a potato masher or ricer. Add cream and parsley and season to taste with salt and pepper. Add nuts, nut oil or butter if you are using them and stir to combine. If the mix is too stiff, add a bit of the water that the vegetables were cooked in.

MY NOTES:

Moroccan Couscous

4-6 Servings

About This Recipe

The classical way of making couscous, which takes a couple of days, is, in my opinion, crazy. You can make delicious couscous at home in a relatively short period of time without compromising the taste and texture. The secret is to ignore the recipes printed on the box. If you use them, you will be very unhappy with the gluey mess that will result.

Ingredients

3	Tbs Butter
3	Shallots, sliced thin
2	Cloves Garlic, minced or pressed
2	Cups Couscous
2	Cups Chicken stock
1	Tsp Salt
2	Tsp Lemon juice
1	Tsp Grated lemon zest
2	Tbs Chopped parsley
¾	Cup Toasted pine nuts or slivered almonds

Procedure

In a medium pot, melt the butter and cook the shallots until they begin to caramelize. Add the minced garlic and cook 30 seconds. Add the couscous and toast it, stirring constantly for about 5 minutes until it turns golden. Add the chicken stock and salt and bring to the boil. Cover the pot, take it off the heat and let it stand for 7 minutes.

Finish the dish by stirring in the lemon juice, lemon zest, chopped parsley and toasted nuts.

MY NOTES:

Piadine

Yields 4-12 Piadine depending on size

About This Recipe

Piadina (plural piadine) is an Italian flatbread that is easy to make because it doesn't need to rise and be kneaded to death. Traditionally, piadine is made with lard, but I've substituted butter. If you want to be traditional, by all means use lard.

This bread is traditionally cooked on a grill or in a skillet rather than being baked. Once cooked, you can top it with all sorts of things. Cheese is obvious, but anything you can conceive of that would make a good pizza topping will work. Instead of topping, you can roll the piadene and fill the resulting tubes or cones with goodies. In Italy a combination of sausage and cooked onions is commonly sold by street carts. Let your imagination be your guide.

Ingredients

3   Cups Flour
½   Tsp Baking soda
1   Tsp Salt
4   Oz Butter, cut into cubes at room temperature
1   Cup Hot water or less
     EVOO

Procedure

A standing mixer with a dough hook will make this recipe easy. Put all the dry ingredients in the bowl and turn on the machine at low speed to combine. Add butter and incorporate. Add enough hot water to pull the dough together. The amount you use will depend on the humidity of your kitchen. When the dough pulls together, form it into a ball and knead it on a floured marble or wooden surface for a couple of minutes. Divide the dough into 2, 4 or 6 pieces, depending on the size you want of the finished bread. Roll out each piece to a thickness of about 1/16". Paint both sides of the pieces with EVOO and grill, about 2 minutes per side. Allow to cool and you are done.

MY NOTES:

Pooris

Yields 4 Pooris

About This Recipe

There are five types of Indian flatbreads that I know of: chipatis, pappadums, pooris, parathas and naans. Although they are all pretty much the same, consisting of flour and water (or milk) and a little oil, there are subtle differences. I wouldn't bother making pappadums at home because you can buy them in a can at an Indian market. Neither would I bother with naan because you can get very good naan frozen or fresh in most supermarkets. Chipatis, pooris and parathas are a different story because they need to be eaten freshly made. The techniques are similar, so I'll just describe how to make pooris and you can look up the other variations.

By the way, this is a fun recipe for kids. They are always amazed at how these flat pieces of dough puff up.

Ingredients

⅓   Cup Flour

⅓   Cup Whole wheat flour

¼   Tsp Salt

¼   Cup Warm water

2   Tbs Canola or peanut oil for the dough

     Oil for frying

Procedure

Mix together the flours and salt in a medium bowl. Add the warm water and mix well. Add the oil and mix to combine with your hands. Take the dough out of the bowl and place it on an oiled work surface. Using your hands, knead the dough for about 5 minutes. Roll the dough into a rough log shape and divide it into 4 pieces. Shape each piece into a ball and then roll out the ball into a 3" diameter circle. Those circles are your basic poori dough.

In a deep pan, heat oil to 365° to a depth of about 1½ inches. Slide a poori into the oil and hold it down with a slotted spoon for about 60 seconds. The poori will puff up. Flip it over and cook it until the top turns golden. Then remove the poori to drain on a paper towel. Repeat for the other three pooris. Serve at once while still hot.

MY NOTES:

Potato Kugel for Gourmets

6-12 Servings

About This Recipe

Although kugel is associated with Jewish food in America, it is native to Lithuania, where it is properly called "kugelis". That said, most of the kugels I've had are pasty concoctions that aren't very exciting. I think it is more tradition than desire that keeps it coming back.

This version of potato kugel is light and airy. The more eggs you use, the puffier the kugel will be, so feel free to add more eggs if you wish. It is flavored with caramelized shallots that add an intriguing element to the dish. In addition, my recipe calls for shredding red potatoes instead of the more traditional grating russets. I also use EVOO instead of plain vegetable oil or chicken fat. You can add herbs if you wish. Thyme would be my first choice. Marjoram and parsley are also good. If you are in an Italian mood, you can add some grated Parmagiano Reggiano or Pecorino Romano cheese.

It is important that you bake the kugel in a glass dish. If you use metal, it will not form a crispy crust. In fact, I recommend cooking the kugel in individual Pyrex custard cups which come in 6- and 10-oz sizes. That way, the crusty surface area is maximized. Just set the cups in a throwaway roasting pan in the oven in case of any bubble over.

The kugel will keep for up to 5 days in the fridge or months in the freezer. Just reheat, but please use a regular oven to maintain crispness, not a microwave.

Ingredients

6	Large red potatoes, about 3 pounds
1	Large Onion, peeled
¾	Cup EVOO
½	Lb Shallots, peeled and diced
4	Eggs (or more)
¼	Cup Potato starch
½	Tsp Nutmeg
1	Tbs Salt (or to taste)
1	Tsp White pepper (or to taste)
2	Tbs Fresh thyme, marjoram or parsley to taste (optional)
½	Cup Grated cheese (optional)

(Recipe continues on next page)

Procedure

Pre-heat oven to 425°.

Peel the potatoes and put them in a bowl of cold water to prevent discoloration.

Heat the EVOO in a skillet or sauté pan and add the shallots. Cook until the shallots have caramelized, about 15 minutes. Remove the shallots with a slotted spoon and reserve them. Place 2 Tbs of the oil in a 13" x 9" Pyrex baking dish and roll it around to coat the bottom and sides. Place the dish in the oven to get hot. Maintain a low heat under the shallot-infused oil to keep it hot.

While the shallots are cooking, beat the eggs in a large bowl and add the salt and pepper, potato starch, nutmeg and optional herbs and cheese. Stir to combine.

Fit the food processor with a shredding blade. Cut the potatoes and onion into chunks that will fit into the feed tube. Process the onion first and drain off any liquid that appears. Then process the potatoes. Add the shredded potatoes and onion, the shallots and the hot oil to the egg mixture. Stir to combine and dump it all into the hot baking dish. If there are any large chunks of potato in the mix, you can discard them. Press the mix evenly in the baking dish, making sure that it is in the corners (the crispiest parts). Bake about an hour until golden brown. Let it rest at least 15 minutes before serving.

MY NOTES:

Spaetzle

6-8 Servings

About This Recipe

Spaetzle is a common side dish found primarily in Germany, Austria and Hungary. It is essentially an extruded dumpling. Easy to make, it can complement almost any meat dish. A spaetzle maker makes the job a no-brainer. You can buy one for less than $7 at almost any cookware store, and it will last several lifetimes.

Most recipes call for mixing the dry and wet ingredients separately and then combining them, meaning that you have to dirty two bowls. I do it all at once in one bowl and can't tell the difference. This recipe calls for a bit of butter in the batter (no pun intended). This isn't necessary, but I believe makes it taste better.

Once the spaetzle are made, you have lots of options. You can sauté them in butter and sprinkle them with herbs. You can cover them with grated cheese and bake in a medium oven until the cheese melts over all - sort of a German Mac and Cheese. Sauté them in garlic oil. Use in place of pasta. Let your imagination be your guide.

Ingredients

3	Cups Flour
2	Large Eggs
	Salt
1	Cup Water
2	Tbs Unsalted butter, melted

Procedure

Bring a large pot of salted water to the boil.

Mix flour, eggs and salt in a large bowl. Add water (up to 1 cup) gradually, stirring to make a smooth batter. Beat the batter with a wooden spoon until bubbles form, then stir in the melted butter.

Place a spaetzle press on top of the pot of boiling water and move the hopper over the holes slowly. The spaetzle will drop into the water. As soon as they float to the top, remove them with a slotted spoon or a sieve. Keep at it until all the spaetzle have cooked.

If you are not going to use the spaetzle right away, rinse them off in cold water to remove the surface starch and help prevent them from sticking together.

MY NOTES:

Sweet Potato Casserole

6-8 Servings

About This Recipe

I hate the word "casserole", which evokes memories of truly awful food, but I couldn't think what else to call this. I thought about calling it a soufflé, but I decided that is over the top. In any event, it is a whole lot better than mashed sweet potatoes and marshmallows and is just as easy to fix.

Ingredients

2	Lbs	Sweet potatoes peeled and cut into 1-inch cubes
½	Cup	Sugar
1	Tsp	Salt
2	Oz	Softened butter
2		Eggs
½	Cup	Half-and-half
1	Tsp	Vanilla

TOPPING

½	Cup	Brown sugar
¼	Cup	Flour
½	Cup	Chopped almonds, walnuts or pecans
¼	Cup	Melted butter
¼	Cup	Shredded coconut

Procedure

Pre-heat the oven to 325°. Nuke the sweet potatoes or bake them until soft. Remove the skins and mash them. Put them in a standing mixer bowl and, beating slowly, add the remaining ingredients one at a time. Beat until everything is combined and smooth. Pour into a 9"x9" baking dish or pan.

Mix together the topping ingredients and sprinkle over the sweet potatoes. Bake 30 minutes.

This dish will keep for many weeks in the freezer.

MY NOTES:

Chapter 18: Vegetable Side Dishes

This chapter includes 16 recipes for vegetable side dishes. Many of them are extremely easy to prepare and take only minutes. I think that you will find all of them to be a departure from the ordinary.

Broccoli with a Thai influence

4 Servings

About This Recipe

Like the first President Bush, I do not care for broccoli. However, my wife loves the stuff, so I am virtually forced to eat it once in a while. I am always on the lookout for ways to make broccoli palatable. This one works reasonably well for me, and I'll be interested to know what you think of it. I use a couple of Thai ingredients although my Thai friend tells me that broccoli is not normally grown in Thailand. Fortunately, the Thai ingredients are available in the Asian section of many markets or online.

To me, no matter what you put on it, broccoli has no redeeming character if it is overcooked. It needs to be crunchy in my view. This recipe calls for steaming the broccoli, so make sure that you stop the cooking before it turns mushy.

Ingredients

1   Lb Broccoli florets
2   Tbs Thai fish sauce
2   Tsp Sugar
       Thai Fried garlic

Procedure

Steam the broccoli florets no more than 5 or 6 minutes. Put the hot florets in a bowl and sprinkle on the remaining ingredients. Toss and serve at once.

MY NOTES:

Cauliflower "Twice-Baked Potatoes"

8-12 Servings

About This Recipe

Everybody knows about twice-baked potatoes. You bake a potato, scoop out the innards and mix them with sour cream, butter and herbs, stuff the mixture back into the skins and bake them again. This recipe, which I adapted from one I found in a Costco magazine (of all places) substitutes cauliflower for the potato. The idea is to emulate a baked potato with a healthier alternative. That is not my objective - mine is to make something that tastes great, thus the addition of butter and full fat sour cream.

In the magazine, "cups" were formed from slices of Canadian bacon pressed into a muffin pan. Not a bad idea, but if you want to serve this dish as a side to, for example, a steak, the bacon will clash. But for the dish to work, you need some sort of shell. What to use? A dilemma. My choices are 1) shells made of filo dough; and 2) baked potato skins. If you use the latter, save the innards for future mashed potatoes.

The recipe calls for topping with cheese. Use what you like that melts. Some recommendations are Parmagiano Reggiano, gruyère or cheddar.

Ingredients

1	Package of filo dough, or
3	Russet potatoes, baked and slightly cooled
1	Head Cauliflower, cut into florets and steamed
2	Tbs Butter
2	Tbs Sour cream
1	Tbs Chopped chives
1	Tbs Chopped parsley
	Salt and pepper to taste
½	Cup Grated cheese

Procedure

If using potato skins, scoop out the insides and save for another time. Process the remaining ingredients together and stuff into the potato skins. Top with grated cheese and bake in a 375° oven for 15 minutes.

If using filo dough, pile up 3-4 layers and cut into pieces large enough to line the insides of a muffin pan. Brush the insides with melted butter and bake for 15 minutes in a 375° oven until crisp. Fill cups with the cauliflower mixture, top with cheese and bake for 15 minutes.

MY NOTES:

Fennel Confit

4 Servings

About This Recipe

If you like the licorice flavor of fennel, you are going to like this dish which goes will with red meat, pork or dark meat poultry.

The licorice flavor is boosted with the addition of anise-flavored liquor, such as Pernod, Ricard, Arak, Kasra, Ouzo, Ojen, etc.

Ingredients

2	Tbs Butter
2	Tbs EVOO
2	Medium Fennel bulbs
	Salt
2	Tbs Anise-flavored liquor

Procedure

Trim off the tops and the root ends of the fennel bulbs. Cut them in half the long way, remove the hard core and then thinly slice them cross-grain.

In a large skillet or sauté pan, heat the butter and EVOO on medium-low. Add the fennel and salt, stir well, cover and cook, stirring occasionally for about 15 minutes. Remove the cover, increase the heat to medium-high and cook until the fennel has caramelized and is a deep golden brown color, 10 - 15 minutes more. If the fennel begins to stick during this process add a little water to the pan. Add the liquor and deglaze the pan. Serve immediately or keep in the refrigerator for up to 5 days and reheat as needed.

MY NOTES:

Fried Green Tomatoes

8 Servings

About This Recipe

Fried green tomatoes are a Southern (more specifically New Orleans) dish that is amazingly good. Originally, the frying medium was bacon grease, and no doubt that is delicious. I've substituted the more conventional cooking oil, but, if your constitution can handle it, by all means go for the original.

The best way to cook these is to deep-fry them, but sautéing them in a skillet also works pretty well, although it won't develop a thick crust. If you do sauté them, add a bit of butter to the oil for more flavor. You can easily italianify this recipe by eliminating the cornmeal and using more breadcrumbs, using EVOO instead of a neutral oil and adding some dried oregano and basil to the breadcrumbs.

Although I've put this recipe in the Vegetable Side Dish chapter, it could be served as an appetizer or even a finger-food. In New Orleans, it is often served as a brunch dish topped with a crabcake topped with remoulade or with a slice of ham smothered in hollandaise sauce. Zowie!

Ingredients

4	Large Green tomatoes
2	Eggs
½	Cup Milk
1	Cup Flour
½	Cup Cornmeal
½	Cup Seasoned breadcrumbs
2	Tsp Salt
¼	Tsp Pepper
	Oil for frying

Procedure

Slice tomatoes ¼" - ⅓" thick. Discard the ends. Beat eggs and milk together in a bowl. Mix cornmeal, salt, pepper and breadcrumbs together and place on a deep plate. Put the flour in another deep plate.

To deep-fry put the oil in a large pot at least 3" deep. Heat it to 365° on a deep-fry thermometer. Dredge the tomato slices in the flour, shake off any excess, then coat with the egg/milk mixture and dredge in the cornmeal mixture. Fry until golden on both sides. Drain on paper towels before serving. If you are going to sauté them, put a little oil and butter in a large skillet and sauté until the coating is crusted on both sides. Just before serving, garnish with chopped parsley.

MY NOTES:

Gin and Orange Juice Braised Endive

6 Servings

About This Recipe

I put a recipe for braised endives in Volume I. It is very good, but this one is a very different alternative. It was created by Chef Tory Miller of L'Etoile restaurant in Madison, Wisconsin . It is so good, I didn't change a thing. I encourage you to look at L'Etoile's menu online for some great gourmet ideas. It changes every day.

Ingredients

2	Tbs EVOO
6	Medium Belgian endives, halved lengthwise
2	Tbs Gin
	Salt and Pepper to taste
½	Cup Orange juice
3	Tbs Butter
1	Tbs Honey
1	Tbs Scallions, white parts only
1	Tbs Toasted pumpkin seeds
	Aged Balsamic vinegar for drizzling

Procedure

In a large skillet sauté the endives in the EVOO, cut side down until they are browned, about 5 minutes. Pour the gin into the skillet and cook until it is reduced by half. Turn the endives over, season with salt and pepper and pour in the orange juice. Cover and cook 15 minutes, turning once.

Transfer the endives to a warm platter, cut sides up. Add the butter and honey to the pan and cook until the sauce is syrupy, about 4 minutes. Pour the sauce over the endives and sprinkle with scallions and roasted pumpkin seeds. Drizzle with balsamic vinegar and serve.

The endives can be prepared ahead of time up to the point where you add the honey. Just refrigerate them in the liquid for up to a couple of days. To serve, gently reheat and finish the recipe.

MY NOTES:

Ginger Sesame Carrots

6 Servings

About This Recipe

This is a simple recipe, sure to please carrot lovers. If you can get them, use whole baby carrots with a bit of the green tops on. If not, just cut up regular carrots into sticks, roughly ¼" x ¼" x 4".

Ingredients

24	Baby carrots or equivalent regular carrots
½	Tbs Canola oil
½	Tbs Sesame oil
½	Tbs Fresh ginger, minced
1	Pinch Ground cinnamon
¼	Tsp Cayenne (optional)
½	Cup Chicken stock
1	Tbs Butter
1	Tbs Lime juice
1	Tbs Toasted sesame seeds

Procedure

Blanch the carrots in boiling salted water for 1-2 minutes. Drain them.

In a large skillet, heat the oils and add the carrots, ginger and cinnamon. Cook 2-3 minutes until ginger is fragrant. Add the chicken stock and bring to the boil. Cook until the stock is reduced by half. Stir in the butter and lime juice.

Put the carrots in a serving dish and pour over the pan sauce. Sprinkle with toasted sesame seeds.

MY NOTES:

Green Beans and Curly Celery

6 Servings

About This Recipe

I got the idea for this recipe from Iron Chef Ann Burrell. She served it underneath baked halibut, but I think it does well as a side dish with almost anything you can think of.

The trick to this recipe is to make long, thin shavings of celery with a vegetable peeler. Placing the shavings in lemon-infused cold water for several hours will make the shaving curl up and get very crispy.

You can use any kind of stringbeans you like. Anne used the little French haricot verts.

Ingredients

6   Stalks Celery
        Salt
        Juice of half a lemon
        EVOO
1   Lb Stringbeans, cleaned
3   Cloves Garlic, crushed
1   Pinch Red pepper flakes (optional)

Procedure

With a vegetable peeler create stalk-length shavings of the celery. Put the shavings in a bowl of ice water with half a lemon and its juice. Place in the refrigerator for at least an hour, better overnight. The shavings will curl up during this process and become quite crispy.

Blanch the beans in boiling water. Remove from the water and plunge them immediately into a bowl of ice water to stop the cooking. When cool, drain the beans and discard the water.

A few minutes before you are ready to serve, heat some EVOO in a large skillet. When the oil is hot, add the garlic and red pepper flakes and cook until the garlic starts to brown. Discard the garlic and add the beans. Cook until they are heated through. While the beans are cooking, dry the celery curls in a salad spinner, then add them to the beans. Sprinkle over some salt and toss everything to heat through. Serve at once.

MY NOTES:

Grilled Marinated Vegetables

About This Recipe

Super simple. Prepare an easy marinade, soak cut up vegetables in it for a couple of hours and grill them for a couple of minutes on each side. It makes for a great side dish to accompany grilled steaks or lamb chops.

If you do this dish on an outdoor grill, make sure that you use an appropriate grate or the pieces of vegetable will tend to fall through.

You can make this dish with different flavor profiles by substituting a different type of vinegar or herb. Try using white balsamic vinegar, for example. Rosemary or oregano are other good choices for herbs.

Good choices for vegetables are zucchini or any other summer squash, eggplant (especially the small Japanese variety) and green or red bell peppers.

Ingredients

2	Tbs White wine vinegar
2	Tbs Lemon juice
⅓	Cup EVOO
2	Cloves Garlic, pressed or minced
1	Tbs Fresh thyme, chopped
	Vegetables, cut up or thickly sliced as appropriate

Procedure

Mix together all the ingredients except the vegetables and pour into a gallon freezer bag. Add the vegetables, seal the bag, squish it around and leave sit for a couple of hours. Grill the vegetables about 2 minutes per side.

MY NOTES:

Moroccan Cauliflower Latkes

6-8 Servings

About This Recipe

I've been making latkes out of cauliflower for years, simply substituting mashed steamed cauliflower for the grated potatoes. But I ran across a recipe in the Vegetarian Times that went another step further by flavoring the latkes with middle-eastern spices. Since I am a sucker for middle-eastern flavors, I decided to try it. The result is a bit different from the original, but I think is at least a slight improvement. Give it a shot.

The original recipe suggests serving yogurt flavored with fresh mint and garlic on the side. I like them plain with a little salt, but you might try the yogurt, especially if you add any hot stuff to your latkes. The original also called for adding raisins, but I think that detracts from the finished product.

Ingredients

½   Cup EVOO, more if needed for frying
1   Large Onion, chopped fine
3   Cloves Garlic, pressed or minced
1   Tbs Curry powder or Ras El Hanout
1   Tsp Ground cumin
1   Tsp Ground ginger
1   Large Cauliflower, cut into florets
1   Egg
½   Cup Mayonnaise
1½   Cups Coarse breadcrumbs
2   Tbs Flour, cornstarch or potato starch
1   Tsp Harissa (optional)

Procedure

Heat 2 Tbs EVOO in a Dutch oven or large pot. Sauté the onions in it until they turn golden. Add garlic, curry powder or Ras el Hanout, cumin and ginger and cook 30 seconds. Add cauliflower and 2 cups water. Cover and bring to a simmer. Cook 20 minutes or until cauliflower florets are soft. Uncover, turn up the heat and cook off the liquid. When cooled, mash the cauliflower.

Whisk together the eggs and mayonnaise in a large bowl. Stir in the mashed cauliflower, bread crumbs, and flour. Season with salt and pepper to taste. Heat the remaining oil in a large skillet and fry the latkes, about 2.5" in diameter, in batches on both sides until brown and crispy. Drain on paper towels.

MY NOTES:

Mushroom Ragoût

6-10 Servings

About This Recipe

This dish can be served as a side dish or as a topping for grilled meat or poultry. It can also serve as an omelet filling, added to a risotto or as a pasta sauce. Truly versatile. You can make it with ordinary button mushrooms or with more exotic types like chanterelles or morels. Either way, reconstituted porcinis must be included.

You can make this dish with a dry white or red wine or with a fortified wine such as Marsala or Madeira. My personal favorite is dry Marsala. The ragoût can be made a few days ahead of time and reheated, although you may find it necessary to add a bit of water or cream to get the sauce consistency the way you want it.

Ingredients

1	Oz Dried porcinis
1½	Cups Boiling water
3	Tbs Butter or EVOO or combination
2	Lbs Fresh mushrooms (any kind), sliced
2	Cloves Garlic, pressed or minced
2	Medium Shallots, finely chopped, or
½	Onion, finely chopped
½	Cup Marsala or other wine
2	Tsp Chopped thyme
	Salt and pepper to taste
¾	Cup Heavy cream
2	Tsp Chopped parsley for garnish

Procedure

Soak the dried porcinis in the boiling water for 20 - 30 minutes, then chop them coarsely. Reserve the soaking liquid. Strain it through a coffee filter if it contains any dirt particles.

In a large skillet or sauté pan, heat half the butter and/or EVOO. Add the sliced mushrooms and cook over medium heat until the mushrooms have released their juices. Turn up the heat and cook until the mushrooms are quite dry and well-browned, about 8 minutes.

Add the other half of the butter or EVOO and the garlic and shallots. Sauté about 2 - 3 minutes. Add the wine, thyme, porcini and 1/4 cup of the porcini soaking liquid. Cook until most of the liquid evaporates, about 2 minutes. Add the cream and cook until the sauce reaches the consistency you want. Season with salt and pepper to taste and stir in the chopped parsley or sprinkle it on top. If the sauce gets too thick for your taste, just add a little more of the soaking liquid.

MY NOTES:

Mushrooms with Red Wine Sauce

6 Servings

About This Recipe

Mushrooms and red wine - a combination designed by the Gods. This is a terrific side for steak or prime rib. You can make it very rich with butter and/or cream - or not. I prefer the former!

You can use any kind of fresh mushrooms, alone or in combination. The sauce tends to overpower the mushroom taste, so I recommend you use the least expensive available.

The recipe calls for the addition of a small amount of Chinese black bean sauce. If you don't have any, you could substitute demi-glace and it will be just as good.

Ingredients

	EVOO
1	Cup Onions, finely chopped
1	Tbs Chinese black bean sauce
1	Tsp Pressed garlic
1	Stick Butter, cut into 6 pieces
1	Lb Mushrooms, cut into bite-sized pieces
	Salt and pepper to taste
¼	Cup Minced shallots
1½	Cups Red wine
1½	Cups Chicken stock
2	Tbs Heavy cream
	Cornstarch slurry

Procedure

Sauté the onions in a little EVOO for a couple of minutes. Add the black bean sauce and garlic and cook 1 minute. Add 1 piece of the butter and the mushrooms and cook until the mushrooms give off their water, about 8 minutes. Season with salt and pepper. Reserve mushrooms.

Add red wine and shallots. Bring to a simmer and reduce liquid by 2/3. Add stock and reduce to 3/4 cup. Add the cream and simmer 30 seconds. Whisk in remaining butter, a piece at a time. Bring to a simmer and add cornstarch slurry, a little at a time until desired consistency is reached.

Add the mushrooms to the sauce, heat and serve while hot.

MY NOTES:

Parmagiano Zucchini Rounds

4-6 Servings

About This Recipe

Very easy and absolutely delicious. In addition to employing it as a side to an Italian meal, you could serve them as an appetizer or a cocktail party finger-food.

Instead of baking these rounds for half an hour, you could deep-fry them, which will take only a couple of minutes. Just make sure that the oil is around 375° and don't cook too many at once. Drain on paper towels before serving.

Ingredients

2   Zucchinis, ½ Lb each, sliced ¼" thick
1   Tbs EVOO
¼   Cup Grated Parmagiano Reggiano
¼   Cup Seasoned bread crumbs

Procedure

Pre-heat oven to 450°. Spray a baking sheet with a non-stick spray

Put the zucchini slices in a bowl and drizzle in the EVOO. Mix it all around with your hands until both sides of each slice are coated with oil.

Mix the cheese and breadcrumbs together. Dip the zucchini slices in the dry mix. Press the coating into the slices to make sure it sticks. Lay the slices on the baking sheet and cook for 25-30 minutes. The zucchini should be crispy. Serve while hot.

MY NOTES:

Quick Ratatouille

About This Recipe

Ratatouille is not the name of a rat. It is a stewed vegetable dish that originated in the south of France. It typically takes an hour or so to make. This recipe takes less than half that time, and is just as good in my opinion. I didn't list any amounts because the proportions aren't important.

Ingredients

EVOO

Onion, coarsely chopped

Garlic, pressed or minced

Eggplant, chopped

Herbs like thyme, basil and parsley, chopped

Bell peppers, any color, chopped

Zucchini, chopped

Tomato sauce, preferably home-made

Procedure

Heat the oil in a large sauté pan. Add the onions and cook 5 minutes. Add the garlic and cook 30 seconds. Add the eggplant and some of the herbs and cook 5 minutes. Add the zucchini, bell peppers and the rest of the herbs and cook 5 minutes. Add the tomato sauce and cook to heat through. Serve at once.

MY NOTES:

Sugar Snap Peas with Thyme and Shallots

4 Servings

About This Recipe

Sugar snap peas are a fabulous vegetable that are as good eaten raw as they are when cooked. Unfortunately, they are only available fresh in the late winter and early spring months. This is a side dish recipe I concocted myself one day just because I had some shallots and fresh thyme. I think you will agree that it turned out pretty well. The caveat here is not to cook the peas too long. Essentially, you want to just heat them through so that they retain their "snap".

Ingredients

1	Lb Sugar snap peas
1	Tbs EVOO
1	Medium Shallot, thinly sliced
1	Tbs Chopped fresh thyme
	Salt and pepper to taste

Procedure

Nip off the tips of the pea pods if necessary (a thumbnail is a great tool for this purpose). Heat the EVOO in a skillet and sauté the shallots until softened, about 3 minutes. Add the snap peas and thyme. Season with salt and pepper. Cook over high heat, tossing frequently, until the peapods are heated through, 2-3 minutes. Serve at once.

MY NOTES:

Sweet and Sour Onions

6-8 Servings

About This Recipe

This is an easy side dish that will go great with turkey, goose or pork roasts. The trick is to find small fresh onions and/or shallots which may be hard to find in your average market. Pearl onions, mini red onions and cipollinis all work well. The shallots should not account for more than 25% of the mixed onions by weight.

This dish can be made days ahead of time and reheated before serving.

Ingredients

2	Lbs Small onions and/or shallots
¼	Cup Butter or EVOO
	Fresh thyme sprigs
2	Bay leaves
8	Fresh sage leaves
	Salt and Pepper to taste
⅔	Cup Port
½	Cup Apple cider vinegar
2	Tbs Honey
2	Cups Chicken stock

Procedure

Peel the onions and shallots. Halve them if they are too big.

In a Dutch oven, melt 2 Tbs butter and add the thyme, sage and bay leaves. Stir to coat the herbs and then add the onions. Season with salt and pepper.

Add port, vinegar, honey, dried fruit and chicken stock. Bring the mixture to a simmer, cover and cook for 10 minutes.

Remove the cover, stir and cook until liquid has reduced to a syrupy glaze, about 20 minutes. If the onions are still not tender, add a little more stock and cook a little longer.

Reserve onions and discard the herbs, Add 2 Tbs butter and cook over high until liquid reduces to a glaze. Return onions to pot and stir to coat evenly with the glaze.

MY NOTES:

Tomatoes Stuffed with Cheese, Herbs and Breadcrumbs

8 Servings

About This Recipe

This is a terrific side dish for any kind of meat or sturdy fish like halibut or swordfish. It is amazingly simple and allows for countless permutations and combinations of ingredients. Basically, you fill a tomato half with a stuffing made from cheese, herbs and breadcrumbs, then bake them. By changing the type of cheese and herbs that you use, you get different results - never boring.

Here are some cheese recommendations: Parmagiano Reggiano, provolone, gruyère, asiago, dry cheddar, Manchego, Emmenthaler. Essentially, any cheese you like that can be grated will work. Here are some herb recommendations: Italian parsley, oregano, thyme, marjoram, basil, garlic, rosemary, cilantro, cumin, dill. I suggest that you try and match up the cheese and the herbs. For example, use Italian cheeses with Italian herbs such as oregano or basil, a French cheese with thyme or a Swiss cheese with dill. You get the idea.

It goes without saying that your tomatoes should come from your own garden or a reliable farmer's market. The breadcrumbs that you can buy in any market will do fine for this dish. Of course, if you want to make your own, I won't stop you.

Ingredients

4	Large Tomatoes
2	Tbs Chopped fresh herbs
1	Cup Grated cheese
¾	Cup Dried breadcrumbs
	EVOO

Procedure

Pre-heat oven to 375°. Cut the tomatoes in half and squeeze out the seeds. Scoop out the pulp and put it into a large bowl. Place the tomatoes into a greased baking dish.

To make the stuffing, add to the pulp the cheese, herbs and breadcrumbs along with some salt and pepper. You want the mixture to be slightly damp. If it is too dry stir in a bit of EVOO.

Fill the tomato halves with the stuffing, drizzle a little EVOO over the top and bake in the oven for 20 minutes. If the top is not nicely browned, put the tomatoes under the broiler for a minute or two. Serve immediately (best), reheat for later or eat at room temperature.

MY NOTES:

Chapter 19: Sandwiches

In the mood for a sandwich? Here are 7 recipes that will put the usual ham-and-cheese to shame.

Fast Pork Fajitas

4 Fajitas

About This Recipe

A fajita is reminiscent of Middle-eastern gyros, but the cooking technique is identical to Chinese stir-fry. The key ingredients are the meat, the bell pepper and the onions. I recommend that you use loin chops or the tenderloin. The bell peppers can be red or green or a combination. If you want heat, add some jalapeños or other hot peppers or you could toss in some red pepper flakes.

Common condiments include shredded lettuce, pico de gallo, shredded cheddar cheese, sliced avocado and sour cream. To make a fajita, put a couple of large spoonfuls of the meat mixture in the middle of a flour tortilla and add your condiments, just like you do with moo shu pork in a Chinese crèpe. Then make a roll and fold up the ends so that the filling doesn't fall out. Get the tortillas in the 12" diameter size.

Ingredients

2	Tbs EVOO
1	Lb Pork tenderloin, sliced thin cross-grain in strips
	Salt and pepper to taste
2	Bell peppers, any color or mixed, cut into strips
1	Jalapeños, seeded and sliced (optional)
1	Onion, halved the long way and cut into strips
4	Cloves Garlic, minced or pressed
2-3	Tsp Fajita seasoning
	Juice of a lime
4	12" Flour tortillas
	Condiments (optional)

Procedure

Warm the tortillas. You can do this in the oven, but the microwave will work just as well. Once heated, cover with a slightly damp cloth and keep them warm. A tortilla keeper is useful. Heat EVOO in a skillet on high heat. Add pork and stir-fry 2 minutes until browned. Add peppers, onion, garlic and fajita seasoning. Stir-fry until peppers and onions are crisp-tender, about 2 minutes. Add the lime juice and cook 1 minute. Serve piping hot with a selection of condiments.

Grilled Cheese Sandwiches

1 Sandwich

About This Recipe

"What on earth is a grilled cheese sandwich doing in a gourmet cookbook?" I'm here to tell you that the right combination of bread and cheese, coupled with the right cooking technique, will turn the ordinary into a gourmet treat. This recipe is adapted from the *Cowgirl Creamery*, a prominent artisan cheese maker.

The filling concept is to use a combination of hard and soft cheeses. The bread has to be first class, and the sandwich has to be cooked to perfection. Accomplishing this is ridiculously simple!

I suggest using three cheeses, one soft, one hard and one in between. The harder cheeses should be grated so that they can be mixed together and will melt evenly.

Ideally, you would make these sandwiches in a Panini press, but a frying pan will do although the cooking will take a few minutes longer.

One variation I've seen is to coat the bread with a mixture of mayonnaise and Dijon mustard and incorporate chopped cooked bacon with the cheese. I haven't tried it, but it sounds good.

Ingredients

4   Oz Mixed cheeses

1   Tbs Fresh basil, parsley or chives, chopped

2   Slices of Artisan sourdough or other bread

1   Tbs Butter at room temperature

Procedure

Grate the harder cheeses. Mix the cheeses together with the chopped herbs.

Butter the inside surfaces of the bread and fry until golden. Spread one piece of bread with the cheese mixture and top with the other piece of bread. Butter the outside surfaces of the sandwich and fry until golden brown on both sides. Don't sweat it if the cheese oozes out.

MY NOTES:

Hong Kong Pork Wraps

6 Wraps

About This Recipe

Ninety-nine out of a hundred Chinese restaurants in America serves Moo Shu dishes. This dish is similar in that it is meant to be eaten in a wrap. The wrap can be the traditional Chinese pancake or a lettuce leaf. In contrast to Moo Shu, this recipe has very few ingredients. Easy to fix and inexpensive.

If you want to use Chinese pancakes, I recommend that you go to a local Chinese restaurant and get them on takeout. If you choose lettuce wraps, I suggest butter lettuce. You can also use romaine or head lettuce leaves, but you will need to blanch them so that they will be soft and easy to wrap.

Ingredients

1	Lb Ground or finely chopped pork
1	Red bell pepper, finely chopped
1	Clove Garlic, pressed or minced
1	Tbs Thai sweet chili sauce
1	Tbs Thai fish sauce
1	Tsp Sesame oil
1	Tbs Canola or peanut oil
1	8-oz Can of water chestnuts
2	Tbs Oyster sauce
2	Tbs Chopped cilantro
6	Lettuce leaves or Chinese pancake wraps

Procedure

Combine the pork, bell pepper, garlic, ginger, chili sauce, sesame oil and most of the canola oil.

Heat the remaining canola oil in a large skillet and stir-fry the pork mixture until the meat browns, about 3-5 minutes. Stir in the remaining ingredients except wraps and cook until heated through. Transfer to a serving bowl and serve along with the wraps. Spoon the pork mixture onto a wrap and eat with your fingers.

MY NOTES:

Merguez Burgers

6 Burgers

About This Recipe

Merguez is the name of a lamb sausage that comes from North Africa. In this recipe, the merguez spices are used in a burger made from ground lamb. Cook these burgers the way you like, but try them medium rare. If you don't like it, you can always cook it longer on the grill.

Most merguez sausages have bit of heat, some of them a lot of heat. You can make these burgers as mild or as hot as you wish. If you really want to sweat, add some Harissa, which is a mind-blowing chili paste from Morocco that comes in a little can and is not too hard to find.

Instead of mustard, ketchup and/or relish, try the trivial-to-make yogurt-based sauce I've suggested, especially if you have made your burgers with a lot of heat. The coolness of the yogurt makes a nice contrast with a spicy burger.

The yogurt needs to be fairly "stiff." If you use regular yogurt, drain it through cheesecloth to get rid of excess water. A good quality Greek, Bulgarian or Iranian yogurt is already thick and doesn't need to be drained.

You can serve these burgers with any sides that you like. Potato or pasta salads, French fries (Pomme Frites of course), etc. etc. all work. If you have some good tomatoes, try the tomato cucumber salad described in Volume I.

Ingredients

BURGER

2	Lbs Ground lamb
1	Tbs Garlic, pressed
¼	Cup Fresh cilantro leaves, chopped
¼	Cup Red wine vinegar
1	Tbs Paprika, hot, smoked or sweet as desired
2	Tsp Ground cumin
2	Tsp Ground coriander seeds
2	Tsp Salt
1	Tsp Cayenne (optional)
½	Tsp Cinnamon

(Recipe continues on next page)

SAUCE

1	Cup Plain yogurt
2	Tbs Cilantro leaves, chopped
2	Tbs Mint leaves, chopped
	Dry Romaine lettuce leaves
	Thinly sliced cucumber
	Thinly sliced tomatoes

Procedure

Mix all the burger ingredients together. Form into patties and grill just like regular hamburgers.

To make the sauce, just mix the yogurt and chopped herbs together. Let stand at least half an hour to infuse flavors.

To assemble the burgers, place a piece of lettuce on the lower bun, add cucumber and tomato slices, the burger, the yogurt sauce, another piece of lettuce and then the bun top. Eat.

MY NOTES:

The Ultimate Steak Sandwich

4 Sandwiches

About This Recipe

Steak Sandwiches are an American Institution. They come in many different guises. Sometimes they use thinly sliced meat and sometimes whole steaks. Some are open-faced, some are closed. In Philadelphia, cheese is added. When I was a kid, I lived near Revere Beach, once New England's premier amusement park, now condos. There were little stands along the beach serving steak sandwiches containing shaved meat, onions and green peppers served in a grilled hot dog roll. I recollect that one cost a quarter. This recipe is a takeoff on the Revere Beach formula.

By the way, New England hot dog rolls do not have any crust on the sides, so that they can be grilled. Unfortunately, they are not sold outside of New England. If you live elsewhere, you do not know what you are missing.

The key to my recipe is, as usual, dependent on the quality of the ingredients. You need tasty steak that you can slice thin. I recommend either tri-tip or flank steak. Partially freeze the steak before you cut it, use a sharp knife and you will be able to get very thin slices with ease. Just make sure that you cut the steak across the grain. You also need a great bread. An artisan ciabatta (Italian "slipper" bread) is ideal.

Here are a couple of other variations you might want to try. 1) Instead of sprinkling salt and pepper on the meat, try a season salt such as Lawry's. 2) As soon as the meat has browned, add some Worcestershire Sauce and/or Tabasco Sauce. 3) Add some cheese to the meat and vegetables at the end of cooking and cook until the cheese melts. That said, and with all due respect to my Philly friends, I'm not crazy about using cheese because I think it obscures the flavor of the meat.

Many condiments will go well with this sandwich, although you can do without and still be happy. Plain mustard, garlic infused mayonnaise, horseradish sauce (prepared horseradish mixed with mayo or sour cream), Asian hot sauce (sriracha) all work, but please, please don't use ketchup.

Ingredients

	Sandwich Bread, enough for 4 sandwiches
4	Tbs Butter
1	Lb Steak, sliced thin
2	Tbs EVOO
1	Clove Garlic, sliced
	Salt and pepper to taste
1	Onion, thinly sliced
1	Green bell pepper, cut into strips
½	Lb Mushrooms, sliced
4	Tbs Red wine or dry sherry

(Recipe continues on next page)

Procedure

Slice the bread in half lengthwise and cut into sandwich size pieces. Butter the cut surfaces and grill or broil until golden. Set bread aside.

Heat the EVOO in a large skillet and add the garlic. Cook for 60 seconds to flavor the oil and discard the garlic. Salt and pepper the meat and cook it just long enough to brown it. Reserve the meat. Add the onion, mushrooms and bell pepper and sauté for about 3 minutes. Add the meat to the pan and the wine. Cook on high heat until the wine has evaporated.

Spoon the meat mixture on the bottoms of the sandwiches, add condiments if desired and serve at once.

MY NOTES:

The World's Best BLT

About This Recipe

I adapted this recipe from one created by Chef Cheryl Burr at Pinkie's Bakery in San Francisco. Her version is great. Mine is better. In this version, the bacon is candied and the tomatoes roasted. It also calls for great artisan bread. I suggest using Ciabatta (Italian slipper bread) because its flat shape lends itself to grilled sandwiches. Costco sells a sandwich bread they call "torta" which is also very good. This recipe is for one sandwich, but you will likely want to make more or make extra bacon and tomatoes for future use.

Here is a tip I'll bet you don't know: Rinse your bacon before cooking in cold water and it won't shrink as much!

Ingredients

Ciabatta bread

Melted butter

Miracle Whip® dressing

Freshly ground black pepper

3 Slices Bacon

Paprika

Brown sugar

Roma tomatoes

Romaine lettuce leaves

Thin cucumber slices

Procedure

Cut the Ciabatta into sections the size you want for your sandwich and then slice each section in half. Brush both sides of the bread with melted butter and grill them in a Panini press or on a griddle until well toasted. Coat the inside of each bread slice with Miracle Whip® that has some freshly ground pepper mixed into it.

Mix together a little brown sugar and paprika. You can use hot, sweet or smoked paprika as you wish. Rub the mix into each slice of bacon. Pre-heat the oven to 425° and bake the bacon strips on a rack set over a drip pan for 15-18 minutes. Drain the bacon on paper towels.

Cut the tomatoes in half lengthwise and remove the seeds and gel. Place then on a baking sheet, drizzle with EVOO and sprinkle with salt and pepper. Bake 15 minutes. You can do this at the same time you cook the bacon.

Assemble the sandwich, in the following order: bread, lettuce leaf, bacon, tomatoes, cucumber slices, lettuce leaf and bread. Put it into the Panini press for a minute to warm it up if you wish.

MY NOTES:

Vegetable Panini

4 Panini

About This Recipe

Don't bother with this recipe unless you can get some great rolls. The idea is to make a sandwich filling out of grilled veggies and cheese. Within that blanket definition, you have a million choices. I'm presenting just one.

It is nice to make these sandwiches in a Panini press. If you don't have one, you can grill the sandwiches or fry them in a skillet, but make sure that you put weights on top of the sandwiches to press them. When one side is done, flip the sandwiches and do the other side. If you don't have a suitable weight in your kitchen, wrap a brick in clean aluminum foil.

Ingredients

2	Tbs Balsamic vinegar
2	Tbs EVOO
2	Cloves Garlic, pressed or minced
	Salt and pepper to taste
1	Red bell pepper
1	Yellow bell pepper
1	Zucchini
4	Portabella mushrooms
⅓	Cup Basil chiffonade
4	4" Diameter rolls
4	Oz Goat cheese

Procedure

Whisk together the vinegar, EVOO, garlic and salt and pepper. Cut the peppers in half and remove the seeds and membranes. Cut the zucchini strips into 4" lengths. Coat all the vegetable with the vinaigrette mix and allow to stand at least 15 minutes.

Grill or broil the vegetables on both sides until lightly charred. When cool enough to handle, cut the peppers into thin strips.

Cut the rolls in half and spread the goat cheese on one half. Assemble the sandwiches with a mushroom cap, a couple of strips of zucchini and several pepper strips on each one. Brush the bottom and top of each sandwich with EVOO or melted butter and cook in a Panini press until the rolls are toasted to your liking.

MY NOTES:

Chapter 20: Miscellaneous

Here are a few items that I think you should know about that don't fit into the other chapter categories. It includes things you might need to make some recipes in this cookbook and others. They are all things that I use occasionally and don't want to forget.

Clarified and Brown Butters

Clarified butter is regular butter from which the milk solids have been removed. It is a handy thing to have in your pantry. It will last at least six months in the refrigerator and some claim that refrigeration isn't necessary.

The primary benefit of clarified butter is that it can be heated to a much higher temperature than regular butter without burning. The Indians call it "ghee", a staple of their cuisine. You can buy ghee in jars, but a lot of it has been flavored with various spices, so be careful to buy what you want.

That said, it is easy to make your own. You want to start with a good-quality unsalted butter. Good quality means a low water content. In the US, I recommend the Plugra® brand, which is reasonably priced. Figure that you will lose about 25% of the amount of butter that you start with. So if you start with 8 ounces, you will wind up with 6 ounces of clarified product.

Cut the butter into chunks and melt it over low heat. Bring to the simmer and cook until the foam rises to the top. Remove from heat and skim off the foam as best you can, but there is no need to be too fussy. Pour the warm butter though a couple of layers of cheesecloth that has been set in a strainer. That will remove any remaining solids. That's all there is to it. Pour it into a jar and use it as you wish.

If you let the butter cook until it turns brown, leaving in the milk solids, you will have what the French call "beurre noisette" and the Italians call "burro nicciuola" which mean "hazelnut butter." It has a nutty flavor that is delicious. It is commonly used in pastry making, but is also drizzled over cooked vegetables and used to make brown butter pasta sauces. When making the brown butter, stir constantly to make sure that the milk solids don't stick to the pan and burn. Using a light-colored pan is also important, because you will want to stop the cooking as soon as the butter turns brown which is difficult to see if the pan is a dark color.

MY NOTES:

Kreplach, Wontons and Purses

This recipe is all about dumplings made into pockets that hold a filling. They can be either savory or sweet. The wrappers can be made from pasta dough, wonton skins, or puff pastry. They can be cooked by boiling, sautéing or baking. Some of them work well in soup, some as finger-food, some as main courses and some as dessert.

For savory dumplings, I recommend that you use pre-made wonton skins which are sold in most markets today. For sweet purses, use frozen puff pastry or 4 layers of filo dough. That takes care of the outsides.

For the insides, you will typically need ½ - 1 teaspoon of filling. The fillings are easy to make in a food processor, and you can control how coarse or smooth the filling will be. I think it is fun to invent your own fillings, but in case you are lazy, here are a few classics:

Kreplach: This Jewish specialty consists of a pasta shell filled with well-cooked pot roast, onions and carrots with seasonings. Kreplach are most often boiled for 5 minutes, then served in soup, but you can sauté them in butter or oil and serve as a main course. Use wonton skins.

Wontons: Finely chop some chicken, shrimp, pork or a combination, add some finely chopped garlic, and ginger, a bit of soy sauce, oyster sauce or rice wine, seasonings, and a touch of sesame oil. If you want some crunch, toss in some water chestnuts. Wontons are invariably served steamed or in soup. Use wonton skins

Thai Purses: Combine cooked shrimp with Thai chili sauce, garlic, coriander, scallions, soy sauce and fish sauce. Use wonton skins and fry them in peanut oil, turning often until they are golden all over.

Beggar's Purses: Combine goat cheese, chopped chives and bacon bits to make the filling. Use filo dough for the wrapper. Bake 10 minutes in a 400° oven until golden.

Fruit purses: Use apples, pears, bananas or any fruit you like that doesn't have too much water in it. Cut fruit into thin pieces, set on precut puff pastry squares, sprinkle with sugar and cinnamon, make into purses, brush with maple syrup and sprinkle on more sugar and cinnamon. Bake 20 minutes in a 400° oven.

Wonton skins are ready to use. Filo is made with multiple sheets (usually 4 is enough) brushed with melted butter between each sheet. Puff pastry dough should be rolled out to the thickness you desire and then cut into squares or triangles depending on the shape you need..

To make purses fold up the sides of the dough and then twist to make it look like a purse. That may not be the traditional shape for a wonton or kreplach, but it is the easiest method. If you are using wonton skins be sure to brush the interior edges with water or beaten egg so that the edges will stick.

MY NOTES:

Macerated Berry Topping

About This Recipe

This is an all-purpose dessert or breakfast topping. Serve in on top of ice cream, angel food cake, French toast, pancakes, waffles, etc.

If using strawberries, they should be hulled and cut into small pieces.

Ingredients

1	Tbs Honey or maple syrup
1	Tsp Vanilla
2	Tbs Orange juice or Marsala wine
1	Tbs Aged Balsamic Vinegar
1	Lb Berries.

Procedure

In a medium bowl, combine all the ingredients except the berries, making sure that the honey or maple syrup is well combined.. Add the berries and stir to coat. Allow to macerate at least 30 minutes, but a couple of hours is even better. The berries will give off some of their own juices, so be sure to stir everything before serving.

MY NOTES:

Mock Clotted Cream

About This Recipe

In the British Isles, you can buy clotted cream, also known as scalded, clouted, Devon or Cornish cream, everywhere. In the US, you can probably find it in New York if you look hard, but it ain't going to be cheap. This recipe approximates clotted cream. Is it the same? Of course not, but it is reasonably close.

To make real clotted cream, you heat cow cream using a steam bath and then let it cool slowly. The cream rises to the top and forms "clots" with a fat content over 50%. Clotted cream is essential in a classic English "cream tea."

Unless you can get sour cream with a low water content, you will need to drain the excess water out of it. Put the sour cream in cheesecloth, set it over a bowl and allow to drain overnight in the refrigerator.

Ingredients

1   Cup Heavy cream, whipped to stiff peaks
⅓   Cup Drained sour cream
1   Tbs Powdered sugar (more or less to taste)
½   Tsp Vanilla extract (optional)

Procedure

Whip the cream. Add the sour cream, vanilla and sugar. Combine well.

MY NOTES:

Phony Mascarpone

About This Recipe

Mascarpone is an Italian spreadable cheese that is made from cream curdled with an acid, usually citric acid. It is a key ingredient in tiramisu and some English trifles. The problem with it is, for inexplicable reasons, expensive. You can easily make a mascarpone substitute that tastes very similar and is actually creamier than the original. All you need are three easily available ingredients, a food processor and about 3 minutes.

Here are some great ideas for using mascarpone:

1. Smear it on toasted bruschetta. Top with prosciutto and a drizzle of EVOO.

2. Mix it with orange juice and sugar and use as a topping for fresh berries.

3. Mix with EVOO and fresh herbs and use is as a stuffing or topping for fresh veggies such as tomatoes, cucumbers or peppers.

4. Use it in ice cream, especially French vanilla.

5. For breakfast, spread it on toast or English muffins, top with preserves.

6. Make a pasta sauce by adding it to sautéed sausage, mushrooms and onions.

7. Mix it with a little sugar, cinnamon and ground allspice and stuff dates with the mixture. Top with chopped pistachios.

8. Make a lemony fresh fruit topping out of it by mixing it with limoncello (See Volume I) and grated lemon zest.

If you like, you can use low-fat or non-fat ingredients. The results won't be as good, but you already know that.

Ingredients

½   Lb Cream cheese at room temperature, cut into small cubes
¼   Cup Sour cream
2   Tbs Heavy cream

Procedure

Unless the sour cream has a low water content, you will need to drain it overnight. Line a strainer with cheesecloth and set it on top of a bowl. Put the sour cream in the cheesecloth and refrigerate for at least 12 hours. Discard the liquid.

Put all the ingredients in a food processor and process until smooth.

MY NOTES:

Poor Man's Seafood Stock

About This Recipe

Consider making a seafood stock out of shrimp shells. They come free if you buy shrimp in their shells. In fact, they may be cheaper than free because shrimp in their shells are usually less expensive than peeled shrimp. You can use this stock in place of clam juice or other fish stock with good results.

Ingredients

Shrimp shells

Carrot

Onion

Celery

Peppercorns

Procedure

Peel the shrimp and toss the shells into a stockpot. Add a peeled carrot, a celery stalk, half an onion and a dozen peppercorns. Cover with water. Bring to a boil and simmer for half an hour. Strain the stock and discard the solids. You can reduce the stock if you want it stronger. Add a bit of salt if you think it needs it.

MY NOTES:

Preserved Lemons

About This Recipe

If you are going to make many dishes from the middle-east, you will need preserved lemons. You can buy them in markets specializing in Mediterranean food, but you can make your own quite easily by following these instructions. Once made, they will keep six months or more without refrigeration.

Preserved lemons are reputed to last for years, but the flavor will change over time. If you keep yours around for a very long time, you might want to make notes about the taste as the months and years roll by.

Ingredients

Lemons

Salt

Water

Procedure

Cut each lemon into four or six wedges and remove any seeds. Place them in a baking dish, sprinkle them generously with salt, cover them with water and cover the baking dish. Bake 3 hours in a pre-heated 250° oven. Put the lemon wedges in a canning jar of appropriate size and cover with the water they cooked in. Wait at least 2 weeks before using.

An alternative is to juice enough lemons to supply the liquid in the canning jar. If you do this, you can skip the water baking. Just make sure to generously salt the lemons.

MY NOTES:

Ras El Hanout

About This Recipe

Ras El Hanout, which means "top of the shop" in Arabic, is a blend of spices used in Moroccan cuisine. You can make it ahead as it will keep several months in an airtight container. Think of it as Moroccan curry powder.

This recipe makes about 6 tablespoons but can be scaled to any size you want. You will typically use 1 tablespoon in a dish.

Ingredients

1	Tsp	Cumin seeds
1	Tsp	Coriander seeds
2	Tsp	Peppercorns
2	Tsp	Ground cinnamon
1	Tsp	Ground allspice
1	Tsp	Ground cardamom
1	Tsp	Ground cloves
1	Tsp	Ground ginger
1	Tsp	Ground nutmeg
1	Tsp	Turmeric
1	Tsp	Dried thyme
½	Tsp	Cayenne pepper (optional for heat)

Procedure

Grind the seeds in a spice grinder or mortar and pestle. Mix all the ingredients together and store in a tightly sealed container.

MY NOTES:

About the Author and This Book

Cooking has been a long-time hobby. For more than 40 years, I've collected recipes that I personally love. The sources of these recipes are friends, family, and restaurants from around the world as a result of extensive travel when I was working for a living. Some of the recipes are of my own invention, and most of those sourced from others I've modified to fit my cooking style or to use ingredients that are readily available in America.

Having retired from my professional life, and having nothing better to do, I decided to share my recipe collection with people who like to eat. The results are contained in these books, *Mikey Likes It!, Volumes I and II.* I hope you do too.

Deciding how to format these books was an agonizing exercise. I consulted many publishing "experts". Most of them said (after expounding in depth on the virtues of various fonts that nobody ever heard of) "Use whatever looks OK." I tried dozens of serif and non-serif fonts, and, after essentially throwing up my hands, wound up choosing the classic Times New Roman for the textual articles and Arial for the recipes and headings. These are the same fonts that I used for decades writing business letters and reports. Since a cookbook is, in a sense, a business document, I think those fonts serve the intended purpose as well as any.

I made the type large enough to be read from a few feet away to make it easy to read in a typical cooking environment. I recommend that you get one of those clear plastic book stands that will hold the book open to the recipe page(s) you are using. In addition, if there is enough space on a page, I left room for you to write in your own notes.

This book is also available in Amazon Kindle and epub editions, the latter through such places as the Apple iStore and Kobo.

I welcome comments and input. You can reach me through the website www.mikeylikesit.us.

To quote one of the culinary giants, Jacques Pepin, "Happy Cooking."

Made in the USA
San Bernardino, CA
26 September 2015